A2 MEDIA STUDIES:
The Essential Introduction

D1151249

Developing key topics in depth and introducing students to the notion of independent study, this full-colour, highly illustrated textbook is designed to support students through the transition from AS to A2 and is the perfect guide for the new AQA A2 Media Studies syllabus. Individual chapters, written by experienced teachers and examiners, cover the following key areas:

- introduction: from AS to A2
- developing textual analysis
- critical perspectives
- issues and debates: case studies
- passing MEST3: critical perspectives
- research and production skills
- passing MEST4: media research and production

Especially designed to be user-friendly, *A2 Media Studies: The Essential Introduction for AQA* includes activities, key terms, case studies, sample exam questions and over 100 images.

Antony Bateman is Head of Media and Film Studies at Wardle High School and was previously Creative and Media Diploma Programme Director for Rochdale. He is co-author of *A2 Media Studies: The Essential Introduction for WJEC* (2010).

Peter Bennett is Senior Lecturer at the University of Wolverhampton's School of Education. He is the co-author of *A2 Media Studies: The Essential Introduction for WJEC* (2010), *AS Communication and Culture: The Essential Introduction* (third edition, 2008), *A2 Communication and Culture: The Essential Introduction* (2009) and *Framework Media: Channels* (2004) as well as co-editor of *Communication Studies: The Essential Resource* (2003) and *Film Studies: the Essential Resource* (2006).

Sarah Casey Benyahia is a teacher and examiner of Film and Media Studies. She is the author of *Teaching Contemporary British Cinema* (2005) and *Teaching TV and Film Documentary* (2008) and co-author of *A2 Media Studies: The Essential Introduction for WJEC* (2010), *AS Film Studies: The Essential Introduction* (second edition, 2008) and *A2 Film Studies: The Essential Introduction* (second edition, 2009).

Jacqui Shirley is a teacher at Cheadle and Marple Sixth Form College in Stockport, Manchester and Principal Examiner for GCE Media Studies.

Peter Wall is Chair of Examiners for GCE Media Studies. He is co-author of *A2 Media Studies: The Essential Introduction for WJEC* (2010), *AS Media Studies: The Essential Introduction* (third edition, 2008) and *Framework Media: Channels* (2004), co-editor of *Media Studies: The Essential Resource* (2004), *Communication Studies: The Essential Resource* and *Film Studies: The Essential Resource* (2006), and author of *Media Studies for GCSE* (2007).

The *Essentials* Series

This series of textbooks, resource books and revision guides covers everything you need to know about taking exams in Media, Communication or Film Studies. Working together the series offers everything you need to move from AS level through to an undergraduate degree. Written by experts in their subjects, the series is clearly presented to aid understanding with the textbooks updated regularly to keep examples current.

Series Editor: Peter Wall

A2 MEDIA STUDIES:
The Essential Introduction for AQA

Second edition

Antony Bateman, Peter Bennett, Sarah Casey Benyahia, Jacqui Shirley and Peter Wall

Routledge
Taylor & Francis Group

LONDON AND NEW YORK

First edition published 2005

This edition published 2010
by Routledge
2 Park Square, Milton Park, Abingdon, Oxon OX14 4RN

Simultaneously published in the USA and Canada
by Routledge
270 Madison Ave, New York, NY 10016

Routledge is an imprint of the Taylor & Francis Group, an informa business

© 2010 Antony Bateman, Peter Bennett, Sarah Casey Benyahia, Jacqui Shirley
and Peter Wall

Typeset in Folio and Bauhaus by
Keystroke, Station Road, Codsall, Wolverhampton
Printed and bound in Great Britain by
Bell & Bain Ltd, Glasgow

British Library Cataloguing in Publication Data
A catalogue record for this book is available from the British Library

Library of Congress Cataloging-in-Publication Data
A2 media studies : the essential introduction for AQA / Antony Bateman . . .
[et al.]. – 2nd ed.
        p. cm.
    Includes bibliographical references and index.
    1. Mass media. I. Bateman, Antony, 1970–
    P90.A22 2010
    302.23–dc22   2010020708

ISBN 13: 978–0–415–45733–0 (pbk)
ISBN 13: 978–0–203–83896–9 (ebk)

CONTENTS

ILLUSTRATIONS

ACKNOWLEDGEMENTS

Every attempt has been made to obtain permission to reproduce copyright material. If any proper acknowledgement has not been made, we would invite copyright holders to inform us of the oversight.

Images

0.2   Courtesy of Company © The National Magazine Company Ltd
0.4   © Corbis
2.4a   © Getty Images
2.4b   © AFP/Getty Images
2.7   Courtesy of Cosmopolitan © The National Magazine Company Ltd
2.9   Lizzie Miller, as pictured in *Glamour* magazine © Walter Chin/Marek & Assoc/trunkarchive.com
2.14   © Jerry Slater
2.17a   © Getty Images
2.17b   © AFP/Getty Images
2.19a   © Express Syndication
2.19b   © The Sun/nisyndication.com. Picture by: John Stillwell/PA Wire/Press Association Images © PA Wire/Press Association Images
3.1   © AFP/Getty Images
3.2   © Andrew Williams
3.3   © Tim Graham/Getty Images
3.5   Men's Fitness © Copyright Dennis Publishing Limited
3.6   Men's Fitness © Copyright Dennis Publishing Limited
3.7   © EMAP
3.8   Heat © Bauer Consumer Media Ltd
3.9   Heat © Bauer Consumer Media Ltd
3.11   © Ben Piggott
3.12   © Getty Images
3.14a   © WireImage

3.14b   © Redferns

3.14c   © WireImage

4.1   Heat © Bauer Consumer Media Ltd. Images © Rex Features: Sandrine
        Dulermo & Michael Labica

4.11   © AP/Press Association images

5.1   © Saga Publishing Ltd

6.5   © Saatchi & Saatchi LA

Text

AQA examination questions are reproduced by permission of the Assessments
and Qualifications Alliance.

All commentary and advice on tackling papers and questions is the responsibility
of the authors of this book and has neither been provided nor approved by AQA;
furthermore the advice given does not necessarily constitute the only possible
solution.

'Illegal downloading is here to stay' by Sean Michaels, 4 August 2008 © Copyright
Guardian News & Media Ltd 2008

'Jordan and her big boobs should just bounce off' by Caitlin Moran, 7 December
2009 © The Times and 7 December 2009/nisyndication.com

'Man sues over lack of lynx effect', 30 October 2009 Orange News

The team of authors would like to give thanks to the following people who have
all contributed to the making of this book: our editor at Routledge, Aileen Storry,
our copy editor, Ann King, our production editor, Anna Callander, and Paul Marlow
and Stephen Kruger for their helpful insight and guidance.

HOW TO USE THIS BOOK

As an A2 student you should by now have some experience of using textbooks. You will realise that they are not constructed or meant to be read as straightforward linear narratives as you might a novel. Rather they are like works of reference which allow you to dip in and out according to your specific needs at specific points in your study.

We thought it would be useful to you, however, to offer some indication of what different sections of the book are intended to do and how they relate to the AQA specification which you are studying. This specification, by the way, is available to you as well as to your teacher. You can go to the AQA website and download it. It provides valuable information about precisely what you need to know and do in order to succeed in your A2 course.

This book is also accompanied by a website provided by our publisher, Routledge. This website is intended to provide some of the support that cannot be offered in a print edition. It also allows you to keep up to date with developments in the media in a way that a textbook cannot. So basically you need to use the textbook as a source of ideas and stimulus for your A2 study and supplement this with visits to the website for some of the fine detail.

So how is the book organised?

We begin by looking at the idea of developing textual analysis because it is a key theme for A2 study. In this chapter we encourage you to look beyond your immediate concern with texts or media products, very much the theme of AS work, to explore some of the wider issues relating to media output. At A2 your concern should be with discovering why media products are the way they are by exploring the different pressures and protocols which determine the nature of media output: wider contexts as they are sometimes called. Chapter 1 on developing textual analysis offers you examples of how you might do this.

You should be able to see a logical connection to Chapter 2 on critical perspectives which is designed to help you ease yourself into an understanding of some of the key theoretical perspectives that may be used to inform our study of the media. We have tried to make this chapter as accessible as possible so that you will feel confident in understanding some of these important perspectives. Of course, theory for its own sake is of little use. What you need to do as you read the chapter on theory is to consider some of the ways in which you can apply the insights that these different perspectives offer.

Chapter 3 on issues and debates offers you a look at some of the core areas of study that you will need as part of your A2 study. The topics we explore are crucial to your understanding of the A2 course. We have offered a series of case studies which we hope will exemplify for you how to tackle these topics in preparation for your exam. As with all aspects of the book, they are not intended to do the work for you. Rather they are there as a stimulus to encourage you to go out and explore your own examples which you can then use to support your answers in the MEST3 exam.

We then take a close look at the exam in Chapter 4, on passing MEST3. We take you through the exam itself and offer some strategies for ensuring that you feel well prepared when you go into the exam room, or that you do at least know what to expect.

The focus of Chapter 5 on research and production skills is primarily your MEST4 coursework. It will provide important guidelines on these processes in a way that we hope will support the work you do in class with your teachers and on your own. The Routledge website (www.routledge.com/textbooks/a2mediastudies) is especially important in relation to the production component as it has links to many resources where you will find support to enhance your technical production skills.

Chapter 6 on MEST4 should then guide you through precisely what you need to do to succeed in the coursework unit from choosing a topic to investigate through to submitting your work for assessment.

Mapping the book to the specification	
1. Developing textual analysis	This chapter is designed to help you with the transition from AS study to A2 and develops the ideas offered to you in the introduction by looking at how you can move from a study of texts into wider contexts and theoretical perspectives.
2. Critical perspectives	This is the unit title of MEST3, so it is an important aspect of preparing you for this exam. It also relates to MEST4, most specifically the critical investigation.
3. Issues and debates: case studies	These case studies are directly linked to the MEST3 topics you need to prepare for your MEST3 exam.

4. Passing MEST3: critical perspectives	Does what it says on the tin.
5. Research and production skills	Designed to help support you with your MEST4 coursework but the research aspect will also be of value in preparing your MEST3 case studies.
6. Passing MEST4: media research and production	Specifically written to help you with MEST4 coursework.

After that it only remains to see if you can get a decent price for the book on eBay.

INTRODUCTION: FROM AS TO A2

In this chapter we will examine:

- What kind of student you have become
- What you learned at AS level:

    - Key concepts
    - Production skills
    - Evaluative skills
    - Some autonomy
    - Basic research skills

- The additional demands of A2:

    - A more imaginative approach to production work
    - Greater autonomy
    - Wider contexts
    - Theoretical perspectives.

What kind of student have you become?

In most occupations, there exists from time to time the necessity to review your performance. For education professionals this takes place through lesson observations, inspections and performance management. Health professionals are likewise given the once over every so often in order to assess their work and to ascertain their suitability to continue practising. The purpose of these review processes can generally be summarised by asking the question: What kind of teacher/doctor/advertising executive/film editor (delete as appropriate) are you?

Although you are probably several years away from entering a profession in which you need to undertake one of these appraisals, there is, as you commence the next phase of your course as a media student, the necessity to ask yourself a similar question. So here goes: 'What kind of student are you?'

We divide students into two categories – active and passive. It is often felt that passive students are a real pain to teach because they can be so heavily reliant on their teacher. They expect their teacher to do everything for them, including thinking, and ideally they would quite like their teacher to take the exam for them, providing of course that they managed to get a decent grade. Passive students are as a general rule less likely to do as well as they might expect at AS level because Media Studies is a discipline which seeks to reward students who do not rely on their teacher too heavily. It rewards the student who is prepared to think independently.

These students who think for themselves are called active students and you may be forgiven for forming the impression that teachers of Media Studies like active students. Well, you would be right. Active students are a pleasure to teach (although they can also be a pain, but for different reasons) because they want to know. They have enquiring minds that enjoy finding out about things. In Media Studies this should translate into a desire to go and seek out media texts and to try applying some of the ideas that have been explored in class to them. Always bear in mind that you are very lucky to be able to study the media. Media texts are nearly always accessible and nearly always enjoyable. These are the raw materials of your programme of study. This is certainly not bad when you can spend an evening watching Ant and Dec or going to the cinema and you can call it homework, provided of course that in this endeavour you are active and not passive!

With any luck, if you started without the level of autonomy that you need to be an active student, you will have developed this to some degree by the time you are studying at A2. If you have not, then here is a serious suggestion: go and do something else. Without the ability to learn independently, you are wasting your time doing A2 Media Studies. The whole of the A2 assessment is geared towards your ability to get up and do things for yourself. Relying wholly on your teacher is a great way to do badly.

INFORMATION BOX

Students who are willing to find things out for themselves and develop their skills of inquiry and independent learning are far more likely to thrive in Media Studies than those who rely solely upon what they learn in the classroom.

Figure 0.1 Students researching in the library

So why is this the case? Well, as you will read in the following section, the transition from AS study to A2 study is marked by a shift from textual analysis to an application of wider contexts and theoretical perspectives. Put simply, you are shifting away from textual study in its own right and looking at media texts in a broader way. You will have to look at the context in which media texts are produced and consumed. You will also have to look at some of the theoretical issues that underpin our study of the media at this level. This is a tall order.

Finally, in your AS level you have probably been nursed through your study by a caring teacher prepared to spend time with you when you needed extra help. This may continue over the next year as you embark upon your A2 course but the next stop is university where members of teaching staff are very unlikely to spend extra time with you. It is sink or swim once you get there. Active students make much better swimmers than do passive students.

What you learned at AS level

If you are embarking upon an AQA A2 course in Media Studies, you will have already studied the subject at AS level and possibly at GCSE level before that. In the future, you may well continue studying to degree level and go on to postgraduate level thereafter. As with all subjects, as you progress upward to a higher level it is always good practice to reflect upon your prior learning and remember that it forms a foundation for your current and indeed future learning.

Any A2 course of study is not simply more of the same; there is a significant upward step from the AS level. Although there are similarities between the two levels in terms of content, the AQA A2 course in Media Studies poses a greater challenge and the subject is examined in more depth. This book will guide you through the transition and help you to meet the challenges of the A2 level course. However, to begin with, let's recap on some AS level learning.

Key concepts

The key concepts of Media Studies are the tools of the subject. In order to produce either a practical production or to analyse a media text or an issue, you need to be able to use the key concepts in much the same way that you need skills with woodworking tools before you can produce a table or a chair. It is knowledge of these key concepts and the ability to apply them which have enabled you to make the progress you have. The concepts and theories found in the study of media act as tools for production and of analysis and they help you to understand the media world.

The main concepts employed in advanced media may vary slightly depending upon the specification you are following but they can be broadly identified as language **(including text, genre and narrative), audiences, representation, institution** and **values and ideology.**

Language is the most fundamental concept in Media Studies as it is through the use of language that meaning is attached to texts. Language incorporates all of the ways a text communicates its messages to the consumer. This communication may be both verbal (what is said or what is written) and non-verbal (all other ways of communicating including in the use of colour, font, body language, facial expressions, etc.).

ACTIVITY

Verbal and non-verbal language on a magazine cover

How much of the overall meaning of this magazine cover comes from verbal communication and how much comes from non-verbal communication?

The verbal communication is quite literally the words. The masthead tells us what the magazine is called and the use of strap lines at the sides of the cover tells us about the content.

However, the body language and facial expression of the model in the feature article photograph in the image and the use of colour and fonts also play an important part in communicating meaning to the consumer.

Figure 0.2 Hayden Panettiere on the cover of *Company* Magazine, September 2009

Recognition of what is verbal and non-verbal communication is only the first step in using the concept of language to analyse a media text. In order to deconstruct a media text and analyse the constituent elements such as colour, facial expression, use of font, etc., further tools are required and we must look to the study of semiotics for this. Each element of a media text has both a physical part (the signifier) and the meaning which is applied to the physical part (the signified). These two features may be equated to the terms 'denotation' (what is actually there in the text) and 'connotation' (the meaning).

So, for the cover of *Company*, we can use semiotics as shown in the following example.

Signifier or denotation	Signified or connotation
The background is white but different shades of pink are used as the main colour on the cover.	The primary connotation of pink is femininity. This is the most likely use of the colour here given the nature of the magazine. However, it would be wrong to simply say that pink is used for femininity alone. The darker pink, almost red colour of the model's dress coupled with her confident and sexy stance suggests a

much more self-assured and modern
connotation of femininity than the more
'girly' pink used in some of the written
text. The connotation of a stronger, more
confident and sexy femininity offers an
interesting juxtaposition to the more sober
masthead and background, a simple font
in black on plain white.

When analysing texts in this way, it is highly likely that there will be a degree of disagreement among your fellow students over your interpretations. This is perfectly fine as there are often texts which have more than one possible connotation or meaning. Such a text is called an open text as opposed to a closed text where the meaning is more obvious. There is no doubt that all of the constituent features come together in the *Company* magazine cover to produce a text with little or no ambiguity. Therefore it is a closed text. However, the meanings behind some texts are less obvious and so different interpretations are likely. The important point when analysing a text and concluding that there is a certain connotation is that you are able to provide evidence or a justification for it. Figure 0.3 will help you through the process of applying meanings to texts.

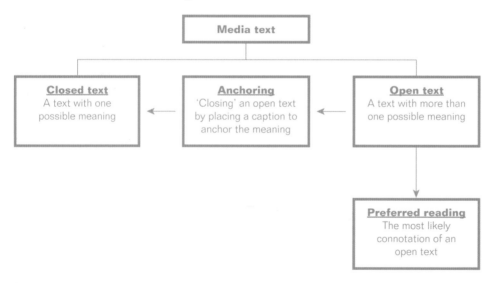

Figure 0.3 Applying meaning to texts

DECONSTRUCTION studying a media text by 'taking it apart' into its constituent elements and explaining each element.

SEMIOTICS the study of signs and their meanings. First used by Ferdinand De Saussure in his Course in General Linguistics at the University of Geneva (1906–1911), semiotics is an important part of media study, as it is a device by which meanings are attached to the signs we see in media texts.

JUXTAPOSITION placing two contrasting elements next to each other in order to increase the impact of each (e.g. darkness seems to be darker when it is placed next to brightness and in a film, or a sudden increase in volume makes it seem much louder due to the contrast).

CLOSED AND OPEN TEXTS a text with only one possible meaning is said to be a closed text, whereas a more ambiguous text with more than one possible interpretation is an open text. An open text may also be called **polysemic**, literally meaning many signs.

ANCHORING when a caption is placed in an open text to anchor meaning.

PREFERRED READING the most likely interpretation of an open text.

A further tool of analysis of media texts using the concept of language is to be found in the study of **genre**. At this point in your studies you will already be aware of the term 'genre' and that a genre consists of a group of media texts with common or shared features. These common features, called the repertoire of generic elements, are referred to as icons or visual signifiers, and so the generic elements associated with the musical genre of rock, for example, would include denim and leather, long hair, references to motor bikes, road journeys and love, and music which is driven by powerful drums and guitars.

INFORMATION BOX

The generic signifiers of rock include leather, long hair and music with loud guitars.

continued

Figure 0.4 Left to right: Kiss, Iron Maiden, ACDC and Foo Fighters all demonstrate a certain similarity generically

In modern media, there is a tendency for texts to demonstrate the features of more than one genre. If you were to look at a reality TV show such as *Big Brother*, for example, you would find the features of at least three television genres. It is part game show, part documentary, and with its human emotional content, even part soap opera albeit less scripted.

Media texts which include elements from more than one genre are called **hybrids**, as they are not truly one genre but have features of many genres.

We tend to think of the term '**narrative**' as referring to the story or the plot of a film. Indeed, one of the most common applications of narrative as a concept is to examine a film text and analyse the structure of its narrative using a theory such as the equilibrium theory of Tvetzan Todorov or a more recent theory such as the classic five-part narrative theory of Robert McKee. A further analysis of narrative comes when comparing the closed narrative of a film with a tight reading in which the audience expects the plot to unfold gradually, although the time in the film's story is usually compressed into the two-hour duration of the film itself and the plot ultimately ends with a sense of resolution, while the open narrative of a TV soap opera has a much looser reading where time corresponds more to real time and resolution gives way to the need for a cliff-hanger ending.

Todorov's equilibrium narrative structure	Robert McKee's classic five-part narrative structure
Equilibrium (peace)	Inciting incident
Disruption of equilibrium	Progressive complications
Recognition	Crisis
Repair	Climax
Restoration of equilibrium	Resolution

The most common form of narrative is a linear narrative, in which the story unfolds chronologically. However, a number of film texts employ a non-linear narrative whereby the action in the film takes a more random chronology. This is often used to add an extra level of meaning to a narrative and to offer the audience something which differs from the accepted method of telling a story in a film. The director

Quentin Tarantino is renowned in his films such as *Pulp Fiction* and the *Kill Bill* films for using non-linear narratives.

However, narrative is not a term which refers exclusively to film or TV; an analysis of articles in magazines or newspapers and the construction of news on TV will also reveal that the narratives tend to follow a structure.

ACTIVITY

How useful is the concept of narrative when applied to new media products such as websites or viral advertising by mobile phone or email? Try analysing the narrative that emerges when you browse the web. Consider, for example, how clicking on a link can open up a whole range of narrative outcomes.

Audience as a concept means considerably more than a group of people in a theatre or a cinema. You will already be familiar with the term 'target audience', which refers to the group of people a media text is aimed at in terms of its content. In reality, however, most media texts will be consumed by many more people than those who make up the target audience, and not everyone who belongs to a target audience will consume each text. The concept of target audience therefore is of more use when analysing the content of a media text than the consumption of it. Figure 0.6 shows the relationship between the target audience and the wider audience groups of actual and potential audiences.

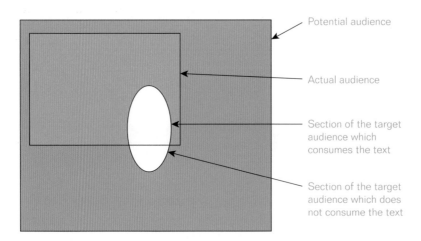

Figure 0.6 Diagram showing the relationship between the target audience and the wider audience groups of actual and potential audiences

Recently, with the emergence of new media, the idea of measuring audiences has changed, and while organisations such as RAJAR continue to measure radio listeners and the Audit Bureau of Circulation count sales in newspapers and magazines, measuring how many people see pop-up advertisements on the internet or who actually read the adverts they are emailed is more of a challenge. Nevertheless, internet marketing is a huge growth industry since the internet has brought media to a global audience. Banking is seen as a particularly important area of the sector as the number of people opting for online banking rather than the traditional visit to their local branch increases. Logging on to your online bank page allows the bank to bombard you with a number of related products which, since they hold such a lot of personal information about you, is geared specifically to your needs (see Activity below).

Audience as a concept is far more than identifying patterns of consumption and marketing of media texts to certain audiences. One of the most important elements of the study of audience lies in the effects that media has on those who consume it. These effects are by no means certain but few would argue that an effective advertising campaign can lead to increased sales for a product, and there are many critics of violent films and video games which have been the subject of many studies in an attempt to ascertain the effect that consumption of them can have upon an audience.

ACTIVITY

Internet marketing or E-marketing is one of the largest areas of growth in marketing, as it is seen as an effective and relatively inexpensive method of marketing. Conduct some research into the use of the internet for marketing purposes. Find out what is meant by:

continued

- Pay per impression
- Pay per click
- Pay per action
- Geomarketing
- Blackhat marketing

Internet marketing is cost-effective and can be very productive due to its success in targeting the products and the right customers. Nevertheless, it does raise concerns about safety and security. Do you feel that internet marketing poses a threat to those who are targeted in terms of data protection or even simply receiving the goods or services you actually pay for over the internet?

The concept of **representation** in media deals with how people, either groups or individuals, places or things (a seemingly vague term but one that is needed to cover the array of subjects such as a human emotion, a religion, a building, a charity, etc. which can be shown in a text) are portrayed in the media. It is useful when analysing representations to have a set of questions, rather like a checklist, to refer to as you analyse the subject.

- **What** is being represented?
- **How** is it being represented?
- **Who** is responsible for this representation?
- Is it an **accurate** representation? (Before you can assess accuracy, at least a basic knowledge of the subject in the real sense is required.)
- Does the representation **challenge** or **reinforce** the existing **stereotypes** which exist about the subject? In order to be able to answer this final point, you will of course need to have some knowledge of the commonly held beliefs, the stereotypes, which exist about the subject of the representation.

A representation is a means of **encoding** a message for transmission. Upon receiving the message, the audience **decodes** the message and applies meaning to it. In this respect, representation is closely linked to language insofar as it is concerned with the creation of meaning. It is therefore one of the main devices through which an audience makes sense of the messages within the text. As this decoding is an individual action, the meanings people apply to the representations can vary enormously. This helps to explain how, for example, one person may interpret a certain meaning behind a representation in one way whereas another may interpret the meaning in a totally different way. In short, a representation, through its use of both verbal and non-verbal communication, speaks to the audience and helps the text to have meaning to those who consume it. In addition to occupying a position among the key concepts of Media Studies, representation is a topic in its own right. Even though events may happen naturally, how they are shown is the result of a production process and the media we consume is constructed; somebody somewhere has exerted a certain creative input into the media product. This is fairly obviously true of fictional media, music and computer games, but even those which claim a close relationship with reality such as documentary or a live sports event still have an element of construction about them. In the case of sport, interactive TV has led to greater control over the choice of camera angle you watch or whether to have the commentator's soundtrack, the noise of the crowd or a discussion between fans, but the fact remains that a decision is made about where the cameras are located and how the sound is produced; in short, there is still, even with live sporting events, an element of representation. Representation as a topic is an area which is covered in several places throughout the book and in some detail in Chapter 4 which examines the MEST3 assessment.

ACTIVITY

Representation is usually identified as the way people, places or things are shown in the media. The increase in opportunities for self-representation on the internet through personal websites (popular among singers, actors and footballers) and YouTube means that there is more self-representation now than at any other time in history. What does this mean for representations? Conduct a discussion with other members of your class and consider the following questions:

- Will the increase in self-representation opportunities on the internet lead to a general increase or decrease in accuracy in the way people are represented in the media?
- Given the fact that the internet is not subject to the same levels of regulation and control as mainstream media, does this pose a danger for a society in which radical, racist or extremist representations are readily available in the public domain?
- To what extent are websites like YouTube an embodiment of free speech and should people be free to use them as they wish?

As a general term, '**institution**' has several meanings. In Media Studies, it refers to the organisations which are behind the production, marketing, distribution and regulation of media output. The producers, marketers and distributors, a group of organisations which might be seen as forming a media **industry**, work very closely to ensure that the media output is varied, interesting, has the potential to create revenue, is advertised appropriately and that it reaches the correct audiences. Efficiency and value for money are key phrases in the media; an industry renowned for being volatile and unforgiving to those producers whose output fails to be profitable.

Regulatory bodies such as OFCOM, the ASA (Advertising Standards Authority) and the BBFC (British Board of Film Classification) can act as a kind of governing body for the media form they are associated with by establishing codes of conduct. They may also act as a censor and require the removal of items deemed inappropriate or as a point of contact for complaints in the event of a media product causing offence. In this final capacity, the regulatory body may then act as an adjudicator and may force a producer to take remedial action such as issuing an apology or paying damages.

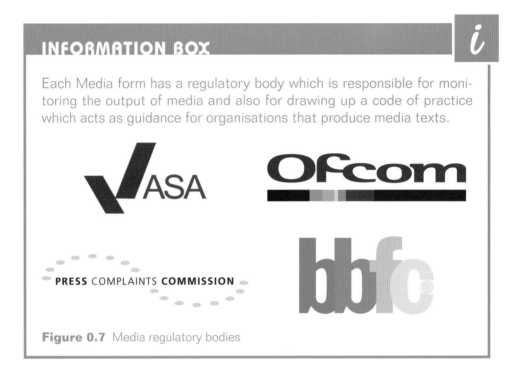

INFORMATION BOX

Each Media form has a regulatory body which is responsible for monitoring the output of media and also for drawing up a code of practice which acts as guidance for organisations that produce media texts.

Figure 0.7 Media regulatory bodies

The final concept in Media Studies, **values and ideology**, is arguably the most complex. Although it influences the overwhelming majority of media output, ideology is rarely singled out as a key concept prior to advanced study. However, it certainly now forms part of the AQA GCE courses, especially at A2 level, and students need to show knowledge and skill in employing ideologies in both analytical work and creative work.

A media ideology is an idea or a belief which influences or underpins a media text in some way. At its most basic level, a simple media text such as a TV advertisement for a car which is designed to make an audience aware of the car's main features with a view to influencing them to buy one is based upon the capitalist or consumerist ideologies which are part of our society. In this way, most media texts are influenced by or are a product of at least one ideology. In studying ideology, you will no doubt have heard terms like 'capitalism', 'socialism', 'democracy', 'feminism', 'fascism', 'communism', 'postmodernism', 'post-structuralism' and so on, and even 'isms' such as Marxism or Thatcherism which are named after the ideas and beliefs of a certain person.

It is useful to divide these ideologies into broad categories. Capitalism, socialism, democracy and especially Thatcherism are what might be termed political ide-ologies, while feminism, postmodernism, poststructuralism and the relatively new queer theory tend to be regarded as social ideologies. There are some ideologies such as communism and fascism which may be regarded as both political and social ideologies. It may be further argued that religious beliefs such as Islam or Christianity form religious ideologies capable of influencing the content of a media text.

Figure 0.8 Logos from some of the UK political parties

It is worth noting here that the A2 level course of study requires students to engage in a synoptic element and part of this is placing media texts in their contexts when you analyse them. This means accounting for their features based upon the ideologies which influenced them and their historical and geographical origin. This will be looked at in greater detail later in this book.

Production skills

The main function of practical production projects at GCE level is to explore the link between theory and practice, to gain more experience in the planning and decision making which is required when working in the media and for you to embark upon a part of your study which acts as a counterbalance to the more conventional learning you have done in a classroom.

Now that you are studying this subject at A2 level, it is important that you regard the practical elements not as separate from those done at AS but rather as an opportunity to build upon the experiences you had in the AS practical. At AS level, there is a focus on research into the topic of the production, the planning and the actual production elements of the project. For practical work to have satisfying outcomes – and this is certainly true of media products made professionally – good planning is essential. This poses a problem for some students, many of whom see the planning or the pre-production stage as the dull part which, when compared to the fun of filming or using computer programs to produce a vibrant and creative production, is a kind of awkward annoyance which stands between you and freedom with a camera, DTP or animation package and as such needs to be done as quickly as possible.

However, it is important to stress that the planning in an advanced level project is much more than providing evidence that you didn't just make it up as you went along.

Planning is the way you evidence the link between theory and practice and, from an examiner's point of view, the way you demonstrate how you arrived at the decisions which inform your finished product. There are a number of important factors when planning and executing a project:

- Know your target audience.
- Know your target audience. (No, this isn't a misprint. It really is that important.)
- Be comfortable in your decision about working alone or as part of a group.
- Engage in both primary and secondary research. Your research will involve an element of audience research in which important questions about the content of the production for your audience are answered as well as research into existing examples of the kind of media text you are hoping to produce.
- Know your limitations in terms of equipment and content. Explosions, car chases, graphic scenes of violence, expensive photo shoots may all show off your creativity in its best light but these are not feasible for this kind of project. Likewise, professional film cameras, editing equipment and blue screen studios are ideal but it's more likely that a home digital video camera and a basic editing package will be all that is available. One of the main issues that you need to address is getting the most out of the equipment available to you.
- Concentrate upon the fine detail. For example, the opening sequence to an action film which, if done reflecting the codes and conventions of the action genre, will be gripping and exciting as it sets the tone for the film, may seem an appealing project, but one which is very challenging to see through to fulfilment. However, a simple conversation between two characters within the genre of drama or soap which uses a wide selection of camera shots especially over the shoulder shots which in a two-way conversation should really be done

by filming the scene twice from different angles and then editing it together post-production can, despite the simplicity, score highly if done effectively.

Evaluative skills

It is almost certain by now that somewhere in your educational career you will have been asked in a question to 'evaluate' something. Perhaps this was the effect of an event such as the fall of the Berlin Wall or the assassination of John F. Kennedy, or perhaps you were asked to evaluate the arguments that increasing the use of fossil fuels leads to climate change. In addition, as part of your learning thus far in Media Studies, you may have been asked to evaluate the point of view that the increase in popularity of reality TV is stifling creativity and leading to a general 'dumbing down' of TV content. The art of evaluation is important across a number of subject areas and, in subjects like Media Studies which do not always have a definitive right or wrong answer but which throw up a number of arguments representing different theories and conflicting perspectives, it is especially important.

So having seen the importance of evaluation skills have you ever actually stopped and asked yourself what you are being asked to do when you are given the task of evaluating? Many people seem to confuse evaluating issues with simply writing about them; yet an evaluation is focused, it should be balanced and represent all relevant theories, perspectives and arguments before finally concluding with an assessment which includes comments about the usefulness or value of the topic up for evaluation.

Some autonomy

Advanced studies in subjects like Media Studies are full of theories, analyses and points of view offered by a wide variety of writers and professionals. Some of these contributors are very well known, others less so, but the use of this kind of material often forms the basis for answers in essays, in exams and in research tasks, and since it has been produced by people who are believed either through their experience or through their academic study or indeed both to know what they are talking about, it also lends gravitas to the work you produce.

However, what about your own points of view? Well, to put it simply, the more you have progressed over your time as a media student, the more **you** have become worth listening to. Your expertise in the subject is increasing all the time and, through your consumption, analysis and evaluation of media texts as well as your production skills, you will be forming your own valid points of view about a wide range of issues found in the media.

As a student in this position, you are afforded some autonomy; indeed it is encouraged at all levels at GCE and is essential for the very best marks. Examples of how you might be autonomous include offering a critical evaluation of media products, offering personal responses to a theory, a viewpoint or an analysis presented by a media professional or academic, or providing your own reading or interpretation of the content of a media text.

Media Studies is a conceptual subject, and as such there is not often a definitive right or wrong answer, disagreements are commonplace, conclusions can contradict each other, and there are many different ways in which people can read and interpret the messages in media texts. It is important, however, that in your bid to be autonomous you do not simply disagree with another point of view or come out protesting your love for or dislike of a certain media text without any further detail or explanation. You need to ensure that the points you wish to make are valid and are able to withstand a certain degree of scrutiny. Explaining why you have arrived at a certain point of view, revealing your evidence for a criticism or offering the counter-argument which has led you to disagree with a certain theory is just as important as actually writing your point of view, making your criticism or providing your counter-argument.

Basic research skills

Research in its most basic form means finding something out or acquiring new knowledge. This can mean finding out the answer to a specific problem or question; for example, finding out how Rupert Murdoch rose to become one of the world's most influential media magnates, or it can mean adopting a more exploratory approach to a more open-ended issue such as finding out how the coverage of an event in a certain newspaper affected public opinion.

There are certain techniques which you should be familiar with for conducting research, and doubtless you will have employed many of them in your AS studies. In general, Media Studies research usually falls into one of two categories: primary and secondary research. Primary research involves gathering information first hand. This could be through conducting an interview or a survey or through the direct examination of the text or texts which are the subject of the enquiry or study. As such, primary research is one of the best ways to achieve a level of autonomy as it requires analysis and evaluation of the actual texts being studied. Secondary research is that which involves using existing material which has been produced by someone else. This includes, for example, books or articles and interviews in magazines or newspapers. Naturally, the more experience the person has or the better their reputation is perceived to be, the more weight the material will have, so an interview with Steven Spielberg on a DVD 'extras' disc will most likely carry more weight than a journalist with no access to Spielberg writing their own thoughts on one of his films in a newspaper, unless of course that writer happened to be someone like Barry Norman or Mark Kermode, who have built up something of a reputation as film journalists.

If you were researching a topic, let us say the use of computer generated images (CGI) in Hollywood films, you could approach your research in the following way:

■ Primary research could involve studying a selection of films which chart the use of CGI for special effects work starting with, for example, *Star Wars*

(1977) which had no CGI and in which the special effects were created through extensive use of models, stop-motion photography, costume and make-up. *Tron* (1982) would be a good example of a film which used CGI in a basic form world followed by *Terminator 2: Judgement Day* (1992) with partial use of CGI to create the scenes when the T1000 Terminator character changes shape and in his natural liquid metal form. *Star Wars Episode 1* (1999) had the very first completely CGI principal character in Jar Jar Binks and, to bring the research up to date, films like the *Lord of the Rings* trilogy (2001–2003) and *Avatar* (2009) use CGI not only to create characters but the worlds they inhabit. The research might look at the greater freedom afforded directors by the progress in CGI and how the films studied use CGI to create the *mise-en-scène* which is in the script.

INFORMATION BOX *i*

The changing face of computer generated imagery (CGI) in film would make an interesting research topic. Advances in technology have made what was once unfilmable a regular feature in some of the biggest blockbusters in recent years.

Figure 0.9 Left to right: a car race from *Tron* – the early days of CGI; the T1000 from *Terminator 2: Judgement Day*; Jar Jar Binks from *Star Wars Episode 1* (1999), and Gollum from *Lord of the Rings*.

continued

The T1000 from *Terminator 2: Judgement Day* was a major breakthrough in computer generated image technology as the character was seen frequently changing appearance and merged with live action. Characters like Jar Jar Binks from *Star Wars Episode 1* (1999) and Gollum from the *Lord of the Rings* trilogy are principal characters created entirely by CGI.

■ Secondary research would include interviews with film directors and those who work in the field of CGI together with producers (who finance films) from a range of sources including books, magazines, DVD extras discs, websites and newspapers. You should also be prepared to examine the range of existing research done by film writers, academics and film critics which measures the audiences' response to the films they consume.

It is important to remain focused when researching. The material you use for either primary or secondary research must be relevant and reliable. A judicious choice of sources bearing the need for relevance and reliability in mind should ensure that your research yields results of a high quality and which can enhance the overall quality of your work.

The additional demands of A2

As mentioned at the start of this chapter, the AQA A2 level represents an upward step in terms of the level of challenge from AS level; it is not, to put it simply, more of the same. Having identified the main key concepts in the previous section, it is fair to say that at AS level, the concepts of language and representation have been the most prominent, especially in the area of textual analysis. The art of deconstructing a media text by offering an analysis of the constituent parts is very much an AS level skill which, although still important at A2 level, is now complemented by the opportunities to explore these texts in greater depth through looking at the wider contexts in which these texts are produced and consumed. As such, the other concepts of audience, institution, or industry, and ideology become more prominent than they perhaps were at AS level. In addition, the practical work undertaken for A2 level will need to show a greater degree of refinement and attention to detail which will separate it from that which has been completed earlier in your career as a student of media. This practical work will also need to have closer links to the key concepts and to demonstrate more confidently how the concepts are reflected through practical tasks.

While not entirely a theory-led subject, there are nevertheless numerous theories and perspectives offered in Media Studies by a wealth of writers, academics and media professionals, many of which are at least worthy of consideration if not learning thoroughly, in order to enhance your understanding. However, perhaps more so than in many other subjects, theories and perspectives can quickly become outdated as the media world advances relentlessly. It may sound impressive to have a list of theories offered by an array of experts, especially if you have kept them relevant and been judicious in your choice of theory. However, an answer laden with theory and bursting with references could potentially show nothing more than that the writer is good at remembering material gleaned from other sources, whereas a good-quality A2 level answer will combine theory, which may be criticised or challenged in its content, with critical autonomy and a debate about the wider contexts of production and consumption.

A more imaginative approach to production work

The production work you complete at A2 level needs to be different and it must show progression from that which you completed on the AS course. Does this necessarily mean it has to be better? Well, naturally you should be striving to make the quality as high as you can and given that you have more experience of practical work than before, it follows that you are probably capable of producing better work, but the focus really ought to be on trying to be more imaginative both in terms of content and in the use of the resources available. There is also the added incentive for improved work in that there is no longer the need (as there was with AQA MEST2 unit for AS level) to produce two texts; all your efforts can now be focused into one practical production. Furthermore, your practical production for the AQA MEST4 unit must be linked to your critical investigation which narrows the confines in which you work a little more. Hopefully, you were pleased with the finished products which you completed for AS level, so much so in fact that you may find it hard to be more imaginative than you were before. However, you should give some consideration to the following ideas:

▦ Try animation. Software is now readily available which will allow alternatives to human actors. This software is also not as hard to use as you might imagine.
▦ Use a more advanced piece of software which will have more possibilities for editing and desk-top publishing. Manipulation of images is relatively straightforward and the possibilities are much wider than they have been in the past. Adobe Premiere digital video editing software and Adobe Photoshop offer enormous possibilities for you to allow your imagination to roam freely.
▦ Consider the fine detail. When making a video, pay special attention to the sound, which is often overlooked. One way to achieve this is to rerecord certain elements of the video post-production (after it has been filmed) and insert the new soundtrack over your video footage. This is a good way to remove unwanted sound when filming outdoors such as the sound of a siren in the distance or of even a gentle breeze which can sound like a howling typhoon when you play your footage back. Likewise, make sure that any photography has the correct lighting. You should aim to use lighting creatively. Try lighting your subject from a number of different angles in order to achieve the correct look for the image you are taking.

- Consider less popular options such as audio work. Radio is so much more than simply playing songs and talking between them; it offers a wealth of opportunity from documentary to comedy, drama to a debate, and provides a quite different set of challenges from the conventional video or print-based task.
- Do not forget the importance of planning for practical work. It is relatively clear to those with the responsibility of marking work which pieces have been well planned and which have a more made-up feel to them. Planning will focus your mind on the product, it will allow you to envisage it and chart a route towards the fulfilment of the project, and thus, it gives greater opportunity to be creative. You may be forgiven for thinking that creative simply means louder, faster, bigger, brighter, higher or more technological. Well, it can mean this, but it may also mean finding a more imaginative way of achieving something which is more conventional. Consider this example. Let us say that you are working with other students and you are producing a short film. Your script requires that a character is pushed and falls from a balcony. Naturally, this is a hard scene to achieve with safety and you certainly should not even consider attempting it for real. In fact, the danger and potential for injury should really lead you to scrap the scene altogether and replace it with a scene which has the same outcome but which is easier to film, say, the perpetrator tripping up the victim. If you sit down with your group to plan and rather than dismissing the scene, address the question of how the effect of a character falling from a balcony without having to actually film it can be achieved, then your discussion might arrive at the following conclusion. Attach your camera to a piece of string so that the lens points downward. Twist the string round a few times and then, having started recording, gently lower the camera from the balcony on to the floor below. The twisted string will then make the camera turn around as it is lowered to the floor. When you come to edit the scene, speed it up slightly on your digital editing software and place the footage after a scene of the perpetrator walking towards the victim with the intent to push and immediately before a scene of the victim lying motionless on the floor. When edited, the scene will then show the push from our (i.e. the audience's) perspective and will cut to the victim's point of view shot of the fall followed by a return to the audience perspective of the motionless victim: a simple and above all safe way of achieving an effect. Planning gives you a much better chance of overcoming these potential barriers to achieving your practical work.
- You may also find that your creativity flows a little more if you produce a piece of practical work which falls outside your own comfort zone or area of interest. You can find yourself being lulled into a false sense of security by the fact that you consider yourself to be somewhat knowledgeable about the product you are making. Your decisions will be formulaic and, as a result, the product can be dull and uninspiring. If, however, you begin from square one with an unknown kind of text, you force yourself to be creative since you are learning about the text as you go. On the other hand, you may find that working within your comfort zone is more likely to inspire an imaginative approach as you have the confidence to take your product in new directions, but whichever

of these is the case for you, thinking outside of the box is a very good way to nurture creativity and imagination.

▓ Finally, when planning to produce a media text, consider the online version. Magazines and newspapers are now supported by websites which you could use as inspiration and which will allow you to produce a text which is interactive and, some may argue, more relevant in the modern world than the printed equivalents.

You will no doubt have made important decisions about your practical work for the AQA MEST4 unit early on when you started out deciding and planning your critical investigation: literally how the topic covered in the investigation can be covered in a practical task or which media types are best suited to the topic of the investigation. There is also a demand at this more challenging level to produce a piece of work which shows a greater degree of sophistication. A piece of work of the same standard which was completed for the AS course will not score the same marks at A2 level due to the more stringent marking scheme applied by examination boards. Sophistication is achieved by making your work as close to a professional standard as you possibly can within the confines of availability. As technology improves and people become more adept at using such technology, the demands upon students using technology have increased and moderators of practical work have raised their expectations accordingly.

In the real media world, the greatest level of sophistication comes with those texts where the complexities of production are less evident to the general audience. In a professional TV show, we don't tend to notice the editing consciously, or the sound effects in a film. Newspapers and magazines use language so appropriate for their readerships that it simply flows as it is read, and music on a CD sounds smooth and polished and no one instrument drowns out the sound of another thanks to the work of the sound engineers. In short, at this level more than ever before, you need to try to produce a product which demonstrates the kind of sophistication and quality of finish found in professional products to a greater degree.

Greater autonomy

'You are now worth listening to!' So it says in the earlier recap of AS level study. Well, if that were the case as you drew upon your experience as an AS and as a GCSE student, how much more is this the case now that you have completed the AS level modules and find your way through the A2 course?

While some autonomy is encouraged at AS level, greater autonomy is really an absolute must for all students, especially those with aspirations for the top grades. In fact, this is arguably the largest difference between the two levels and the most notable way in which progression is evidenced. Among the main ways you can achieve greater autonomy are:

▓ Continuing to offer your own concise, well-thought-out, relevant and incisive points of view about media texts.

- Building up a catalogue of knowledge from your own media consumption and making sure that your examples are not all those which were given in your lessons.
- When media texts are influenced by other texts in terms of content or style, they are said to be **intertextual**. Companies frequently use intertexuality in the way they advertise their products. Cuprinol, for example, used the song 'We Are the Self-Preservation Society' from the 1969 film *The Italian Job* in their adverts for wood preserver. The company simply replaced the phrase 'self-preservation' with 'wood preservation' in their rendition of the song.

One of the most famous examples of intertexuality is in a scene in a railway station in Brian De Palma's 1987 film *The Untouchables* where the director plays out a scene reminiscent in part through his use of a baby in a pram of the massacre on the Odessa Steps scene in Sergei Eisenstein's The *Battleship Potemkin* (1925). Any further links which can be made between media texts are evidence of autonomy. Try looking at the video for Queen's *I Want to Break Free* and *Coronation Street* or Michael Jackson's *Thriller* and John Landis' *An American Werewolf In London*, or any one of the films from the Zombie subgenre.

Figure 0.11 Intertextuality – *Battleship Potemkin* (left) and *The Untouchables* (right)

An example of intertextuality. Amid the carnage of the massacre on the Odessa Steps in Sergei Eisenstein's *The Battleship Potemkin* (1925) a baby in a pram makes an unexpected entrance (left). Influenced by this, Brian De Palma used a pram in a similar way in the shoot-out scene on the steps of the Chicago railway station in *The Untouchables* (1987).

- Being critical of the theories and the perspectives offered by others. This does not simply mean saying that you disagree or even agree with a theory; rather it means reinforcing or challenging its orthodoxy, highlighting its strengths or weaknesses, which may be many, as theories tend to be frozen in time while media texts are not, and of course giving reasons for your appraisal of the material.

Some students feel uncomfortable with the idea of autonomy, especially if it is at the expense of established theory or perspectives, as this can give the impression that the response is lacking in planning or research and being offered 'off the cuff'. However, this is not the case provided that the autonomy within the response broadly follows the guidance offered above. However, autonomy need not mean this at all. Simply by taking the response in the direction you wish to take it and bringing in the examples you wish to bring in, moving away from a standard and formulaic answer and generally offering your response in a creative and original way, you are also taking steps towards achieving a greater degree of autonomy. This will invariably mean moving away from the texts and issues themselves or the theories and perspectives which underpin them towards the wider contexts which are pertinent to them.

Over the course of your life, it is likely that you will be asked several times to name the piece of music which you think is the greatest ever written. Of course there are several ways to answer this. The most common answer, which is in fact not an answer to this particular question at all, will probably be that you have lots of favourite pieces of music. However, if you were pushed so that you had to pick one, you could answer by saying, for example, that John Lennon's 'Imagine' was the greatest piece of music because of the simplicity of the arrangement, the clarity of the vocals and the importance of the message. You could give statistical evidence to support this by the fact that Channel 4 voted it the best number one single of all time (see http://www.channel4.com/entertainment/tv/microsites/ G/greatest/singles/results.html for the full list). Since your reasons for this answer relate entirely to the actual text itself, in this case a song, this is a text-based answer.

Consider someone answering the same question by saying that their favourite song was Madonna's 'Crazy for You' because it was the first song they danced to with a boyfriend, or 'The Shock Of The Lightning' by Oasis, as it reminds them of the last year they were at school which was up to that point the best year of that person's life. These responses have little to do with actual text, but they do make reference to the wider contexts.

In Media Studies, a context can refer, as these examples do, to the conditions of consumption, but a context is also defined as the circumstances which exist at the time a text is produced and which may be seen to have influenced it. Since media texts are produced all over the world and at different times throughout history, the main contexts which you will be dealing with are social, political, historical and cultural. In order to be successful at assessing the wider contexts and the significance of them for the text, it is often necessary to cease consuming the text with your own twenty-first-century experiences in mind and try to place yourself elsewhere; for example, by our modern standards and after the experiences of recent shock horror films such as *Saw* (2004) and *Hostel* (2005) and their sequels, an early 1930s horror film such as *Dracula* (1931) may seem anything but frightening. However, to the 1930s audience with no experience of colour, prosthetic special effects, digital technology and whose experiences of film were limited by censorship which seems very strict by modern standards, *Dracula* was at the cutting edge of thrills and chills in the cinema. By this same rationale, the range of computer games, music and films which engage young people today will seem outdated and tame in terms of content and limited technologically in comparison to those available to future generations.

So placing texts in their contexts can help you to analyse their content more deeply, give further insight into how they are likely to be consumed and can also tell us something about the circumstances which affected their production. Contextualisation is a very valuable tool for comparing media texts, especially when they have been produced in different places or at different times. In the film *The Longest Day* (1962), for example, there are several scenes which show

American soldiers landing on the beaches of Normandy on D-Day during the Allied invasion of Europe towards the end of the Second World War. The same event is shown in *Saving Private Ryan* (1997) and although they both tell of the same event, visually there is a wealth of differences. The death of soldiers in battle as they land on the beach is shown in both films, but there is a visceral, gritty realism in the scenes in *Saving Private Ryan*. Limbs are blown off, wounded soldiers cry out in agony and the use of the handheld camera is highly effective in giving the audience a sense of participation. Overall, the effect is much more shocking and disturbing, and many critics praised the film as giving an accurate portrayal of the horror of war and of that particular event in particular. In one particularly emotive scene, a soldier who has lost one of his arms searches the ground for his lost limb. Upon finding it, he picks it up and continues further on to the beach. For added effect, the scene is played in slow motion and with muffled sound to emphasise the loss of a sense of reality experienced by Tom Hanks' character who witnesses the event. The fighting by contrast in *The Longest Day* seems much more sanitised, with action which contrasts vastly to those in *Saving Private Ryan*, most notably when an American general played by Robert Mitchum runs unarmed on to the beach and even has time to smoke a cigar throughout the battle. Fewer soldiers are shown dying and those who do appear to do so die immediately and in much less pain.

Some of these differences in this example may be attributed to the texts themselves; for example, the Normandy Landings is shown as an opening sequence in *Saving Private Ryan* while it is the climax of *The Longest Day*, but most of the differences are attributed to reasons which become evident upon examining contextualisation. *The Longest Day* was released only 18 years after the events of D-Day. Many of those who had participated in the war and the parents of the soldiers who had died would have been alive and formed part of the potential audience. It would be inappropriate to have shown such appalling and gruesome deaths to an audience for whom memories of the war and loss would have been so fresh. Furthermore, in 1962, the technology to allow complex special effects had not been developed, nor would the censors have allowed scenes of such violence and suffering. However, by 1997, the Second World War was less fresh in the filmgoing audience's mind, massive advances in special effects allowed for highly realistic scenes of injury and death, and the tolerance for violence and suffering in film from both the audiences and the censors had risen.

Although showing scenes from the same event, the Allied landings on the beaches of Normandy in June 1944, the films *The Longest Day* (left) and *Saving Private Ryan* (right) have many differences which may be explained in a number of ways. Most of these can be contextualised by taking into account the circumstances surrounding each film's production.

Figure 0.12 Scenes from *The Longest Day* (left) and *Saving Private Ryan* (right)

There is however a further context in terms of how war itself is represented in these two films. *Saving Private Ryan* was released at a time when many Americans had started to question the wisdom of their country's involvement in foreign wars. The overwhelming conclusion on the Vietnam War was that it had been a disaster for the USA whereas the outcome of the Second World War owes much to American involvement. To most commentators America came out of the Second World War somewhat more positively than it did from Vietnam, and after that campaign, war itself had become the enemy, and the madness and futility of war is one of the key areas explored in *Saving Private Ryan*. In *The Longest Day* war was represented much more positively. The soldiers go into the battle more willingly while war is shown as glorious and as a necessary means to achieve an end.

In addition to looking at the features of a media product which are shaped by historical contexts, as we have done with the previous example, the study of wider contexts can embrace the same period of time and look at how a product can impact upon other media types. Garnering much critical acclaim for its gritty and realistic representations of war, *Saving Private Ryan* seemed to reinvigorate the war genre and lay the foundations for further film releases such as *The Thin Red Line* (1998) and *Black Hawk Down* (2001), and also for the genre to embark upon a journey which would embrace a number of different media platforms. In a further collaboration between the film's director and star, Steven Spielberg and Tom Hanks joined forces to bring both *Band of Brothers* (2001) and *The Pacific* (2010) to TV screens. According to Spielberg, the medium of television removed the two- to three-hour time constraint that film imposed and allowed for much more story development. Widening the context of the war genre even further, technological improvements in the world of computer gaming have led to the same level of gritty realism in recent computer role-play games like *Modern Warfare* series in which players can interact with the war environment, make decisions with life-and-death consequences and experience the role of combat soldier from the safety of their own home. At the end of the first decade of the twenty-first century, with Britain and the USA engaged in war in Iraq and Afghanistan, the wider contexts which inform the war genre across a range of media types are still an important factor in their continued popularity.

INFORMATION BOX – NEW MEDIA IN ACTION *i*

Call of Duty 4: Modern Warfare, the computer game, shares features and is intertextual with films and TV shows which traditionally at least are perhaps more associated with the war genre.

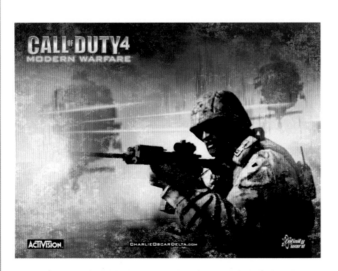

Figure 0.13 *Call of Duty 4: Modern Warfare*

Theoretical perspectives

The word 'theory' is used often enough to either send shivers down the spine of students or to instil them with a sense of boredom and tedium which does little but detract from the hands-on parts of the subject. To the modern student, theories in all subjects seem to fall into one of two categories: they have the reputation of appearing either blindingly obvious on the one hand or so complex that rather than providing elucidation, they muddy the water and make the topic about which the theory has been written even less easy to come to grips with.

The irony is that both of these points of view are equally valid. On the surface, some theories are fairly obvious while others are undeniably complex. Helpfully, or perhaps not, many of the theoretical perspectives relevant to Media Studies are found in other subjects, and so a GCE student of Media and, say, Sociology, Film Studies or English will find some cross-curricular links. It is likely that the discerning A2 level student will probably treat the wealth of theoretical perspectives in Media Studies with respect and disdain in equal measure. Once again, as we saw in the section on autonomy, there are opportunities for theories to be both praised and criticised so long as you can justify your stance within the relevant context of your area of study.

Whatever your own opinion of theory, there can be little doubt that the challenges which are posed in the final year of an A level course require you to have not only the knowledge of some key theoretical perspectives but also to have the ability to use them appropriately and with relevance in your work. It is useful to think of these perspectives as forming part of a toolkit into which you delve to take out the required tool when it is needed. When you are studying a certain medium, say, newspapers, it is not enough to simply write about the content, to comment upon the use of language, the political ideology implicit in the articles or to identify that there seems to be a large amount of American news without pulling out the required theoretical perspectives from your toolkit and linking them to the points you are making. It is these theories which will give your work a sense of substance. However, before looking more closely at these theoretical perspectives, it is worth noting at this point that overuse of theories, especially when it appears to be simply for the sake of it, is to be avoided, not least because without the knowledge and the correct application, your work can appear naive if not simply incorrect. There are many theoretical perspectives and, to be honest, there is unlikely to be a time when you will know all of them, since they have a tendency to emerge and evolve as time passes. Nevertheless, there are a number of key theoretical perspectives which A2 level students should be aware of and have at their disposal in their toolkit to draw upon while working at this level. The main theoretical perspectives which you will find the most relevant to your study of media are discussed more fully in Chapter 2.

References

McKee, R. (1997) Classic five-part narrative taken from McKee's story seminar at Northern Alberta Institute of Technology.
Todorov, T. (1969) *Grammaire du Décameron*. The Hague, Mouton.
Winship, J. (1987) *Inside Women's Magazines*. London, Pandora.

DEVELOPING TEXTUAL ANALYSIS

In the Introduction we explain some of the ways in which you need to move up a gear in your approach to the media in converting your AS approach to new A2 thinking. The purpose of this chapter is to help you make that important transition. Note that the title is 'Developing textual analysis', not replacing or abandoning but developing. That means that textual analysis is still important. Media products, or 'texts' as we will call them when we are talking about analysis, are important forensic materials in any discussion of the media. Just as a biologist relies on working with laboratory specimens to support more abstract hypotheses, so a media student needs to work closely with the actual output of the media both to begin any critical investigation and to support any hypothesis that may emerge from such a study. What this chapter should show you is how you can take a text or group of texts as a starting point and then move to a broader understanding by considering some of the wider contexts that make media productions the way they are. This is an especially important skill that will help you in tackling the first part of the MEST3 exam paper where you will be asked to make a comparison of two texts the starting point for further investigation. (See Chapter 4, p. 178).

So in the transition from AS to A2 Media Studies you need to reflect on what your course has thus far added up to, what it has equipped you to do: 'What does it enable me to do that I couldn't do already?'

One answer to this question will almost certainly concern critical skills. You have, in fact, spent much of your AS year dealing with the different ways in which mass media products, from 'SUN SAYS' editorials to computer game covers, can be approached, seen and analysed. These 'readings' may be semiotic (see Introduction), focus on the technical codes of a specific medium (e.g. framing or *mise-en-scène*) or concerned with genre (such as soap opera or teen drama) or issues of representation (age and gender).

What you will have developed are your skills in reading texts. You know you are a Media Studies student because you are able to respond to the text below in a particular way.

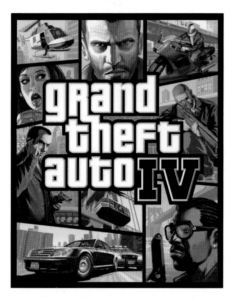

Figure 1.1 *Grand Theft Auto IV*

ACTIVITY

As an AS student you will be able to construct a detailed analysis of the cover of *Grand Theft Auto IV*.

Initial response:

- Look at the cover as a whole – what are the most prominent features?
- What other media forms does this layout of scenes remind you of?
- What is the relationship between words and image?
- Do the images appeal to you?
- Are you familiar with the imagery – with the game itself?

Textual analysis:

1. Choose three of the scenes from the cover, and for each scene make notes on the following: subject matter, *mise-en-scène*, framing and angle.
2. Using your notes, identify three key points on the representation of gender (male and female) on the cover. Consider whether you think the representations reinforce or subvert stereotypes.
3. What narrative is set up in the front cover? Make reference to typical characters, setting, actions.
4. How would you categorise the game by genre? There is more than one approach to this – consider the media form, the type of game, as well as the plot, setting and character.
5. What does the front cover tell you about the audience? Analyse the mode of address (with reference to words and images) of the cover – who do you think the target audience is? In identifying the audience, make reference to segmentation and psychographic variables.

Moving on from an AS approach

As an A2 student you will need to develop this analysis further, taking into account a range of contexts and approaches which can add to your understanding of the text. In other words, what doesn't the detailed textual analysis of the cover of *GTA IV* tell us?

One of the most pressing contexts is that provided by the internet and new digital media, which has eclipsed our thinking about almost every aspect of media and culture. For a discipline that has sought always to address those forms where the mass audience gathers, the latest figures for computer gaming may come as an unpalatable shock. The fact that unprecedented numbers of teenagers (of all ages) (in excess of 95 per cent of 14–17-year-olds) are contributing to an industry worth twice as much as the music industry has led to a debate among academics and teachers about exactly what Media Studies is as a subject.

Wider contexts: production and distribution

The text that you have begun to analyse in the previous activity is the cover of a leading computer game franchise and as such is the product of a particular set of contexts. The contexts of production and distribution will be a major part of your study at A2 and cannot be understood just by analysing the front cover and these issues.

> **PRODUCTION** the production stage refers to the developers or pro-
> ducers of a media text (e.g. Hollywood as the producer of blockbusters,
> the BBC as the producer of TV news programmes).
>
> **DISTRIBUTION** the distributor is an organisation which mediates
> between the producer and exhibitor to make the text available for
> consumption by an audience. For example, in film the distributor is the
> link between a film producer and the exhibitor (cinema, DVD, TV, etc.),
> who ensures that the film is seen by the widest audience possible. In
> media the term 'distribution' also refers to the *marketing* and advertising
> of media texts.

In the contemporary media world of global conglomerates it has become more difficult to distinguish between these stages – this is clear when looking at our example of *GTA IV*.

ACTIVITY

Production and distribution of *GTA IV*

How would you research the production and distribution contexts of this computer game?

■ Which institution produced GTA IV? There may be more than one (clue – the company logos are usually on the cover). Can you make a distinction between the institution which produces the game and the technology it's played on?

Analysis of the production context of *GTA IV*

The *GTA* series was designed and developed by Rockstar North. This is a British company – the headquarters are in Edinburgh – which has also designed other popular games including *Manhunt* and *Lemmings*. The company is a part (a subsidiary) of a larger company, Rock Star Games. Rock Star Games is a publisher of games developed by other people rather than an originator of material. In turn Rock Star Games is owned by Take Two Interactive, an American developer, pub-lisher and distributor of video games.

Distribution context

A study of the distribution contexts of games includes some of the key contemporary media debates:

■ The competition between a few dominant conglomerates
■ The effects of new technology on revenue and profits.

The distribution context here is concerned with the future of online technology. How long will games be distributed on disc and sold in shops or online? The position of game distribution today is similar to film and music industries 10 years ago.

In considering the effects of this changing distribution context you could start by asking who would benefit from the move to entirely online distribution and who would lose.

ACTIVITY

Distribution and new technology

How would new distribution techniques affect:

■ Consumers?
■ Manufacturers of games consoles and discs?
■ Game publishers?

Some suggestions:

Consumers:

■ Online distribution should be cheaper than the purchase of discs (unlike films or music, games are difficult – though not impossible – to illegally copy due to the large amount of memory required for sharing and storage). There would no longer be the need to buy a console.
■ Greater variety – gamers can play a range of games without having to purchase them.
■ Instant access – select and play through the TV, so no longer a need to buy a disc first.

continued

Manufacturers:

- Loss of revenue from obsolete consoles. The companies (Sony, Nintendo, Microsoft) also sell games which are exclusive to their own consoles – they will lose that captive audience as online gaming is not restricted to a specific console.

Publishers:

- Publishers would probably be able to keep a greater portion of the revenue from digital downloads as the revenue no longer needs to be shared with the console manufacturer.
- Because digital distribution has no disc there will be a reduction in the used game market – this is also good for publishers.

From the reference to distribution and production contexts it should be clear how at A2 textual analysis is merely the starting point for a reading of a text. The next development is in the study of the audience. Building on the work on target audience that you are used to from AS, Media Studies has developed new ways of talking about audience.

Performance context: how is a media text used?

This context represents a shift in our approach to reading a media text; rather than analysing the text from a distance (as we did with the cover of *GTA IV*) the performance context is a reflective approach, asking how people use a text and how it works. This relies much more on the idea of participation – how real people respond to media texts.

In their work on the experience of gaming, McDougall and O'Brien have devised a list of categories to suggest the different experiences participants have in playing games. Many of these refer to the way gamers use the world of the game to create and 'try on' new identities.

- *Gaming as performance*
  Gaming is conventionally seen as a solitary occupation but the idea of 'gaming as performance' suggests that the experience is as much to do with performing skilfully and developing a particular style of gaming for the benefit of those watching. The knowledge of being watched playing *GTA IV* is likely to change the way in which the game is played.

  The performance aspect of gaming is also affected by where the game is played. The 'video' arcade, although seemingly an old-fashioned place to play games, provides some of the best opportunities to perform – and to watch. The blogger *chewingpixels.com* writes about the particular pleasures of the arcade:

> **a perceptive gamer can tell a great many things about the men competing at Street Fighter. And Street Fighter, like Dance Dance Revolution, or Raiden 3 or any other game that allows the performer the chance to exhibit flair, technique and character, is a game best played in public. Here the stakes are raised and the narrative becomes a communal one; the resulting stories are unforgettable.**

▓ *Carnivalesque*
One of the pleasures of any kind of play is the aspect of pretending; escaping to the world of 'what if?' This form of escapism can provide a period of freedom from the rules of conventional behaviour. In this definition of experience gamers are in an ambiguous place – neither real nor completely fantastic.

▓ *Frivolity – playing, picking and mixing*
Games are often assumed to focus on darker, more violent aspects of society but participants discuss much lighter, more frivolous aspects to gaming. Examples of this may be seen in the way gamers discuss the enjoyable aspects of the games – flying, pet battles, fashionable 'vanity' clothes to wear over armour, designing tattoos, etc.

▓ *Morality*
The assumption is that the world of most games is morally corrupting. In fact many gamers talk about the moral dimension of their game identities and performances – for example, see the discussion 'Should Morality be Applied to Gaming' at http://www.cheatcc.com/extra/moralityandvideogames2.html. The arguments around morality and gaming will be familiar to you from effects debates in film. It is important to consider these debates within the specific context of the game – the reward for a violent act is about power in the game – not an ethical debate.

▓ *The 'Baroque Showman'*
Baroque originally refers to a style of architecture and music from the seventeenth century which had a flamboyant and highly ornamented style. The term has come to be associated with any form (e.g. in art, fashion, writing) which is elaborate, decorative and extravagant.

In your analysis of the representation of gender on the cover for *GTA IV* you probably noted the reinforcement of gender stereotypes – the rugged, macho man with big guns, the attractive female with long hair and pouting red lips. Your ideas about genre and narrative would probably also make reference to the expected roles of gangster and sex object. The idea of the 'Baroque Showman' suggests that there is a different way of interpreting these roles – the gender characteristics are so extreme and exaggerated in their traditional roles that they can no longer be taken seriously. This then allows gamers to try on and play with these representations – as subject (first-person position) and as object.

This research into games emphasises the way in which players experience the world of the game, how they play it. This is clear in the following extract with a player writing 'in' rather than just 'about' *Liberty City*. He begins:

> **Starting the game from scratch isn't easy. Anyway, in between trying to sort this, this being a GTA game, I decide to take a walk down the street and fight some random passers-by. Got beaten up by a girl at one point couldn't learn how to fight fast enough. Once I master the art of street fighting, it's back to driving the car round Liberty City. By now, about 40 minutes into playing, I'm picking up the thread a bit I can drive, I can fight and this starts to impress the ladies.**

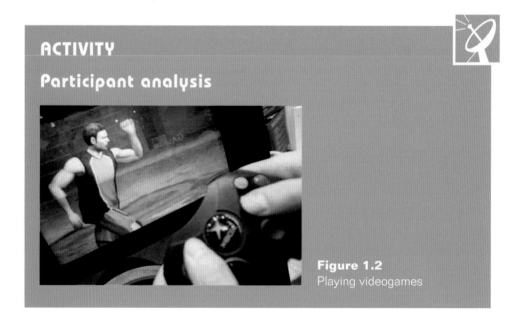

ACTIVITY

Participant analysis

Figure 1.2
Playing videogames

1. Choose two games which you regularly play. They should be contrasting in some way – the difference might be the genre, format or platform (e.g. RPG and a Strategy game, a PSP and Xbox game).

   Your aim is to produce a commentary of your experience of playing the two games. The following are some suggestions of areas that you could consider.

   - When do you play the game? Is it a particular time of day? Do you choose the game depending on what kind of mood you're in?
   - Where do you play? Are you usually alone or with friends?
   - Which aspects of the game do you find easy? Does this make playing the game more pleasurable or boring?
   - Are you aware of the games designer's plans as you play? If so how do you respond to this?
   - If it's a game which includes violent actions how do you respond to these?
   - How would you describe your relationship to the central character in the game?

   Finish your commentary by writing up – or recording – your thoughts (300 words).

2. Choose a film that you're familiar with and watch the opening sequence and try the same exercise. How is the experience of watching different to playing?

   Consider the following:

   - What are the differences in your responses to the characters? Think about identification, sympathy. Are the characters attractive (appearance and actions)? What do you know about their personality?
   - What is the difference between narrative in film and computer games? Do you know what will happen next? How does this affect the way you play/watch?
   - Are you aware of the filmmaker's intentions as you watch?
   - Do you think the term *participant* applies to you when you watch a film?

   The final stage of the activity would be to summarise your ideas in a comparison of the different experiences of the 'audience' for games and films.

Suggestions for further work

Reception context

A further way to develop our understanding of a media text would be to analyse its reception – how it was received by fans, critics, non-users:

▥ Like films, games are extensively reviewed on release (see *Official Xbox Magazine, Game Spot*, etc.).

▥ There are many online forums where gamers discuss their reactions to new games (e.g. gamerforums.proboards.com, computerandvideogames.com).

▥ Games are a controversial media form in the wider society and there will be press coverage of games as well as reports produced by various interested groups such as psychologists, educationalists and politicians (e.g. see *The Byron Review* into the effect of games on children at http://www.dcsf.gov.uk/byronreview and 'Video Games are Good for Children' at http://www.guardian.co.uk/technology/2009/feb/12/computer-games-eu-study).

Developing an analysis in this way demonstrates the different ways in which media texts are appropriated and used by their audiences. It helps us to understand that texts are polysemic, capable of different meanings for different audiences. It also suggests that these different interpretations are never neutral but always shaped by particular experiences and interests.

To read more about new developments in Media Studies and the theories which underpin them go to the companion website.

Take a look back at what we said in the Introduction about A2 study. One thing you need to learn to do is to take a step back from analysing media products in themselves and take a step forward into looking at the contexts that influence the production and consumption of these products. A very simple way of reminding yourself of this is to think about not *how* products are constructed but to consider *why* they have been constructed the way they have. *Why* is always a more difficult question in Media Studies and probably life in general.

So the case studies in this chapter will exemplify this approach. We offer a set of common prompts which provide your agenda for A2 Media Studies.

Products are meant to be starting points for broad and varied discussions and explorations, and not simply stores of information to be visited on guided tours. We have, of course, carefully chosen our set of examples to lead certain discussions that we are interested in having with you. When it comes to making your own choice of products to explore, you should bear in mind the discussions you want to have and the ideas you want to consider. Making an appropriate choice from the start can have a positive influence on the outcome of your study.

These worked-through examples provide a foundation for A2 study but must be supplemented by examples of your own. Go to our website for more prompts for further investigation. Shared texts provide a starting point which, in the case of this chapter, show how arguments about a given industry or platform can be developed. These 'maps' will require further features to be added.

All media texts contain coded information about everything, from the way in which they were made and 'sold', to their outlook and values and ultimately to the values of the culture that produced them. However, this information can only be meaningful within the contexts of other texts. It makes little sense, for example, to give an analysis of the radio experience provided by Chris Moyles without some appreciation of what else radio is doing and can do.

The 'discipline', and ultimately the real value of Media Studies, is provided by the key concepts, a set of good ideas that often reveal about media products what we thought we already knew. These are the critical tools that will always give us a starting point for any investigation of 'media'. They explain and reveal what A2 study is all about. One way to consider them as a whole is to create a simple description of what it is that we do.

> Media texts REPRESENT the worlds we inhabit through multiple NARRATIVES, FORMS and GENRES. In doing so they epitomise INDUSTRIAL practices (production, marketing, distribution) which are bound up with media TECHNOLOGIES and their development. These processes provide AUDIENCES with experiences that shape their IDENTITIES and are shaped by them.
>
> At the same time much is revealed and constructed about the VALUES and IDEOLOGIES of contemporary culture.

Of course in this digital age of increasing convergence texts are often trans-media and cross-platform carrying multiple identities.

Dr Who, for example, has become a flagship show for the BBC by being what former Director-General Mark Thompson claimed was 'the BBC's most successful attempt at turning a transmedia strategy into a successful and sustainable reality'. This is not merely about marketing but about storytelling which finds form in novelisations, fan fictions, webcasts, radio versions, multichannel television, even TARDISODES (for mobile phone use) as well as the re-established Saturday evening slot. Websites have become a staple for most TV and film presentations with ITV's *A Touch of Frost* recently ending a run of 18 years with online alternative endings.

A seemingly simple franchise like *The X Factor*, for example, demonstrates why A2 study is principally a series of starting points, of issues and *debates*.

Primetime Saturday evening programme *The X Factor* features the progress of a nationwide talent competition from mass regional auditions to a pre-Christmas spectacular final over two nights. Working principally within the formats of reality TV, a generic hybrid of documentary and variety show, it offers multiple narratives wrapped up inside an old-fashioned rags-to-riches story. It is, however, as much about its Kingpin Simon Cowell and his new Geordie queen Cheryl Cole as it is about the contestants. Cowell's concept is a business model using trans-media 'storytelling' to substantiate the X factor experience and market it as a thing in itself (a show with, as it were, the X factor). The 90-minute show has increasingly become a small if vital part of an experience that happens 'around it' in spin-offs and across social networks and blogs.

At a time of falling primetime audiences, the show boasts typical viewing figures in excess of 19 million while reinforcing a secondary audience for ITV's own digital channels widely available via Freeview. Moreover, its importance as a media text is confirmed by the negative responses of media analysts and cultural critics. It is often dismissed as 'Cowell's Karaoke'.

INFORMATION BOX – THE PRICE OF FAME?

A popular campaign against its domination of the Christmas charts resulted in an unexpected championing of the unlikely but aptly titled Rage Against the Machine to number one in December 2009. 'Killing in the Name' contained a clear message to Cowell and his like: 'FUCK YOU! I won't do what you tell me!'

Clearly *The X Factor* has the potential to open up a wide range of discussions not only about the state of contemporary television but more widely about media technology and about our culture and its values. Some of these issues will be explored across the rest of this chapter, in one case with the programme itself as a marginal context (see pp. 53–4).

We begin our 'developing' textual analysis with an understanding of what this 'developing' is making visible. The texts are arranged in groups according to the media industries that produced them and each is prefixed by an introduction identifying what we might consider interesting and significant themes and trends.

film: computer-generated infancy?

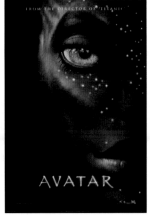

Figure 1.3 Left to right: *Twilight: New Moon*, *Avatar* and *Looking for Eric*

When watching *Avatar* it has become important to distinguish which version you saw. This is no longer a matter of which print (director's cut, uncut, fancut) but a matter of context and equipment (and therefore opportunity). Is this 2D, 3D or full iMax experience? If we want shock and awe, we may need to go where the critics went to see it:

Avatar: what the critics said (when they liked it):

> For true cinematic spectacle, *Avatar* is out of this world.
> Anita Singh (*Daily Telegraph*)

> Is *Avatar* worth seeing? Yes, on a big screen in 3D because it really is spectacular. The Na'vi are more expressive than any previous examples of motioncapture technology, except Gollum in *The Lord Of The Rings*.
> Christopher Tookey (*Daily Mail*)

> *Avatar* truly is something else, a wondrously-detailed visual extravaganza quite unlike anything you've seen before.
> David Edwards (*Daily Mirror*)

> The effects of *Avatar* are certainly something to see, especially on an Imax screen the size of an upended football field. But it's difficult to tell if the game has really been changed or not.
> Peter Bradshaw (*Guardian*)

On the popular film criticism site Rotten Tomatoes, *Avatar* received positive approval ratings 80 per cent-plus from both the site's users (film fans of various kinds) and from 'Top Critics' like those above. However, an interesting issue which arises from these and from those below who didn't quite get it is the degree of predictability in all these responses. What is being discussed here is an issue, not a text, and there is a strong feeling that the taking of sides is based as much on principle as on response.

Avatar: what the critics said (when they didn't like it):

Avatar is overlong, dramatically two-dimensional, smug and simplistic.
Andy Morris (*GQ Magazine*)

Avatar is a phenomenon you can't ignore, monumentally imposing and done with extraordinary expertise – but the same could be said of the Dubai skyline, and I'm not sure that represents any future worth investing in.
Jonathan Romney (*Independent on Sunday*)

It's an achievement to make 3D look as good as it does here, but that counts for little if the characters are all in 1D. The film is a triumph of effects over affect.

Sukhdev Sandhu (*Daily Telegraph*)

ACTIVITY

How special are these effects?

At some level the history of cinema is the story of a developing technology delivering ever more 'special' effects. These 'how did they do that?' moments are on the increase in contemporary films but are a feature of even the earliest films. Spectators of the 1920s, for example, marvelled at Buster Keaton's apparently underwater encounter with a gigantic (and obviously rubber) swordfish in his film *The Navigator*, for which he'd borrowed a ship from the US Navy. However, any film that is chiefly remembered for such issues is possibly not a very good film.

Make two lists of films with particular visual impact from your life collection (all you've seen), headed 'Spectacular failures' and 'Specially effective' and then discuss the difference between the two sets. You might like to start with *Avatar*, which has been put in both columns in the reviews above.

It's as if the 'spectacle', the sum of the film and all its works, has swallowed the film. Created by the budget, the backstory (Cameron waiting 16 years until the technology was in place: a tale without a tale), the jaw-dropping special effects (leaked in part but also kept under wraps) and more particularly an orgy of marketing and merchandising, this film's story was monomaniacal. Forget the actors, forget the motion capture, I'm the new game, stating the art, redefining the 'immersive experience of cinema': I'm style, I'm form, I'm (for the second time) 'King of the World'. And so we need to take sides, and by doing so the spectacle and what it means are confirmed.

How often has the thought crossed your mind when watching the latest Hollywood blockbuster: 'That must have cost a packet!'/'I can see where the money was spent!' This is not to make any judgements about the film, any more than many of the critics above were doing. At best what is being responded to is effect, its 'awe'. We are to be 'immersed', amazed, overawed and certainly impressed, all of which are things done to us, if we allow.

Avatar is of course much more than a slice of mainstream consumption; it is an event, a phenomenon. With the lines drawn before the film premiered it feels almost impossible to return the film to the status of a text that might in some way be useful to us, let alone be reasonably evaluated. Andrew Pulver summed up this mood in the *Guardian* when he wrote:

> Whether *Avatar* is any good barely seems to matter. When the film was first released, reviewers appeared unable to resist the mounting anticipation, and disgorged oceans of admiring prose. I can't say I joined in the acclaim. I felt compelled to write a less-than-complimentary review, which resulted in streams of abuse on aggregator sites such as Rotten Tomatoes, and I've since been tagged, not entirely correctly, as 'the guy that doesn't like *Avatar*'.

Avatar, whatever its merits, exists partly in this context which has little to do with film as such and much to do with a society and culture that is becoming progressively infantalised. The shades between childlike and childish are progressively less clear. Visiting the *Avatar* official website we are greeted by 'the thrill of it all', this primitive event for which the world has been long awaiting. We are also alerted to the merchandising potentials of the film, particularly 'Avatar: the game', which blurs the line further. Five years ago barely anyone knew what an avatar was; now it represents, through online gaming, the emergence of computer gaming from nerd-backwater to mainstream. 'You've watched the game now play the game' it might intone, as we contemplate the number of computer game films we've watched in recent years. The world of the Na'vi, Pandora, gets opened for us by the film and we step, almost literally, into another world where we get to see things differently. This is partly a cleansing of the doors of perception moment but it is more 'trippy' than trip. Yes, we can learn something from these guys since in Disney terms they 'paint with all the colours of the wind'.

ACTIVITY

Film as computer game/computer game as film

Ever since Disney's groundbreaking but virtually unwatchable *Tron*, cinema and gaming have existed hand-in-hand. Action films all seem to have the obligatory first-person shooter, which sell around the time of the film's release and then disappear. From about the time of Super Mario Brothers, games have also provided characters and stories for a range of films.

Which films are there specifically which use games as their 'template'?

Why are they not very good?

How are films like and unlike computer games?

It's a little cheap to write the film off as 'Pocahontas in space'. With so few stories to tell it's inevitable that every film has a narrative displaced from somewhere else. *The Lion King* was, after all, 'Hamlet in Africa', and no one minded. I guess the more critical point is the one about the Disneyfication of culture, which is not so much 'dumbing down' as 'schmalzing out'. The mass audience is not so much becoming younger as younger at heart, with a little help from the Hollywood machine. Five years ago the criticism was that mainstream had become 'teen'. Interestingly the other 'monster' (pun intended) hit of 2009 was a (bona fide) teen movie, the second in the Twilight franchise.

It's fair to say that *New Moon*, as a film experience, has very little of the quirky charm of its independently made 'older sister' *Twilight*, though it did boast the biggest opening night of any film in US history. It is interesting though because it tells another version of the 'where film is now' story. Here is a film with a niche market, specifically 'teen' and 'girl', confounding the market and spawning a merchandising feed-frenzy. Its 'niche-ness' is best proved by the fact that not many outside of that audience seemed to get it at all. I suspect this bemusement is shared by the town of Forks (population 3,000), the film's setting, which has reputedly welcomed 67,000 'Twi-hard' film-tourists.

It prompted the *Independent* less than a week after the film's opening to employ a teenage girl, Ella Thorold, to explain the phenomenon to its readers. This was juxtaposed in the paper with a piece detailing the money being made by the franchise and largely deriding the talents of *Twilight* author Stephanie Meyer, 'a devout, somewhat reclusive, 35-year old Mormon, who lives in small town Arizona'. Consider this as a piece of representation alongside the expectation 'what successful media folks are meant to be like'!

It also did little to endear itself to a demographic that the quality press are supposed desperately to need (anyone under 40) by dismissing the USP of the tetralogy (there are four of them) as a 'breathless girly perspective'. Furthermore they got their 'middle-aged white bloke' feature writer John Walsh to write a fairly unfunny piece on what is meant to happen to teenage girls in vampire films. This view may have fairly identifiable ideological implications. John Walsh: 'The vampire tale used to be a mix of bats, blood, cleavage and snobbery.'

> **Vampires never did much in the way of chat or charm, but they trapped women in the palms of their manicured hands simply by looking at them, and left them either dead or gibbering with lust. Serving wenches with chests that strained against drawstring blouses went weak at the knees when confronted by these sneery aristocrats, and wound up dead behind the counter at The Inn. Posh teenage girls (for which read 'virgins') in skimpy peignoirs were mesmerised by the implicit threat of sexual jiggery-pokery, and became transformed into wanton sluts.**

In this context Walsh finds *New Moon* inexplicable. He presents the plot as follows:

> **Edward cannot shag Bella, for fear of making her join the undead. Bella takes up with Jacob, a secret were-wolf, who cannot shag Bella for fear of tearing her throat out. So Bella spends the film undebauched, untransformed and staggeringly uninteresting. She's defined only by what she can't (or won't) do. Eventually, you start to wonder, ungallantly, how much fun Bella would be in the sack, with her permanent sulk and her air of injured propriety.**

Staggeringly, Walsh, though tongue in cheek, complains that 'it's shocking to see a noble tradition being monkeyed about with, in order to persuade nervous teen girls that modern boys – even modern monsters – are full of conscience, responsibility and remorse.' Ella Thorold unwittingly provides a right to reply with an unpretentious and elegant account of what its audience might think. She starts simply:

> It is easy for me to see the appeal of this film. First and foremost, *New Moon* contains two of the most lustworthy male actors in the world in the form of Robert Pattinson (Edward) and Taylor Lautner (Jacob).

She admits these appeals are 'shallow', but there's more than enough 'shallow appeal' served up by Hollywood to teenage lads (of all ages). Her further analysis raises more interesting questions (alongside *Avatar*) of where film is going at the beginning of the second decade of century twenty-one:

> *The Twilight Saga: New Moon* is essentially an old-fashioned love story, which somehow incorporates attractive vampires and werewolves into the mix. It is ironic how the actors are sexualised to the extreme in this film, when the underlying theme is essentially abstinence. This theme, which openly clashes with today's society, is part of the allure of *New Moon*. In any other teen flick, two 17-year-olds who didn't have sex would be quite a novelty, but for *New Moon*, it separates itself from its clichéd counterparts in its genre. It is for this reason that the audiences of these books and films have such a wide age range. Young girls can watch this film while maintaining their innocence, teenagers can watch this film and allow themselves to feel the pain yet excitement of a first love secondhand, and older women can reminisce about true love.

There is potentially an awful lot of wisdom here about mass media audiences. She is also interesting on the issue of perspective ("breathless girly"):

> Bella in the book is very relatable, and this again is another reason for the popularity of the books, but Stewart has managed to capture this incredibly well. She is not cool, or popular, or a cheerleader, she is simply a normal girl, and this is what teenage girls can

relate to so easily. So many young girls can project themselves on to her, and her introverted, shy, unassuming character is something I feel was needed in the world of teenage cinema before it was completely taken over by the likes of Vanessa Hudgens (*High School Musical*) and Miley Cyrus (*Hannah Montana*), and Stewart has allowed this to happen beautifully.

Here is some evidence to perhaps begin to make our analysis more balanced. Perhaps then we can take seriously Ella Thorold's conclusion that 'To many, *New Moon* is not just a cheesy, teenage love story with vampires and werewolves, but instead something which they can relate to, and really understand.'

At least if we wanted to take *New Moon* 'on board' it was not difficult to do so. A surprise, and limited hit of 2009 which offers a further alternative view on mainstream film was harder to find. I went to see *Looking for Eric*, the hilarious and critically acclaimed collaboration between veteran British auteur Ken Loach and footballing genius and style icon Eric Cantona at a hideously theme-parkish multiplex on the outskirts of Birmingham in the middle of the night. Distribution, or lack of it, was the most significant issue, meaning the film had very much a 'dedicated' audience. Given this film was getting four- and five-star reviews across the popular press (*Heat* magazine called it a 'wonderful feel-good hit'), this suggests a set of commercial expectations which find it difficult to adapt to variations in film fayre.

ACTIVITY

Multiplex playlists

What we see at the cinema depends on more than our inclination. Not every film is shown everywhere. Audience statistics often record the number of screens at which the film is being offered. This is something of a self-fulfilling prophecy as those films with most screens crudely get most spectators, thus proving it was right to give them so many screens! This means that in any given week the average multi-screen cinema may be delivering a little less than its '20 screen = 20 films' 'logic'.

Get hold of a weekly multiplex film listing and record against each billed film the number of screens it's being shown on. Now rank the films according to the number of screenings that week and crudely calculate the percentage of total screenings for each of the five most widely screened films, both individually and as a set of five. Now write about how multiple the multiplex offer really is.

This suggests a continuing set of fairly rigid delineations between different kinds of film 'categories' which are meant to provide different kinds of film experience to different kinds of film audience. The lines are drawn in terms of progressively unclear and imprecise understandings of what once was 'mainstream' (popular, commercial) and 'alternative' (independent, arthouse), not only in terms of a public debate but also in terms of production, distribution and exhibition. Thankfully Loach has always been better appreciated on mainland Europe than in Britain, hence the variety of revenue streams contributing to the film's production, but it is somewhat depressing that this "beautiful story about loyalty, trust and friendship" (*News of the World*) didn't find a wider audience.

Loach made his name in the early 1960s with the much-talked-about *Cathy Come Home*, which highlighted the problems of homelessness and was credited with changing the law in this area. Television at that time, with only two channels, was able to offer thoughtful quality stuff to a mass audience intensively. In 2009 this "warm, witty and wise" film (*Daily Mirror*) enjoyed only a limited release despite working through similar contexts as a film like *The Full Monty* (which might also have deserved the warm, witty and wise tag). While the footballing connection may have attracted a few inquisitive film novices, *Looking for Eric* is not really a film about football at all. It is a lovingly bleak reflection on ordinary life in our increasingly brutal inner cities, where many, to take Thoreau's words, "lead lives of quiet desperation".

One of the problems is that Loach doesn't use stars, and stars are the most valuable commodity in the marketing of films, both as concepts and as finished products. Aside from the wayward French footballer, the most recognisible face in the film is John Henshaw's, and he is best known for a series of Royal Mail commercials on TV. This means that despite the significant slice of fantasy (where even Cantona is 'measured'), a grainy northern realism pervades the film, which is grounded, human and, consistently foul-mouthed. Given the villain is an all-too-believable Manchester gangster, it's hardly going to be polite! However, while we have a place for the 'motherfucker' street gang film and the 'Life's grim oop North' gig and the 'will-they-won't-they' rom-com we don't have much of a context for all of them together. In addition, stories of not very attractive types seem always harder to sell, however 'heart-warming' they are.

Again there's a sense in which genre is becoming less and less viable as a critical tool. This is not about genre but rather about narrative, and about complexity and intensity. In the end the story is simple but the experience is substantial and intense; many critics talked about 'heart and soul'. The message is delivered with pathos by one of football's great individualists. When postman Eric Bishop asks Cantona to name his favourite football moment he chooses not a goal but a pass which led to a goal for a team mate. "You must trust your team mates," the Frenchman intones: "without this we're lost."

TV: the art of re-invention

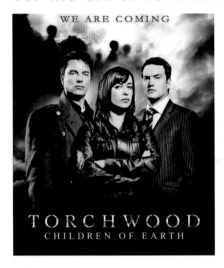

Figure 1.4 Left to right: *Torchwood Series 3: Children of Earth*, *The Apprentice* and *Peep Show*

Most English town centres of the 1970s bore a variation of this graffiti: 'SAVE OUR CINEMA'. Stourbridge, a middle-sized town between Birmingham and Worcester, had three picture houses; now it has none. Yet cinema was not killed by TV any more than TV, despite the power of Buggles' argument in *Video Killed the Radio Star* (and the crazy video), killed radio, or the internet has killed magazines. Amazingly, we've gone in 40 years from worrying about what television is doing to society to worrying about what social and technological changes have done to 'our' television. Was it television's fate to become merely a reminder of a former time, like those electric and gas fires in centrally heated houses that people buy and never use? Some have called it the nation's 'hearth'. After all, the fire and television do for the home what the church and pub do for a rural village.

The reasons that television survives as a mass cultural experience into the new century's second decade are many and complex, but one stands out. It is the fact that television occupies a specific, one might say special, position within our culture, and in this singular sense it did usurp radio. While it has been mythologised as much as the piano in Victorian homes around which the family would sing, no social history of the twentieth century could ignore the impact of TV. Whether you visit a living museum of the twentieth century or your local IKEA, rooms, our 'living' spaces, are orientated around the 'gogglebox /all-seeing eye/etc.' No other medium has so many different names, which suggests something with which we have an uncomfortable perhaps love–hate relationship. When we speak of television therefore we are addressing very much an extended signifier, which operates semiotically something like this.

Television

Denotes: the technical equipment, all of its output, a mass medium.

Connotes: something oppositional: a source of information and entertainment, an asset and a danger, a social activity.

Myth: much of the above is enshrined, in particular the dichotomy of 'help' and harm'. Television presents 'social values not social reality' to which others have added 'as if there were' as a substitute for 'not'. This unhelpfully reduces TV to its content and makes all of its issues issues of representation.

Marshall McLuhan wrote cleverly about technology and, even when his arguments don't quite convince, they pose interesting questions. He was particularly interested in the ways in which communication technologies developed in relation to one another and in relation to our needs and intentions. He theorised these relationships in a model he dubbed 'the tetrad' (because it has four parts). Actually they are four questions to ask of any communication technological innovation:

■ What will it enhance?
■ What will it impair?
■ What will it recover/rejuvenate?
■ What will it make obsolete?

Following a succession of innovations it seemed, on the surface, that television as we had known it was likely to find itself in slot 4's obsolescence. We'd had ever more affordable and powerful home computers and ultimately laptops, films and now even the programmes themselves on demand, ever-more powerful games machines, mobile phones and internet access, personalised video recorders (like Sky+) and on top of all this the internet itself, an unassailable visual archive. All of these devices might have rationally contributed to a slow but terminal decline in the importance of television. In fact there is a counter-argument which suggests that television is in a particularly healthy state and that its apparent competitors have paradoxically become its most significant benefactors. To understand why this set of events produced this rather unexpected set of results, we need to first remind ourselves of some key audience theories. We might summarise these as being of three types:

■ Text-based (effects) theories
■ Use and gratifications theories
■ Context-centred theories.

In the context of new, better, more visceral means of communication 'effect' and of infinitely greater access to all the information and entertainment, the first two sets offer little help. Both sets also address television solely as a broadcast medium, a technological means to address the 'general public'. If 'the medium is the message', this one has been outdone, overtaken by better ways to do its turn. Now, from the moment Atari patented the first games machine on which glowing squares were batted around the screen, television has provided a channel for a variety of stuff. And yet we effectively forget that what we watch on television is often not television, and research has suggested that the more we watch television of any kind the more live stuff we are likely to see. Paradoxically, for example, the use of PVRs (Sky+, etc.) actually increased the amount of television watched. Similarly the massive popularity of games machines that need screens, the bigger the better, have in some cases returned TVs to use. The medium once again is the message.

However, there is also something more significant going on that is clear from the work of context-centred theorists like Morley and Lush. Fiske summed up this approach very clearly when he wrote: "The important thing is rather than trying to understand what the text is, is trying to understand how people use it." Lull and his team of observers, for example, watched the behaviour of viewers in 200 American households. As a result Lull makes an important distinction between users of television which he describes as structural and relational.

▨ The *structural* uses are about answering particular needs such as the need for information and entertainment, or even company when alone. Here there is a direct relationship between the viewer and the programming.

▨ The *rational* uses were much more to do with organising the life of the home and the relationships within it. People used television as a regular social ritual, the context for a group discussion, even a way of being alone. Here the relationship between viewer and programming is indirect.

It is the second set of uses that has become increasingly significant both for mainstream broadcast scheduling and for significant innovations like the Nintendo Wii. For the latter the relative crudity and clunkiness of the graphics and game play (in the face of the almost virtual reality of Xbox and PlayStation 3) has been traded royally for the human interaction across demographic barriers. In addition, whereas the home Karaoke machine never broke retail records the game player franchises 'Singstar' and 'Lips', even 'Rock Band', are coining it. And at the centre of it all is the family and the TV: two age-old institutions.

For academic critics, for whom the F word has recently been Fragmentation, there is also the spectre of *The X Factor* and the highest paid performer on American TV, Simon Cowell. First, they find it difficult to appreciate (let alone like) the programme despite the fact that apparently those elusive folk, 'ordinary people', are watching it in literally their millions. 'Fragmentation' is essentially a negative reading of 'segmentation', masquerading as a viable all-embracing theory. It argues that multi-channel TV and all the attendant technologies for personalising viewing will inevitably undermine the mass audience with dire consequences for most of us in the medium to long term. These consequences reach out beyond the media sphere and into the wider society. They include:

▨ The extinction of the PSB tradition/strand, and ultimately, save on subscription to a few, of quality television content. The undermining of the old terrestrial flagship brands (this was also forecast at the original deregulation in the 1980s, along with Italian housewives stripping on TV).

- The ultimate end of the mass TV audience sharing significant experiences 'live'.
- All kinds of social ills resulting from the undermining of the family with each family member retreating to their own viewing station and a bare living.

Obviously this is an exaggeration of the more pessimistic readings but as Adorno pointed out it is often exaggeration that is needed to bring into "bold relief the tensions in a force-field". The force-field in this case is the notion that cultural change can be rationally plotted and predicted. It is precisely the irrationality of people and systems that makes the process so fascinating. When in 2009 *The X Factor* built an audience over a dozen weeks that peaked in the 'live' final at 19 million it ripped up most of the accumulated wisdom on the mass TV audience. Everyone looked for answers, though most looked in the wrong places. Naturally some saw *The X Factor* as a special text (or especially dangerous) and then either over-respected its 'homely charm' or senselessly slipped back to models of mass manipulation, the hoodwinked audience. This analysis didn't get very far simply because the format is in fact fairly simple: a jury consisting of two wise older men and two presentable younger women judge as a dozen champions of the British public (chosen by Destiny) almost literally (and in a positive way) sing for their lives (or at least for the right to trade theirs in for a better one). This is not a new idea: it's *Search for a Star*, *New Faces*, *Opportunity Knocks* (ask your parents).

The key is about finding contexts in which people will want to use your product. Interactivity must mean more than exercising your right to phone in; the challenge is to get your audience members to interact with one another in response to and as a result of their experience of your product. The Wii, for example, persuaded family members of all ages to clumsily take part in a bowling competition without balls and without graphical sophistication. The key is that an assumption of families is that they do things together, even when they largely did not. Anything that successfully taps into this mixture of desire/hope/fear/guilt was therefore likely to succeed: 'book it and they will come'. This interaction is now of course more accessible via the World Wide Web and the cynic would say exploitable. Certainly a franchise like *The X Factor* leaves no stone unturned in its quest for new ways to connect with its audience: text messages, blogs, websites, support programmes on ITV3. The point is that this is more than new places to market, it is more profoundly embracing the reality of convergence culture to create a new model of what might be partly called a trans-media text: though very much with its nucleus on the terra firma of the Saturday night early evening schedule. It's partly also about learning a lot from *Dr Who* and less from *Big Brother*. Ultimately these interactions, this new model, were as confirmed by the internet campaign which made Rage Against the Machine the Christmas number one by the 19 million people who watched the live final. In fact all of this very much corroborates the argument that the internet has changed everything, that, as Ross and Nightingale suggest, "the information age is changing what it means to be an audience". At the same time though it stops short of quite accepting their more strident assertion: "Audiences are learning how to *be* the media, how to net-*work*." Henry

Jenkins still seems to provide the more balanced view: "The inter active audience is more than a marketing concept and less than a semiotic democracy" (semiotic democracy is Fiske's term for the process by which everyone makes their own meanings).

In simple terms where television is succeeding it is negotiating convergence on its own terms, enlisting potential competitor media as significant collaborators. This has necessitated a reinterpretation of the art of scheduling in the face of the decline of the 'static' live audience. Scheduling was once almost entirely about fixing broadcasting experiences to our routines and keeping us tuned to a single channel with a varied diet of favourite genres. Now texts are more discretely packaged, usually commercially endorsed experiences which may be accessed in a number of different formats at the audience's request in what has been called a 'Martini Media' after Martini's famous tagline: "Anytime, any place, any where." And yet, at the same time, they are more open-ended than ever before, seeping across media platforms, trans-media experiences in infinitely different combinations and routines. This new scheduling is partly merely a campaign of marketing and distribution, though now in 3D but more interestingly being alive to the possibilities offered for the textual experience to be more dynamic and open-ended. Henry Jenkins has coined the term 'trans-media storytelling' for this "new aesthetic that has emerged in response to media convergence". The important point is that while scheduling was always an 'art' of sorts, it is now to be considered as part of what Jana Bennett, Controller of BBC Television, called the "creative revolution every bit as ambitious as the technical one we've seen".

If you want a case study look no further than the revival of that old sci-fi chestnut *Dr Who*. In a detailed and readable essay 'Dr Who and the convergence of media', Neil Perryman provides an extensive survey of how the BBC's decision to bring back the cult series unwittingly created a blueprint for addressing the new trans-media landscape. At the centre of the project is a commitment to the creative process, the creation of a 'factory' of ideas based around script writer Russell T. Davies and producer Julie Gardner. However, more telling is BBC Director-General Mark Thompson's admission that "There's a coherent plan in place for the whole audience relationship with the content almost from the start." Here is the new 'scheduling' at the heart of the creative process. The idea is to abandon the linear model in all respects so that this is not simply an extension across platforms or into related products and an attempt to embrace the creative complexity enabled by the trans-media context: not spin-off but back-around-and-through. Perryman writes of "extra-value content and narrative complexity . . . by deploying a series of evolving and challenging story telling strategies across a wide range of media platforms". It could be argued that this new dispensation which foregrounds a kind of formal hybridity renders a traditional concept like 'genre' almost redundant. *Dr Who* bears a factory mark rather more than a generic code and this may be not so much a matter of franchise as of auteurship.

Certainly if you identify something like *Torchwood* Series 3 as a text it is easy to see the Who signature, which is mostly synonymous with that of the chief writer (since he is the easiest 'auteur' fit). As such while there are sci-fi generic aspects to *Children of Earth*, which playfully references a number of 'influences' for sci-fi, genre had become sidelined by issues of form and identity. Although it was a surprise even to star actor John Barrowman, pitching *Children of Earth* into a prime BBC1 slot for five consecutive nights became the item's most significant statement. For here the realities of the 'on-demand' world proved, as Mark Thompson predicted, to be "creatively inspiring and liberating". In the same way that advertisers have been forced to rethink, well everything, Russell Davies and his team attempted a spectacular and unprecedented coup. Experiments with the 'for five nights' had been attempted with a concept very like *24* where the emerging story was, for example, happening over the 'real time' of the five days. Heavyweight crime dramas like *Above Suspicion* and *Silent Witness* do something similar over two and three nights, though the spotlight here is on intensity and focus.

I believe the *Torchwood* thinking was a little more open and creative, and, it must be said, encouraged by a soundtrack record of success: who'd have ever thought that by 2009 *Dr Who* would become an established part of the BBC's Christmas Day schedule? *Torchwood*'s thinking might have run along the following lines:

- Given that we have six hours of TV to make
- And we have an established residual audience who will access this however we package it
- And we have a brand/auteur identity which might at least turn heads
- Where is the sense in the conventional option of BBC2 every Tuesday at 9 p.m. for six hours (or even upping the ante to BBC1)?

Instead, what you get is six hours of old-fashioned 'Earth in Danger' narrative, complete with social comment, political debate, human interest, fantasy, comedy and ultimately tragedy. You get convincing special effects, genuinely frightening aliens and a powerfully implausible ending yet which is thematically consonant with the general humanist and collectivist message of the franchise. But above all you get six hours of primetime 'family drama', a substantial sci-fi narrative, which you know is very unlikely to be consumed 'live' over five nights. This is the antithesis of the argument that PVRs have made all slots potentially prime since it plays on the symbolism of primetime while carrying little risk to the time-shift audience. *Children of Earth* thus becomes an advertisement for and endorsement of the creative factory while at the same time conducting a high-profile argument for quality and variety in mainstream TV.

One of the ways in which this has been reinforced, and which has irked both media commentators and audience members alike, is the BBC's rather more explicit approach to self-promotion. Something very like the old radio play list (where producers decided which records would be played on BBC radio) appears to be operating when guests are chosen for chat-shows and even news magazine programmes (e.g. *Morning BBC*). Stars are identified when they happen to be starring in forthcoming BBC programmes. Equally, as we have suggested above, this is now built into the ways in which programmes converse with their audience.

Thus a hit show like *The Apprentice* offers straightforwardly a weekly one-hour report on hours of action which leaves us and 'Surrallon' to match words and actions in very much a courtroom style, though as a 'who-didn't-do it', since s/he who fails to dare, loses: and before we have time to fully digest Surrallon's verdict (and whether we agree) we are whisked off to BBC2 where a second panel (consisting of a cross-section of the funny, the famous and the business-savvy) subjects these judgements to a kind of lightweight judicial review. And if that's not the end of it, the wheel comes full circle on the following morning with the 'This week's loser' interview exclusive to Radio 5 Live and including a phone-in. This is important because it returns us to real time and to the realisation that reality TV is still 'made', which means 'recorded', 'edited' and neither 'pure' nor 'simple'.

The cult sit-com *Peep Show* continues these arguments about multiple formats and the notion of stylistic identity being individual rather than generic. Here is a show that has always attracted critical acclaim but for most of its six-year run has had very unimpressive viewing figures, not many more than a million viewers until the latest run (2009). Although it has not always been a given, the show has persisted for a number of reasons which include the quality of the work itself, the positive critical reception and the sense that it has an investment in the developing profiles of Mitchell and Webb. A jump in audience figures for series six (to 1.8 million) may suggest that Channel 4's patience is paying off, though the switch to an earlier time slot of 10 p.m. perhaps also suggests accessing a bigger teen audience. However, the other supporter of the programme has been the consistently high sale of series DVDs.

Although it has many of the trademarks of classic situation comedy including a traditional situation (an American version was unsurprisingly called *The Odd Couple*), *Peep Show* works around substantial series-long and trans-series narratives. A series is not just six encounters with our quirky friends but rather six chapters in an ongoing set of stories. The fact that the programme's stylistic signature is the use of point of view to allow us intimate access to what our favourite characters see reinforces the integrity of the show – as innovative and distinctive (it has also been claimed that this artiness prevented the show from finding a wider audience). The DVD 'box-set' format (which in this case is a single, slim, coloured case per series) therefore better suits the *Peep Show* identity perhaps than any evening slot can, even with a catch-up on your PVR.

Todorov argued that a world without a theory of genre was unthinkable since genre integrates the reader into the world of the characters and prepares us for a certain kind of reading. In other words, genre delineates the boundaries of the possibilities of meaning, reducing complexity and enabling the text for us. In this context *Peep Show* appears hardly to have a generic identity at all since all of these functions seem to be delivered elsewhere, through identities that are formed in more specific individual contexts, of form, of style and of performance. Todorov also pointed out that genres exist in historical contexts which allow their particular stories. It may be that the era of television genres is over or at least needs significant renegotiation.

2 CRITICAL PERSPECTIVES

In this chapter we will examine:

- The role of critical perspectives and theory in a study of the media
- Marxist perspective
- Feminist perspective
- Postmodern perspective
- Postcolonialism as a perspective
- Queer theory.

The role of critical perspectives and theory in a study of the media

Media Studies is a discipline full of theories. On one level this is great news because it allows you lots of opportunities for looking at theoretical perspectives. Any text you look at is likely to lend itself to a whole host of different tools with which to prise it open. Marxist, feminist or postmodernist theories are all likely to be applicable to the texts that you want to explore.

However, slavish adherence to what these theories propose or tell you is not always the best way to use them. The hallmark of a really good 'active' Media Studies student at A2 is a willingness to question what has gone before. This does not mean that you have a licence to go around rubbishing every theory you have encountered. There will be theoretical issues that you will feel remain useful and have an important application today. Equally you must realise that it is not an act of heresy to call into question some of the received wisdom that underpins Media Studies. You need to adopt a healthy scepticism about the ideas that you come across. Better still be prepared to test them out against your own experience of texts and contexts.

Your study of the media should have made you aware of the vast extent to which it is used socially. Media output is a common talking point whenever people meet and exchange ideas, be it physically or in cyberspace. Just about everyone has something to say about the media, especially contemporary topics such as the latest reality TV show or a controversial new film showing at the cinema. On this basis, the majority of the population could wander into a Media Studies exam and have a go at many of the questions on an A2 paper. Some of the better informed might even scrape a pass. The reason the majority would probably fail, however, is that their knowledge and understanding of the media would lack the important theoretical framework that is crucial to an academic study of the media. It is your ability to show that you have grasped at least some of this theoretical base that is such an important ingredient of your success at A2.

Of course, there is an argument which suggests that theories exist for no other purpose than to be shot down. Well, perhaps you are not quite at the stage of your academic career when you feel equipped to challenge the major theorists. What you are in a position to do, however, is to question and test out the validity of the theories that you come across. More simply you are in a position to question whether they are theories that are true on the basis of the products and issues that you have studied.

Don't forget that you are studying Media Studies at a time when the discipline is in a state of flux. A lot of the theories and ideas that have been taken for granted for many years are now being questioned, not least because they have become outdated in the face of the vast technological changes that have taken place in the way in which media texts are both produced and consumed.

Of course at this point you are hoping for a list of key theories that you can learn and show off in the exam. You have probably guessed, however, that being Media Studies it is not quite that simple. There is an explanation of some of the more important theoretical perspectives coming up, which you will be glad to hear, but it is not the sort of thing that you can just learn and trot out in the exam.

Most theories or perspectives by their nature are designed to explore texts and issues from a specific point of view. Far from being an objective take, they seek to put forward and support a particular perspective from which to consider media output. One thing you may note is that different perspectives often invite you to look at an issue in terms of how power is distributed within society. In other words, how media output may be seen to serve or not serve the interests of different groups within our society.

A good example of this would be feminist theory which, as you will read, sees media output from the perspective of women. Clearly this is a complex issue, but at a simple level many media texts can be interpreted through their ideological function of supporting, reinforcing and preserving the patriarchal social order in which power is vested in men. Media output may be seen as a mechanism for diverting and controlling women in order to ensure that they remain in a position in society which is subordinate to men. A survey of advertising, for example, by a feminist, would point to the representation of women in advertisements in ways that are very different compared to those represented by men. The conclusion might be that the media do this in order to gain our acceptance that this way of representing women is natural or inevitable, and therefore in some way acceptable or 'right'.

So where does that leave you as a Media Studies student in relation to theory or critical perspectives as they are often called? The simple answer is that if you know and have a basic understanding of a perspective it is a good idea to apply it. However, you should only do this if you are convinced it is appropriate. Nothing looks worse in an exam or coursework essay than a half-understood theory contrived to fit a particular situation in a vain and simplistic attempt to show off some nodding acquaintance with said theory. It is probably better to use no theory at all than to use it inappropriately or merely for the sake of trying to show off.

You might like to think about what is implied by the term 'perspective'. It is a term often used in art to describe the way in which a two-dimensional painting is created to give the illusion of three-dimensionality. That is not to suggest of course that perspective is merely a shallow trick. What a perspective does is offers a vantage point which invites the spectator to see the universe as complex and multi-dimensional rather than merely as a flat surface. So perspectives, or theories, offer to you, the student, vantage points from which to identify the complexities of the media and its output. It is for this reason that they are important. What they allow you to do is to move from the individual or particular to the general. So, in Media Studies, that can empower you to move from close study of one particular product to feeling confident in making broader statements about the cultural, social and ideological functions of the media more widely.

ACTIVITY

Look at the illustration on the right and make a list of some of the issues it raises for you beyond the image itself and into broader cultural and social issues.

What do we learn about the values of our society from looking at what is in the advertisement or perhaps what isn't in it? Or does that depend on what we want to learn about the values of our society? Do you think different social groups within our culture would see different values according to the perspective which forms their point of view? Where do you stand in relation to the advertisement?

Figure 2.1 Advert for Tom Ford for Men

Much of the theory you need you already know from your AS study. One of the chief perspectives that informs any study of the media is that of structuralism. Structuralism suggests that there are certain structures that underpin much of human activity including the production of media output. Look back at the Introduction and you will see that at AS you learned about genre, narrative and semiotics. All are examples of structuralism, a perspective that allows us the vantage point of seeing common and often universal strands in the construction of media products. There is a refresher of these in the Introduction, but if you need more details you could refer back to *AS Media Studies: The Essential Introduction for AQA* (2008).

We have tried to identify and highlight for you some of the key critical perspectives that we feel you will need to enhance your A2 study. This is not an exhaustive list – you can find something akin to that in the AQA specification (weblink) at least for the purposes of your A2 course. What it does offer is a series of accessible ways of applying theoretical perspectives to your study by giving some basic guidance on key perspectives.

For the moment, perhaps a short quotation taken from an earlier edition of this book might persuade you that exploring critical perspectives a little more deeply is worth the effort:

> **Rather annoyingly, theories often suggest that something which had always seemed perfectly simple and straightforward is actually complex. As we shall argue later, the mass media have a particular knack of making things seem so obvious and so natural that it would be just plain daft to criticise or ask for explanations. In those areas, especially, it is important to have theories which never take anything for granted, theories which ask *how* and *why* we see things as obvious or natural.**

(Bennett et al., 2005)

What follows is a brief introduction to some of the key theories that should inform your study of the media. They come in no particular order; none should be considered more important than any other. This introduction should be seen as a starting point to your study of theory, especially if you are intending to pursue media or an allied discipline to another level when you have completed A2.

Marxism

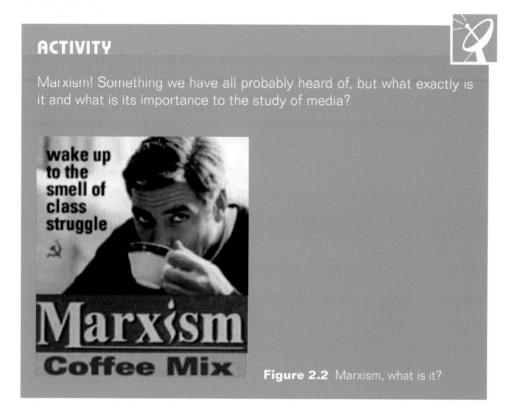

ACTIVITY

Marxism! Something we have all probably heard of, but what exactly is it and what is its importance to the study of media?

Figure 2.2 Marxism, what is it?

Marxism as a theoretical perspective has an almost unrivalled pedigree. It can trace its origins back to the 1840s when Karl Marx began his career as a political writer and philosopher. Few theoretical perspectives have the notoriety today that Marxism has which, given its age, makes it all the more remarkable. Social and political ideas which are products of the Marxist tradition have affected the lives of millions of people, not simply because they are influential in themselves, but because they formed the core of the communist ideology which was central to the Soviet Union until its collapse and which remains part of the social fabric of China and North Korea today.

The writings of Marx gained more widespread acceptance after his death in 1883 than they did during his lifetime, and this influence appears to have continued through the twentieth and into the twenty-first centuries, but in reality, Marxism as a theoretical perspective has evolved and developed over time, and it now incorporates many different perspectives, ideas and theories. The body of Marxist thought is much more than the writings of Marx alone; rather, it is a body of work with many contributors. Although the content has Marx's own writings as a point of origin, there is by no means complete agreement or harmony among all the constituent parts of the Marxist tradition.

So what are these fundamental ideas at the centre of Marxist thought? Well, any detailed examination of the topic of Marxism is a huge undertaking, since the perspective has something to say about almost all facets of human existence and the societies in which we exist. However, a basic knowledge of the main principles of the topic is required to enable a deeper understanding of media theory, not least because the mass media is one of those facets of human existence about which Marxism is concerned.

At its heart, Marxists believe that all societies have an economic 'base', a system through which production occurs or services are offered. From this economic base, people get paid for their work and those who own the means of production take home the surplus, or profit, as it is more widely known. Radiating out from this economic base is the 'superstructure', which consists of the social and cultural institutions such as the family, the education system, the judiciary or legal system and, of course, the media. Marxists argue that the superstructure is shaped and determined by the economic base, so if, as is the situation in twenty-first-century Britain, the economic base is founded upon capitalist and consumerist ideas, then the superstructure reflects this. However, in pure Marxist ideology, the superstructure is not only a reflection of the ideology at the heart of the base, it acts to protect and legitimise the economic base, and it is in this area that Marxism offers most to the study of media.

Marxists believe that in capitalist societies such as ours, there exists a state of conflict between those who own and control the economic base, the 'haves', and those who work for them: the (at least relative to the haves) the 'have-nots'. In Marxist terminology, those who own or exert control are called the bourgeoisie while the workers are called the proletariat. For the proletariat there is relative poverty, a feeling of being exploited, inequality and a distinct lack of power or a sense of control over their own lives, whereas for the bourgeoisie there exists a healthy sense of well-being and satisfaction at becoming wealthier and more powerful thanks to the hard work of the workers who are rewarded with low pay and minimal prestige.

If the picture painted by the Marxist perspective concerning the relations between those who own and control the means of production and those who work is true, then it is hardly a happy picture. Yet, despite outnumbering the bourgeoisie hugely, despite the sense of angst that Marxists believe the proletariat have a right to feel, and despite the certain and inevitable collapse of the social system if the workers downed tools and protested, the status quo is largely maintained and the workers tend to continue to work, the odd strike or two excepted, while the owners, chief executives and directors continue to grow richer. This inactivity on behalf of the proletariat is, in no small part, due to the workings of the superstructure which protects and legitimises the base, and through a process whereby the proletariat seem to succumb to their position which Marx called 'false consciousness', the inequitable and exploitative relationship between the ruling class and the working class is maintained.

The Slovenian philosopher Slavoj Žižek offers an interesting viewpoint on the Marxist ideas in his work on the evolution and development of an ideology. It is useful to consider the development of an ideology rather like a narrative unfolding over the course of a film or a book. Each ideology begins as a 'doctrine' by which it is formed following a set of ideas or beliefs. It is here that the ideology is in its purest state. The next stage is 'belief' whereby the key points of the ideology become apparent in wider society before the ideology finally moves to the 'ritual' point whereby the individuals in a society regard themselves as examples or the embodiment of the ideology.

In the evolution of Marxism, which itself began as an ideology based on the beliefs of Marx, it became accepted as an established ideology and is reflected in the workings of the superstructure, especially in certain communist societies, before finally leading to a feeling of exploitation and powerlessness by the working classes.

In this section, you will notice that so far there has been no mention of the media. This, after all, is a media textbook, so where does the subject fit into this theory? Well, Marxist belief is that the media is one of the key institutions which make up the superstructure.

The relevance of Marxist theory may now quite feasibly be called into question. Writing over 150 years ago and referring to a period of time when industrialisation was in its infancy, Marx saw squalor, poverty, a lack of esteem and low wages among the working classes which are far more a feature of Victorian England than of today's society. The companies and businesses of Marx's time were much more likely to be owned by an individual person or by a small partnership of two or three people. Today's companies are likely to be owned by shareholders who are drawn from a variety of backgrounds. Privatisation and flotation on the stock market of large companies and organisations means that companies can be owned by several million shareholders, many of whom will be the very workers who Marx regarded as exploited. Later Marxist thought then is much more concerned with a 'ruling elite' rather than with the factory and business owners of Marx's day. Members of this ruling elite at the heart of the economic base may not own the means of production or services, but they control it and, through the workings of the superstructure, they ensure their survival as the most powerful and influential group in contemporary society.

Marxists also believe that the objective of survival as the most powerful group can lead to members of the ruling elite acting in their own self-interest rather than in the interests of the wider society. A good example of how the role of those who hold positions of power and influence in media can be affected by their position to the detriment of their society is offered by Edward Herman and Noam Chomsky in their book *Manufacturing Consent* (1994), in which they argue that the decisions which are made by the American news media in setting an agenda – literally deciding the content and the discourse for news coverage in American news – are determined by the need for the news institutions to remain profitable. In the newspaper industry, for example, the main source of income is from advertising, and in some instances this can account for up to 80 per cent of all revenue. The newspapers are less likely to cover items which cause offence to or upset the advertisers if they feel that by covering these items of news, they could jeopardise their relationship with advertisers and thus threaten their own profitability.

BASE in Marxist terminology, the base refers to the economic core upon which a society is organised. It is the central means by which wealth is created and distributed among the people within that society.

SUPERSTRUCTURE this is the name Marxists give to the institutions which exist in a society other than those associated with the economy, which would be part of the base. These institutions include religions, the law, education, the political system and the media. Marxists believe not only that these institutions are shaped by the economic base, but also that the superstructure helps to legitimise the base and ensure its future as the economic system of that society.

PROLETARIAT the name Marx gave to those who work the means of production and provide the services offered in a society – the working classes.

BOURGEOISIE the Marxist name for those who own or control the means of production or services – the middle classes.

FALSE CONSCIOUSNESS a term which suggests the working classes are not fully aware of the exploitation they endure at the hands of the ruling class. It is regarded as a reason why those who are exploited do not rise up and rebel against the ruling elite.

CAPITALISM the economic system in which a society is focused upon the pursuit of capital (wealth). In Britain and other Western countries, capitalism may be said to be at the heart of the economic base. The main criticism is that it does not seek to create wealth for all people. For there to be wealthy people, others have to remain poor. Therefore critics of capitalism argue that while it is good at creating wealth, the unavoidable consequence of capitalism is inequality: the rich get richer and the poor get poorer. As capitalism has spread across the world, this inequality is no longer confined to within a country but is seen on a global scale.

Figure 2.4 The haves and the have-nots: the inevitable consequence of global capitalism

As part of the superstructure, the media plays a pivotal role in the function of maintaining the power and influence held by the ruling elite, according to Marxist theory. First of all, it is worth considering that just as is the case with institutions in other sectors of British society, the media institutions, organisations and businesses are themselves controlled by members of this group of the ruling elite, and those who work in the media industries are themselves exploited by their managers just as they are in other industries. Finally, and perhaps most importantly from the viewpoint of the role of the media in legitimising and perpetuating this unequal state of affairs, the media is used to indoctrinate and influence people into accepting their role. In other words, the Marxist perspective of the media is not only to make money for those who own or control the media institutions, but also to preserve the interests of the ruling elite and to keep the workers in their place and accepting of capitalism as the natural and best way for the economic base to be structured.

ACTIVITY

Despite the glitz and glamour often associated with media industries, not everyone who works in the sector benefits from high-profile, glamorous and well-paid jobs. Conduct some research into the experiences of people who work in a variety of media jobs which lack the glitz and the glamour frequently associated with the media sector. For example:

- Production runner
- Hospital radio DJ
- Freelance photographer
- Fanzine editor
- Local news reporter
- Session musician.

Examples of the Marxist perspective in media

Let us begin to apply this Marxist perspective in a simple way, by looking at the media platform of film. Marx himself claimed, though obviously not by means of a direct reference to cinema, that there is often a disconnection between the maker and what is made. This is perhaps nowhere better illustrated than in the world of cinema. Take a look at the film poster for the 2008 film *Body Of Lies*.

On this poster, as is the case with most film posters, there is a hierarchical approach to the personnel involved in its production not unlike the hierarchy that Marxists believe exists in wider society. At the top of the poster we see the surnames of the two lead actors. Leonardo DiCaprio, by virtue of having his name on the left, is given billing precedence over Russell Crowe. The importance of the two actors to the film can be seen not only by the prominent position of their names but also by the fact that theirs are the only faces we see on the poster's image. Again, in this respect it is DiCaprio who enjoys the more prominent representation; despite Russell Crowe's Oscar success in *Gladiator* it is clear that the producers feel DiCaprio is their most prized asset for marketing the film. The next piece of written information is the film's tagline followed by the details of the director. A kind of ownership is ascribed to him by the term "A Ridley Scott Film".

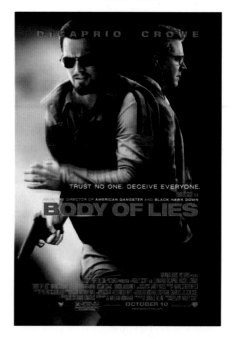

Figure 2.5 Poster for *Body of Lies*

Although in the film industry, Scott is a very influential and successful director with numerous credits to his name, he is less likely to be as instantly familiar to as many people as either DiCaprio or Crowe, and so the audience is reminded of some of his earlier work. Finally, the fourth item of written text from the top is the film's title. Last, we see a billing block with certain key members of the cast and crew, including DiCaprio, Crowe and Scott once again to finally confirm their place among the ruling elite, but if you have ever stayed until the end of a film in the cinema, you will know that several hundred names have been omitted from the poster's billing block who were involved in the film's production.

This is a crude and rather simple application of Marxist theory, and of course the reasons for the layout and design of the poster are fairly obvious. The film was made to make money for those who produced and made it, which in itself can be justified by the capitalist context, that of pursuing profit, in which Western media operates. Under these circumstances, it makes sense to emphasise the selling points of the film; hence the mention of the director's previous successful work such as *American Gangster* and *Black Hawk Down*. However, if it is the case that referring to previous work can help to sell a film, then why just the director? Why does it not make reference to the electrician's previous work or the lighting rigger? Surely the make-up artist, the set designer or the solo violinist for the musical score have a body of work worthy of inclusion for advertising the film. The reason for their omission is simple. They do not form part of the ruling elite of the world of cinema. That accolade is the honour of directors, actors and writers, and herein lies the key point in the Marxist perspective. For a ruling elite to stay as a ruling elite, it must remain a small and exclusive club. If entry into this elite club was open and membership widened, it would by definition cease to be a small and exclusive club.

A further area of media where the Marxist perspective is particularly relevant is in news presentation. Watching a news bulletin on the TV or reading a newspaper, it becomes clear just how much coverage is given to the main areas of politics, business and commerce, which all help to define the kind of society Marxists

believe the UK to be – consumerist, capitalist and 'Western'. The theory of news values which ascribes newsworthiness to events suggests that if an event is deemed to be important it will be given plenty of coverage. Put simply, the dominance of politicians, business leaders and other key members of the ruling elite in news coverage serves to remind audiences just how important they are and to reaffirm their status as that ruling elite.

ACTIVITY

■ Watch news bulletins on TV over the course of a few days. How much of the content involves one or more of the three areas of business or commerce or politics?
■ Now do the same activity, but this time read a newspaper over the course of a few days. Again, coverage of news (as opposed to sport or reviews) should be studied to get a picture of the content.
■ To what extent do you feel that the coverage of the 'ruling elite' from the worlds of business, politics and culture serves to reinforce and legitimise their position as the ruling elite?

It is worth reflecting on the important Marxist concept of hegemony here in the context of news coverage. Hegemony, a term coined by Antonio Gramsci, refers to the power and influence held by an influential and powerful, though usually smaller group over a weaker but larger group. This domination can be on a local scale, for example, the power held by politicians over the rest of a society, or on a much larger scale, such as in the case of the domination of the USA on the world stage relative to the rest of the world. In the case of news, Anthony Giddens writes, "Control of the world's news by the major western agencies . . . means the predominance of a 'First World outlook' " (Giddens, 1993, p. 559). There is also evidence which suggests that this domination, especially by America, takes place on a cultural level too. Consider the huge influx of American culture in British society with American film, music and television. This serves to reinforce America's position as the dominant global force for cultural exports. The media in these examples is being used as a means of ensuring that members of the ruling elite, both nationally, and internationally, can maintain their hold on power and protect their position as the ruling elite.

ACTIVITY

Conduct some research into the TV shows currently airing on British television. Do not limit your research to any one genre; make sure you include comedy, drama, children's shows, documentary and so on. How much of the TV we receive in the UK is American? How well represented are other countries on British TV?

There are, as is the case with every theory, criticisms of the Marxist perspective. It is rather a simple theory, a factor which may make it attractive as a concept, and, compared to some of the more complex and verbose philosophical viewpoints, this is certainly something of a positive. However, its simplicity also contributes to its weakness. What Marxism assumes is that the proletariat are too ill-educated to know that they are being exploited. The belief that the media serves to reinforce the position of the ruling elite to a passive and inactive audience which does not realise it is being duped is rather outdated and has been discredited by a wealth of media theorists. Marxist theory has also suffered somewhat through the seismic changes in British society today compared to when Marx was writing. Social mobility has increased, people born into a working-class family are not as entrenched in this existence as they once were, and for those who hold traditional working-class occupations, there exists an improvement in pay and conditions and a level of contentment and affluence which did not exist in Marx's day.

Marx himself wrote that religion was the opiate of the masses. By this he was referring to his belief that working-class people were held in their place by religion which promised rewards in heaven, and which helped to quell any notion of revolution and revolt by workers against the oppression exerted by the ruling class. To revolt and take up the struggle would have placed that heavenly reward in jeopardy, and through religious doctrine and teaching, the working class was held in its place. Statisticians tell us that religiosity has declined enormously since the mid-nineteenth century, so the promise of redemption following a hard-working life holds less relevance for people today than it once did. Yet we still see no revolution by hordes of hard-working proletarians. Could it be that the new opiate of the masses is the consumerist and capitalist society whereby luxury items such as expensive designer handbags, watches, plasma screen televisions and the latest hi-tech, hi-def 'blu-ray' DVD kit are no longer the preserve of the wealthy and the privileged but are more readily available to everyone? Of course the media with its advertising and marketing of such products helps to promote this. Why should the workers smash their chains and revolt, as Marx predicted they would? They're too busy playing their Xboxes, watching their plasma screen TVs and surfing the internet on their Blackberries looking for the nearest shop to buy a new Rolex.

Feminism

Feminism is the belief that women should have equal rights to men. In consequence, the feminist movement fights for equal rights and opportunities for women.

There are many different kinds of feminism, and feminists themselves tend to disagree about the ways in which women are disadvantaged and what exactly should be done to achieve equal rights. For example, 'socialist feminists' believe that women are exploited by the capitalist system both at work and in the home.

However, it may be argued that there have been some real improvements in the way in which women are now represented in the media, possibly because of the increase in women working in the media, sometimes in positions of power. However, many would argue that women are still represented in a negative and stereotypical way and are still a long way from enjoying equal power in media institutions. Feminists would argue that this reflects and reinforces the unequal social, economic and political position of women.

A brief history

The history of feminism may be divided into three main movements or waves:

- The *first wave* – in the nineteenth and early twentieth century in the UK and US. It won improved rights for women in marriage and property. Its biggest achievement was winning some political power. In the UK the *Suffragettes* and *Suffragists* campaigned for the women's vote, in 1918 women over the age of 30 who owned property won the vote, and in 1928 it was extended to all women over the age of 21.
- The *second* wave – 1960s and 1970s. It extended the fight beyond political rights to education, work and the home. In *The Feminine Mystique* (1963), Betty Freidan argued that women were unhappy because of the feminine mystique. She said this was a damaging ideal of femininity which she called "the Happy Housewife" and it restricted women to the role of housewife and mother, giving up on work and education. This may be seen in the US drama series *Mad Men* in the character of Betty, and similar themes are explored in *Desperate Housewives*. Both of them show women trapped in the stifling role of homemaker and the damage this does to women, men and society. Freidan's book was seen as one of the main forces in of the second wave of feminism. Freidan also co-founded the *National Organization for Women* which concentrated on winning equal legal rights for women, such as the Equal Pay Act and legalising abortion.

  Another important second-wave feminist book was *The Female Eunuch* by Germaine Greer (1970). She argued that women are 'castrated', the eunuch of the title, by society. In particular she attacked the nuclear family, romantic love and the limits on women's sexuality. She argued that gender roles were not natural but learned. They conditioned girls to conform to a very restrictive femininity. The book has been criticised for not offering any realistic solutions to women's oppression, because it proposed action by individual women rather than organised political action.

■ The *third* wave – 1990s to the present. It widened the feminist movement and its ideas beyond middle-class, white women, addressing the different disadvantages women experience because of, for example, their race, ethnicity and class.

Seeing the history of feminism in these three waves can ignore the fight for equal rights and the end to discrimination by women outside the large feminist movements in the UK and US, including working-class women and black and ethnic minority women.

Post-feminism – 1980s to the present

This includes a wide range of reactions to the feminist movement and is often critical of feminist ideas. The word 'post' suggests that feminism is something that has already happened. Some post-feminists argue that feminism isn't relevant any more because women have won equal rights. Other post-feminist ideas argue that younger women don't see feminism as relevant to them now. They may still believe in equal rights for women, but either see themselves as individuals, not part of a feminist movement, or don't want to use the word *feminist*. This has been criticised by feminists as a way of 'manufacturing consent' for the fact that women are still unequal, by getting women to accept their unequal position in society.

ACTIVITY

Some post-feminists would argue that the sexually explicit images of female pop stars are empowering to women because they show them as sexually confident and active, using their sexuality on their own terms. Analyse the images of a number of female pop stars online and list arguments against this.

Recent developments in feminist ideas

ANGELA MCROBBIE

McRobbie has written several books, especially about young women and the media. She argues that many feminist ideas from the past aren't seen as relevant by young women now. Her first famous study was on the teenage girls' magazine *Jackie*. Then, in *Feminism and Youth Culture: From Jackie to Just 17* (1991), she came to more positive conclusions about media representations of young women. She argued that there were some positive aspects to, for example, women's magazines, with ideas that could empower their young female audience, such as how to enjoy sex or learning about their bodies. In *The Aftermath of Feminism* (2008), she explored how the media encourages women to consent to and play a part in negative media representations, for example, lads' mags competitions to appear on front covers or makeover programmes that ask the female audience to be critical of other women's bodies.

Figure 2.7 *Cosmopolitan* Magazine cover, March 2010

ACTIVITY

Analyse the front cover of a women's lifestyle magazine. List the positive and negative representations of women.

Do you agree or disagree with McRobbie's ideas?

THE BEAUTY MYTH (WOLF 1991)

Naomi Wolf argues that women are oppressed by the pressure to fit into a myth or false ideal of beauty. Feminism may have won women new rights, but they are still held back by an obsession with physical appearance and a very narrow definition of beauty, for example, to be white, thin and made up. This beauty myth is socially constructed and helps to maintain patriarchy, where men still have power in society. Women buy into this myth, helping to create hegemony, where the values are accepted even by those who are harmed by them. Wolf attacked the *fashion* and *beauty* industries, and the advertising and media industries that support them for exploiting women. Women's magazines make their profits from advertising that depends on women feeling inadequate and being critical of themselves.

Women can never achieve the ideal of beauty because it is an unrealistic, airbrushed construction. There have been many recent examples of images of women in the media that have been manipulated to conform to this unrealistic ideal. For example, in 2003 Kate Winslet complained that her legs had been made thinner and longer when she posed for the front cover of *GQ* magazine. Keira Knightley was given larger breasts in the marketing posters for the film *King Arthur* and in her Chanel campaign.

Figure 2.8 Keira Knightley on the UK and US film posters for *King Arthur*

In an article in the *Guardian* in 2009 Emine Saner discussed the controversy over *Glamour* magazine in the US publishing a photo of a model that hadn't been touched up. The model Liz Miller said, "People don't ever see images like this in *magazines*. It shows how hungry the world is to see all different body types." At the other extreme, gossip magazines and websites are very critical of celebrities' bodies; for example, www.perezhilton.com calls his website "Hollywood's Most-Hated Web Site!" and scrawls comments all over photos of celebrities, and *Heat* magazine has its famous Circle of Shame. Mark Frith, the former editor of *Heat*, said he believed the reality pictures actually made his readers feel better about themselves.

Figure 2.9 Model Liz Miller's picture was published in the US edition of *Glamour* Magazine without airbrushing

This unrealistic body ideal has been accused of contributing to women's negative body image and leading to physical and psychological problems, such as eating disorders. It has been argued that young women in particular use the media to construct their identity and are especially vulnerable. It is very difficult to prove a direct causal link between the media and audience behaviour, and many active audience theories argue against it.

ACTIVITY

What do you think?

On your own consider the following questions. Alternatively, split into groups, each group discussing one of the following questions, and report back to the class the arguments for and against, and their own views.

1. Does the representation of women in the media lead to women having a negative body image?
2. Is the representation of women's bodies in the media one of the causes of eating disorders? What other contributing factors could there be?

3. Is there increasing pressure on men now to live up to a masculine body ideal created by the media?
4. Are there alternative representations of women in the media or does one body type dominate to the exclusion of others?
5. Why is it in the economic interests of the media for women to feel inadequate and insecure about their bodies?
6. Do you think young women are especially vulnerable to the effects of the beauty myth or not?

Then, as a class, discuss what could be the solution to the problem.

RAUNCH CULTURE (LEVY 2005)

Andrea Levy, in her book *Female Chauvinist Pigs: Women and the Rise of Raunch Culture*, attacks the increasingly sexualised culture that objectifies women. She argues that women are encouraged to see themselves as objects and to see sex as their only source of power. This may be seen in lads' magazines such as *Nuts* and music videos of female artists such as Shakira.

Figure 2.10 Homepage of Katie Price's website

ACTIVITY

1. Is Katie Price a good role model for young women? Is she a successful and wealthy business woman who uses her body on her own terms? Or does she show that society only values women who see and sell themselves as sex objects?

continued

Zoe Williams in the *Guardian* in November 2009 argues, "She colludes with – no, encourages – the commodification of her body, values it out by the pound to whoever pays the most in whatsoever state of undress, and this makes her a very neat icon of raunch culture."

In *Media, Gender and Identity* (2008), David Gauntlett argues that audiences are active; role models "should not be taken to mean someone that a person wants to copy. Instead, role models serve as navigation points as individuals steer their own personal routes through life."

2. List five people whom you like or admire in the media; try to include a range of different people. Then swap your list in twos. What does the list suggest about the other person and the values they have?

3. Divide your class into young men and women. Are their any names that were repeated? What does your list suggest about the values that the media communicates about gender? What exceptions were there?

Feminists argue that sexualised images of girls and young women now saturate the media and are widely available in mainstream media, such as advertising, magazines and television. This damages women's self-image and it also distorts men's views of women. The internet has led to increased and easier access to pornography, whose message is that women are sexually available and their bodies are for sale.

GENDER AND IDENTITY (BUTLER, 1990)

Judith Butler argues that feminism has contributed to a binary view of gender, where men and women are divided into opposing groups, with fixed ideas about what it is to be masculine and feminine. This has narrowed down the choices people could have made about their own identity and excluded people who wanted to be different. She emphasises that because gender is socially constructed, rather than something men or women are born with, it should be flexible, able to change at different times and in different circumstances. She argues that gender is only a performance, it's how we learn to behave, and our society rewards us for behaving in what are seen as gender-appropriate ways. She argues that gender identities should be challenged by subversive action or what she calls gender trouble, where people create or perform their own new identity, so that there are lots of different identities, not one narrow and restricting one. This is seen in queer theory, which challenges what are considered 'normal' ideas about gender or sexuality. You can read more about queer theory on pp. 92–8. The media can be one of the main places where new ideas about gender and sexual identity may be explored.

ACTIVITY

The games industry is dominated by male characters with dominant representations of men as competitive, violent or heroic. In *Gender Inclusive Game Design: Expanding The Market* (2003), Sheri Graner-Ray questions why the game industry is still producing computer games that primarily target males aged between 13 and 25. She argues that game developers must start looking at expanding their market, which means designing titles that are accessible to a female audience.

There are some alternative representations of women in gaming. Collect a range of images from game covers, game websites and shots of game play from games that you think are challenging gender roles.

How are they creating gender trouble, challenging 'normal' gender roles and behaviour?

The game blog (www.vgfreedom.blogspot.com) lists their *Top 5 Coolest Women in Video Games* as

5. Nariko from the *Heavenly Sword* Series
4. Princess Zelda in *The Legend of Zelda*
3. Joanna Dark in *Perfect Dark*
2. Lara Croft from *Tomb Raider*
1. Samus Aran from *Metroid*

Figure 2.11 The coolest women in videogames. Left to right: Joanna Dark, Lara Croft and Samus Aran

Developments in new and digital media have led to an increase in the number of representations of women, some alternative, and an increase in self-representation. There are now lots of feminist webzines that are critical of existing representations of women in mainstream media and which offer alternative representations.

ACTIVITY

Compare the representation of women in the homepage of a feminist website with the homepage of a mainstream women's lifestyle magazine online. For example, www.mookychick.co.uk or www.fbomb.org, with www.glamourmagazine.co.uk or www.graziadaily.co.uk.

1. How do the two websites represent women? What are the main differences? Are there any similarities?
2. What values do they communicate about femininity, how society constructs what it is to be a woman? How is mookychick a feminist product?
3. What effect could this have on their audiences? However, because alternative representations are often only seen by a small audience does this mean they don't have the power or influence of mainstream dominant representations?
4. Is it possible for women to get a negotiated reading from either of the websites?
5. Who is producing the two products and why are they producing them? How does this influence the representations?

Figure 2.12
Homepage of feminist website www.mookychick.co.uk

Figure 2.13 Homepage of *Glamour* Magazine website

Postmodernism

One of the great attractions of postmodernism is that it roundly dismisses almost all the other theories on the grounds of irrelevance. According to postmodernists, any theory which makes claims about universal or underlying truths is just missing the point. Those 'big stories', like Marxism or Christianity, are no longer convincing in a world that is ever more confused and fragmented. Jean-François Lyotard called these discredited 'big stories' metanarratives in his 1979 book *The Postmodern Condition* and stressed the breakdown of values that this entailed.

Postmodernists also reject the idea of cultural value: the notion that some cultural practices and products are simply and intrinsically *better* than others. "We live," said Lyotard, "in a cultural Disneyland where everything is parody and nothing is better or worse." Here the old distinctions between high and popular culture have broken down and the construction of cultural identities is an active process of bricolage, of tinkering with the debris. We have, according to John Storey, "an audience of *knowing bricoleurs* who take pleasure from this and other forms of bricolage". This is a do-it-yourself world of meanings where popular culture is no longer seen as the poor relation but simply as another means of expression. It is a world where William Shakespeare's *Romeo and Juliet* is a gangster movie and *Jerry Springer: The Opera*.

> **BRICOLAGE** the dictionary usefully defines it as "a construction made of whatever materials are at hand; something created from a variety of available things", which is precisely how postmodernists use it, though the constructions are of meaning. 'Bricoleurs' in French are tinkers, people who travel around collecting unwanted items.
>
> Classic bricoleurs on British TV 20 years ago were 'The Wombles', bear-like rubbish-collecting inhabitants of Wimbledon Common, who, according to the song were
>
> > "making good use of the things that we find,
> > Things that the everyday folks leave behind."

We can see evidence of this kind of bricolage and recycling everywhere: pop songs which sample riffs and licks from the 'classics' of popular or serious music, the 'instant nostalgia' of television programmes like *Mad Men* or even *Life on Mars*, advertising's appropriation of the icons of visual arts such as the 'Mona Lisa'. Of course, the meanings originally attached to these 'borrowings' from the past can be accepted, rejected or manipulated, often in the name of 'postmodern irony'. Lads' magazines, stand-up comedians, schlock films and homophobic rap artists have all dismissed the criticism that they are being offensive and tasteless on the grounds that they are expressing a form of 'postmodern chic'.

ACTIVITY

Cultural implosion?

Jean Baudrillard argues for "the implosion of meaning in the media", suggesting that the old structures of 'high' and 'low' have been replaced with something of a 'bombsite'. What examples can you find where high art and popular culture (or 'old' and 'new' culture) are confused or combined (think TV and pop music and film and computer games).

Despite the energy and excitement sparked by this active approach to meaning, both Lyotard and Baudrillard are fundamentally pessimistic, worrying where this succession of breakdowns will lead. Recycling old meanings in new combinations is all very well but it may have implications for our understanding of what is real and particular for our sense of the past. This is Lyotard's point about us inhabiting "a cultural Disneyland", an idea developed in Baudrillard's work on hyperreality and the simulations which create it.

For Baudrillard, we live in an era of media saturation in which we are bombarded with information and signs. So much of our experience is in the form of media texts rather than first-hand, direct experience that the signs become 'more real than real'. This is *simulation*: the part of our lives that is dominated by television, computer games, DVD, Internet chatrooms, magazines and all the other image suppliers. This is a very big part of many people's lives, maybe even the biggest and most important part. Consequently, Baudrillard argues, the distinction between reality and simulation breaks down altogether: we make no distinction between real experience and simulated experience. Hyperreality refers to the condition where the distinction between them has not only blurred, but the 'image' part has started to gain the upper hand.

HYPERREALITY

Here is an example which may help explain the rather baffling concept of hyperreality. Let's imagine that I have never visited Paris. In spite of this I have a huge fund of impressions based on the simulations of Paris that I have seen in films and on television, usually to the accompaniment of accordion music. I have looked at magazines, travel brochures and my friends' holiday snaps. I have read about the entertainment, the food and the nightlife. The

Figure 2.14 A trip to Paris: reality or hyperrreality?

simulated Paris I know so well is a vibrant, exciting and stimulating city. One day, I decide to visit Paris for the first time. It is drizzling, my hotel room is cramped and dirty, nobody is particularly friendly and I get ripped off in a restaurant. Now I have a fund of rather negative 'real' experiences to add to my very positive simulated experiences. Which of these will win out to form my overall impression of Paris? If Baudrillard is right, they will all merge into one undifferentiated set of experiences, but the image-based simulations will be just that little bit more powerful than my direct experience. My Paris is hyperreal.

Baudrillard's argument is that in a media-saturated world, representation has been replaced as the dominant mode by its opposite, simulation. John Storey summed it up well when he wrote, "In the realm of the postmodern, the distinction between simulation and the 'real' continually implodes; the real and the imaginary continually collapse into each other. The result is hyperrealism: the real and the simulated are experienced as without difference" (Storey, 1998, p. 347). If hyper-realism reflects a hyperreality, reality itself is forever lost to us.

Baudrillard revives the biblical term 'simulacrum', which refers to an identical copy without an original. He proposes that we are surrounded by representations which have no real reference to reality; they are images of images. Baudrillard considered representation to be the opposite of simulation, which is interesting to us as Media Studies students. Representation, he argued works on the principle that "the sign and the real are equivalent", whereas simulation divorces the sign from its original subject. This process through which images are degraded works in four phases:

- it is a reflection of basic reality
- it masks and perverts a basic reality
- it masks the *absence* of a basic reality
- it bears no relation to any reality whatever: it is its own pure simulacrum.

(Baudrillard, in Storey, 1998, pp. 353–4)

This is the cut-and-paste world of parody and pastiche which is the modern mass media experience. It is a world in which 'Comic book films' have become a viable (and lucrative) film genre: the reflection of a reflection of a reflection. It is a world in which image and images have lives of their own; unanchored to any 'basic reality', they constitute their own. This is not just about virtual realities and other computer-generated environments but about the worlds represented by film, advertising and television. Think of the Manchester presented by *Coronation Street* since 1960 or the East End offered up by *EastEnders* since 1984. They have become significantly more and less than realistic realisations of reality. Like pubs in living museums or theme parks, the Rovers Return and Queen Vic, for example, are simulations, part of a hyperreality.

In the same way, depictions of female characters in blockbuster Hollywood action films can hardly be seen as representational. In the codes of these films there is a paradigm of female types, which as they are progressively used progressively undermine the motivation of the images.

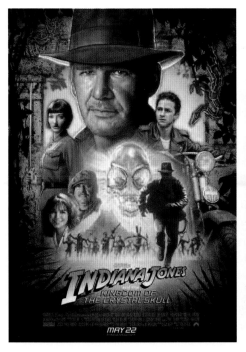

Figure 2.15 Film poster for *Indiana Jones: Kingdom of the Crystal Skull*

Figure 2.16 DVD cover for *Pulp Fiction*

ACTIVITY

Look at the three women depicted on the posters above and decide, irrespective of your knowledge of the films themselves, what you can confidently predict about their character and function. What else do you notice about them?

The representation of women in these texts, Baudrillard would argue, has been superseded by a process whereby mythic features have taken over from the desire to be realistic. Thus what might have started out as a realistic portrayal is soon conventionalised away from its reality and into the service of the hyperreal. Take either of the stock representations of 'evil' women/bad girls above (Cate Blanchett's 'manly' bitch or Uma Thurman's *femme fatale*). Both may have been coined as representations of a perceived aspect of 'womanliness' or of individual women but as they are continually reproduced across media platforms and genre (they will feature just as readily in news as in drama) their link to these realities is eroded. And the precession begins:

- It is a reflection of basic reality.
- It masks and perverts a basic reality; the original image is adapted and developed in a way that moves it further from its basic reality.
- It masks the *absence* of a basic reality; ultimately it comes to be understood as marking the absence of any real 'evidence' of meaning-making.
- It bears no relation to any reality whatever: it is its own pure simulacrum. It is now merely a counter in a world of claim and counter-claim.

One thing that is masked in this process is any sense of where these simulations have emerged from, any historical context. Bricolage may be about plundering the canon of 'great works' and recycling the past but this accumulation happens on the surface and in the present: it has no depth or past. Postmodernism concerns itself primarily with surfaces. As you will be aware, the media consists largely of 'shiny surfaces' that give the illusion of depth, like a film set. The form of a film or an 'alternative' CD may give us the impression that it is weighty and meaningful, but this impression may very well be limited to the form rather than to the content; the text *looks* very significant, but that is as far as it goes. A postmodernist take on this would be to say 'So what? What you see is what you get.' In other words, we shouldn't even expect depth or meaningfulness. Just as there are no 'deep structures' there are no 'underlying meanings'; the signifier has detached itself from the signified. The cultural form which exemplifies this approach perfectly is the pop video. A dense array of suggestive signifiers may be compiled, drawing on all sorts of cultural reference points. But what does it all mean? If you are asking the question, you have already missed the point!

Now this is a very positive take. Most postmodernist theorists are more concerned with the impact that the unreliability of reality as a concept might have. Freed from history the modern audience seeks further simulations and these are primarily fuelled by nostalgia.

> **When the real is no longer what it used to be, nostalgia assumes its full meaning. There is a proliferation of myths of origin and signs of reality: of second hand truth, objectivity and authenticity. There is an escalation of the true, of the lived experience.**
>
> (Baudrillard, in Storey, 1998, p. 354)

Prophetically this is a manifesto for 'Reality TV', that "escalation of the true, of lived experience". In reality a show like *Big Brother* (now axed) has itself gone through a period of 'degradation' as its initial purpose, to teach us something about social interaction, gives way to something far more expedient. Here postmodern playfulness only serves to further expose a further masking of reality.

Postcolonialism

> "Rule Britannia! Britannia rules the waves.
> Britons never, never, never shall be slaves."
> (Adapted from the poem 'Rule Britannia' by James Thompson, 1740)

History books tell us that the British used to have an empire which at one time spanned half the globe. Among the parts of the world which Britain colonised were the USA, Canada, Australia, South Africa, Jamaica, and the areas which now form the countries of India and Pakistan. Patriotic songs like 'Rule Britannia' are replete with references to our domination of the seas and many nations of the world. The building of an empire with such a global reach was made possible by the military might of Britain in the eighteenth, nineteenth and early twentieth centuries. Less-developed countries would be entered, a new system of governance established and the resources and labour exploited by the colonising power. Over time, colonial territories declared their independence, often after war or revolution, and the empire declined. While it is true to say that relative to the position it once held, British influence on the world stage and that of other colonising countries such as Spain and France has declined significantly, there exists a belief that in the aftermath of the empire, the effects of colonisation have by no means vanished completely. This standpoint forms the basis for the theoretical perspective of postcolonialism.

Among the areas where these effects may be seen most obviously are in language, sport and culture. English is widely spoken across all the countries which were once imperial territories just as Spanish is across most of South America following the colonisation of that continent by Spain. Australia, India, New Zealand, the West Indies, Pakistan and South Africa all excel at either cricket or rugby, or in some cases both. These sports were exported by the British to these countries during the times when they were colonies. Although Britain and other Western countries no longer have an empire where through military might they enter and take control of a country in the way they once did, the postcolonial theoretical perspective is concerned with the view that in terms of media and culture there is still a sense of Western domination, or as Marxists would term it 'Cultural Imperialism' and that this echoes the empire building of old. While the tool of empire building was once a sword or a gun, today it is far more likely to be culture, consumer products and media production.

Even in the furthest reaches of Africa, the influence of the American global giant Coca Cola can be felt, as the images below show.

Figure 2.17 The influence of Coca Cola in Africa

Arguably, the most evident sign of cultural imperialism in the contemporary world is the area of cinema, a media platform which is dominated by the USA. Even a cursory glance of the film schedule at your local multiplex at any time will reveal a preponderance of American film showing on the screens. Even countries like France with a well-established national cinema has expressed concern at the effect the influx of American imports might have on its own film industry. The influence of US media and culture may be evidenced in a wide range of other media platforms such as music or television, and also in the organisations which produce the media. However, the US influence is just part of what may more broadly be regarded as Western influence which in addition to the media output of the USA also includes European and Australian media. Through recognising the East/West divide in media, postcolonial theory involves looking at how Eastern and Oriental culture is viewed through the eyes of the dominant Western media. Edward Said in his highly influential book *Orientalism* (1978) argues that Eastern culture is habitually seen as inferior to Western, a phenomenon he calls Orientalism. The West, he argues, terms Eastern cultures as the 'other' and contests that this perception can be traced back to the work of, among others, Shakespeare, Byron and Chaucer. At best, Said argues, when represented by Western culture, Orientalism is seen as exotic, which is relatively harmless, but of more concern is the manner of this representation – a deliberate and aggressive exploitation by Western culture which perceives itself as stronger and which perpetuates a doctrine that has legitimised this imbalance of power and the relative weakness of the East. Elizabeth Poole supports the main points of Said's study in her research into representations of British Muslims in the media. Political Islam, she argues, emerged as a consequence of the oppression of the colonisation of Islamic countries and has "allowed the West to construct Islam as the new enemy" following the collapse of communism in the late 1980s. Within the Marxist perspective, the media are seen to act as a tool of hegemony, a means by which the interests of a powerful group, the West, are both legitimised and enforced over the weaker group, in this case Muslims. Similarly Poole suggests that the media are instrumental in demonising Islam, and both reproducing and sustaining the ideology which subjugates Islam and those who follow the faith (Poole, 2002).

This is perhaps nowhere more evident than in the representations of Islam in Western media. The film *Executive Decision* (1997) portrays a radical Islamic group who hijack a plane with a view to crashing it into an American city, thus releasing nerve gas which will kill millions of people, and, having pitted his wits against aliens, communists, machines and private armies, Arnold Schwarzenegger took on a radical group of Muslim extremists in *True Lies* (1994). Recently, the hit TV show *24* which has been praised by many critics as an innovative and original concept whereby the action takes place in real time has also attracted its critics for its representations of Muslims. During the fourth series of the show, the Council on American–Islamic Relations complained to the show's producers, Fox TV, about the negative portrayal of Muslims in the show. This complaint led the show's star, Kiefer Sutherland, to announce at the start of one of the episodes that "the American Muslim community stands firmly beside their fellow Americans in denouncing and resisting all forms of terrorism. So in watching *24*, please bear that in mind." Nevertheless, the criticism continued when Muslims were again portrayed as terrorists in the sixth series. The eighth series which first aired early in 2010 once again saw radical Muslim characters involved in terrorist plots with dissident Russian characters.

INFORMATION BOX

These characters, from top left Tarin Faroush, Farhad Hassan, Habib Marwan, Ahmed Amar and Abu Fayed, have all attempted to bring terror upon the USA in the name of an Islamic cause in the TV show *24*. This has led to criticisms of the show for the negative and stereotypical manner it portrays Islam, but do such characters demonise Muslims and help spread a sense of Islamaphobia?

continued

Figure 2.18 Muslim characters in TV series *24*

Research conducted by the Islamic Human Rights Commission (http://www.ihrc.org.uk/show.php?id=2493) counters further that the demonisation of Islam is not limited to fictional media but may be found in the way Muslims are represented in TV news, current affairs and more broadly in literature. Coverage of Muslims in TV news seems to be dominated by issues of terrorism, radicalisation, illegal immigration and a general representation as Said argues of Muslims as the 'other'. In his book *Hegemony or Survival: America's Quest For Global Dominance* (2004), Noam Chomsky explains how America sought to portray Saddam Hussein as an imminent threat to the USA and as responsible for the terrorist attacks in New York on 11 September 2001, accusations which with the benefit of hindsight appear to have been inaccurate at best, if not completely false. This was part of the USA's strategy through which it reserved the right to resort to force to protect its global hegemony. Chomsky concludes that this campaign was highly successful in America in shifting attitudes and the media was partly responsible for this. However, it could be argued by taking an institutional viewpoint that the purpose of all media, including those concerned with news and current affairs, is to make money, and so it is simply reporting the events which they determine as newsworthy, a process which is based upon the application of a set of news values to an event. This was a concern of Noam Chomsky in his earlier book *Manufacturing Consent* (1988) where he argues that American news media in its drive to make money reports those events which will attract the largest audiences and so attract the largest number of advertisers upon whom they rely for revenue. Clearly the feeling with this perspective is that the demonisation of Muslims in news media helps to sell news media.

What Elizabeth Poole, critics of shows like *24* such as the Council on American–Islamic Relations and the Islamic Human Rights Commission are referring to here is perhaps better known today as Islamaphobia or a fear of Muslims borne out of the actions of a few radicals who have perpetrated a number of atrocities, including the 9/11 terror attacks and those in London in July 2005, and which has intensified to a fear of the entire faith of Islam. It is argued that the media plays a key role in influencing opinion on this issue; certainly it has been quite widely reported in the press and a wealth of negative coverage has led to the belief among some that Islam is dangerous. Yet the figures do not support this fear. The overwhelming majority of Muslims across the world do not engage in any terrorist activity, nor do they actively seek to be in a state of conflict with the West as has been reported in the media.

This takes us back almost full circle to the Marxist consideration of media as part of the mechanism by which the ruling elite legitimises and maintains its control and power over the rest of society. The postcolonial perspective fits neatly as a parallel to this, since it seeks to explain how the West, which regards itself as the ruling elite, legitimises and maintains its power over the East and exerts its cultural influence around the world. This cultural imperialism is further strengthened when

the West is willing to invade countries and impose Western democratic political ideology upon the population, as is the case in Afghanistan and Iraq. Portraying Muslims in the media as terrorists, a threat to Western values and principles and as the 'other' to be feared and mistrusted becomes an important means by which consent for the dominant ideology and the wider military objectives can be won.

Queer theory and queerness

Queer is an academic theory of popular culture (originally about film). It is the name given to a small range of media texts (queerness) and a radical activist movement which includes groups such as ACTUP and Outrage.

Queer theory and queerness in popular culture is difficult to reduce to one definition. This is partly because one of the arguments of queer theory is that as an audience it is possible to take up queer and straight positions at different times, that media texts can be straight and queer; films with gay characters can be straight (in the context of queerness) while a film about straight characters can be queer. This rather confusing outline does reinforce the fact that queer is not a synonym for gay but rather a position which rejects conventional or mainstream expressions of all types of behaviour – including sexual identity. A characteristic of queer theory has been a debate about what a queer text is and what it should look like. This argument has often been structured around the differences between mainstream and alternative institutional contexts of popular culture – asking whether there can ever be a queer mainstream text.

Theoretical context

Queer theory has a close relationship to feminist theory and gender studies. In some ways queer theory continues the approaches of those areas but it also rejects some of the assumptions underpinning these more traditional perspectives. Like feminist theory and gender studies, queer theory is interested in studying non-normative expressions of gender and sexuality. In opposition to these approaches queer theory rejects the essentialist nature of theories of identity which are expressed through binary oppositions – male/female, gay/straight, etc. Queer theory argues that people do not simply categorise themselves in this way, representations don't conform to either side of these divides – instead there is another space outside of these oppositions and it is this space which is 'queer'.

Queer positions: androgyny, cross-dressing and reception

This concept of a queer space may be applied to the example of androgyny and cross-dressing. A film which has been discussed a lot in queer theory is *Sylvia Scarlet* (Cukor, US, 1935). In this film, Katherine Hepburn, an actress whose star persona emphasised her unconventional gender characteristics (trousers, suit jackets, athleticism, strong features), plays a young woman who dresses as a man (Sylvester) in order to avoid arrest. Straight male audience members who gain sexual pleasure from looking at Katherine Hepburn in male dress are having a queer moment – something which cannot be simply categorised as gay or straight (Doty, 1995).

This analysis could be tested with reference to a more recent film, *Boys Don't Cry* (Kimberley Pierce, US, 1994). The central character – Brandon – is a female who identifies as and performs the role of a heterosexual male. Brandon's girlfriend identifies as a heterosexual female rather than a lesbian, even when she knows that Brandon is biologically female. *Boys Don't Cry* isn't necessarily queer though; Brandon's attempt to 'pass' in society as a heterosexual male could be read as a reinforcement of conventional definitions of gender and sexuality and therefore not queer.

Figure 2.20 Katherine Hepburn in *Sylvia Scarlet* and Hilary Swank in *Boys Don't Cry*

What is a queer text?

Queer texts are defined in two ways:

- Those which deal with explicitly queer themes and characters.
- Those which are read as queer; the accumulation of queer readings 'queers the text' whether it is explicitly queer or not.

The definition of a queer text – or persona – as one which 'has accumulated queer readings' (Doty, 1998) means that texts with gay characters may not be queer but gay, while texts without gay characters can be queer.

There is of course a great deal of disagreement about what constitutes a queer text, but an independent film movement in the US in the early 1990s which was named 'new queer cinema' by critics is generally agreed to be queer. These films had in common a central character that was on the margins of society – an outsider – usually due to their sexuality, but issues such as race, gender, class and physical disability were also referred to. While there had been films which featured gay characters and storylines before, new queer cinema was different in that it rejected the idea of positive representations which would be acceptable to the hetero-sexual, mainstream audience and instead deliberately attempted to shock and anger that audience. In a similar approach, the term queer which had previously been used as a term of abuse was appropriated by some organisations and individuals and used as a positive form of identification.

Poison (Todd Haynes, 1991), *My Own Private Idaho* (Gus Van Sant, 1991), *Swoon* (Tom Kalin, 1992), *Go Fish* (Rose Troche, 1994), *The Living End* (Gregg Araki, 1993) and *Savage Grace* (Tom Kalin, 2007).

Figure 2.21 Film posters for *Go Fish* and *Swoon*

Queerness and the mainstream

The debates around definitions of queerness in mainstream texts can be illustrated by the career of Gus Van Sant. Gus Van Sant was a leading figure of new queer cinema, an out gay director of independent, experimental films as well as star-driven Oscar winners (*Good Will Hunting*, 1997). *Milk* (2008), which is a bio-pic of Harvey Milk, the first openly gay elected politician in the US, has been defined as a gay rather than a queer film. This is partly due to its mainstream institutional context, star performance (Sean Penn won an Oscar for the title role) but particularly because it focuses on themes of equality and acceptance, the idea that everyone is the same and can be assimilated into mainstream society. Queer is instead a celebration of difference and is unapologetic in foregrounding that difference – whether it is uncomfortable for the audience or not. Gus Van Sant's films which deal less explicitly (or not at all) with gay themes are, conversely, queer in their representation of outsiders, drifters, criminals and addicts (see *Drugstore Cowboys* (1989), *Last Days* (2005), *Paranoid Park* (2007)).

This approach to queerness means that films such as *Rebel Without a Cause* (Nicholas Ray, 1955), *Edward Scissorhands* (Tim Burton, 1990) and *Donnie Darko* (Richard Kelly, 2001) are queer due to the focus on and sympathy for characters who do not conform to the conventional expectations of their society.

Queer genres

A diverse range of style and content may be characterised as queer but many queer texts do share a particular characteristic – the subversion of traditional genre rules. This form mirrors the other unconventional representations in the films. *Brokeback Mountain* (Ang Lee, US, 2006), a film which caused controversy for a variety of reasons, has been the focus of a gay vs. queer debate among critics and academics.

BROKEBACK MOUNTAIN AS QUEER TEXT

- The use of melodrama, which is traditionally structured around heterosexual relationships to tell the love story of Jack and Ennis (the central characters in the film), places the audience in a queer position, identifying with characters who are queer rather than gay (they don't self-identify as gay – the concept hardly exists in the world of the film).
- The melodrama – also known as the woman's film or weepie – is intercut with the Western. This placement of the two genres together reveals meanings which had always existed in the Western but which had not been acknowledged. *Brokeback Mountain* takes the homoerotic aspect of the Western and puts it centre stage. This queering of the Western is not the uncovering of a subtext but acknowledging a meaning which had always existed alongside dominant, straight readings (the truth of this analysis is perhaps evident in the delight a variety of audiences and media experienced in describing the film as the 'gay cowboys movie').

- The concept of 'queer space' which is neither gay nor straight is symbolised in the geographical space of Brokeback Mountain.

BROKEBACK MOUNTAIN ISN'T QUEER

- The concept of queer positioning carries with it the idea of pleasure for the audience. As a melodrama the audience is positioned to suffer with the characters.
- Gay relationships are represented as a source of suffering; the best you can hope for is a few weeks of happiness. The silent endurance of Ennis is completely at odds with queerness which refuses to be quiet.
- The audience emphasises with Alma, Ennis' wife, and the misery caused to her by Ennis and Jack's relationship.

Figure 2.22 Heath Ledger in *Brokeback Mountain*

IT'S NOT GAY, IT'S QUEER: *I LOVE YOU PHILLIP MORRIS*

There has been an identifiable shift in the representation of gay characters in mainstream texts in the past 20 years. Stereotypes have been challenged and gay characters (although with the exception of *The L Word* it does tend to be gay male characters who appear) are more common and are no longer defined simply by their sexuality. Popular TV series (*Brothers and Sisters* (ABC, 2006–present), *Glee* (Fox, 2009–present), *Nurse Jackie* (Showtime, 2009–present)) have central and supporting gay characters. Queer theory questions the meaning of these representations though, arguing that too often they are based on assimilation and the need for acceptance by straight society. The recent Hollywood, star-driven film *I Love You Phillip Morris* (Glen Ficarra and John Requa, US, 2009) seems to represent something different; a mainstream film about gay men which is actually queer. The film is based on the true story (as the tagline puts it 'no, really, it is') of Steven (Jim Carrey), a con man who, after a happy marriage and family life, comes out as gay and embarks on a career as a con man. While in prison he falls in love with Phillip Morris (Ewan McGregor) and the rest of the film is about their relationship in the context of Steven's outlaw lifestyle. Despite its mainstream context, *I Love You Phillip Morris* may be read as queer in a number of respects.

INFORMATION BOX   *i*

■ The outsider theme of queer is clearly evident in the poster and plot line; the heroes are convicts who continue a life of crime on release.

■ Sexual desire and the physical pleasures of gay sex are dealt with in a cheerfully frank, explicit way. Gay sex is represented as different to straight – gay films usually try to minimise the sense of difference.

■ There is no moral judgement made about their lifestyle (as criminals or gay men) leading to the film being described as 'morally reprehensible'.

Figure 2.23 Film poster for *I Love You Phillip Morris*

■ The difference between gay and straight lifestyles is celebrated throughout. As an out gay man Stephen lives a totally different life to his straight, suburban existence (he's 'living high on the gay hog'). When he goes to play golf with his boss in order to get on in the corporation, Phillip cries in horror: "*But you're a homosexual!*"

■ This disregard for the conventions and morality of mainstream society is typical of queer.

■ A characteristic of queerness is the subversion of genre conventions. *ILYPM* is a hybrid of romantic comedy, crime film (there are

continued

Figure 2.24 Scenes from *I Love You Phillip Morris*

similarities with *Catch Me if You Can* (Steven Spielberg, 2002)) and the prison film. As with *Brokeback Mountain* the mix of traditionally male and female genres queers the text. The rom-com narrative structure means we root for the happy couple, and the references to the prison film acknowledge the homoeroticism of that form.

■ The use of the comedy genre – rather than the drama or melodrama – constructs an audience response of happiness and celebration. Steve and Phillip's relationship is romantic, joyful and public – in direct contrast to the tortured 'gay cowboys'.

Summary of queer theory

■ Queer is used as an overarching term to describe the way in which a range of identities (sexuality, race, gender, disability) intersect; it is not synonymous with gay.

■ Queer theory shares with feminism and gender studies an interest in unconventional gender characteristics.

■ Queer theory rejects the concept of essentialism and binary oppositions in defining identity.

■ Queer texts can be defined through content and the accumulation of queer readings.

Conclusion

ISSUES AND DEBATES:
3 CASE STUDIES

Preparing case studies for the MEST3 exam

The AQA specification requires you to undertake two case studies to answer your MEST3 paper, Critical perspectives. These will help you to answer Section A questions on unseen media products and will be the basis of your Section B essay. The idea behind the case study is that you will focus on one area of each of the pre-set topics, undertake research and analysis, and then apply what you have learned in one of them to an essay question in the exam itself. This gives you the opportunity to get to know an area in the media especially well so that you can showcase your research and understanding of the topic when you respond to the essay exam question. You will need to investigate the wider contexts, those social, political, economic and historical forces that shape media output, and to show an awareness of contemporary media issues and debates that impact upon the media, as well as demonstrating some theoretical insight, where appropriate. You can read more about the mechanics of how to do this in Chapter 4.

What follows is a fairly detailed work-through of three topics: representation, new and digital media, and media and identity. The latter topic is especially useful as it casts some interesting light on the other topics and is likely to be the sort of issue that will feature in the future.

These case studies are not intended to do the work for the MEST3 exam for you – far from it. They are a means of getting you started on your own individual investigation. By this stage of the course there must be something that interests you sufficiently to want to find out more. Make that your case study. The value of the case studies you have should offer you a way of looking into the topic area through the examples we have used. You should use this chapter in combination with the chapter on MEST3 itself to ensure you have prepared thoroughly for the exam itself. One important tip is to make sure you have plenty of contemporary examples to use when you come to write your exam essay. Over your year of A2 study, make sure you are constantly on the lookout for interesting and appropriate examples to use when you want to exemplify an issue or a point. If you do this, your revision will prove so much easier.

Case study

REPRESENTATION

When you switch on your TV, the images are largely iconic; they resemble the images that you see when you look through your window at the world outside. Indeed, TV is often described as 'a window on the world', which suggests that what we see on our screens is in fact the world outside. However, television is not a 'window', nor could it ever be. Every televised image is the product of many decisions about how reality should be transformed. For this reason, television cannot simply show reality, it can only offer versions of reality influenced by the decision-making processes of media producers and the technical constraints of the medium. This is what we mean by the construction of reality by the media. Because all media messages are constructed in this sense, everything contained within them is a representation. Of course, representation does not just concern pictures; it concerns every aspect of communication. Newspaper journalists, for example, may talk about 'telling it like it really is' or 'transparent reporting'. The implication is that they convey 'reality' exactly as it is to their readers.

Much of the nature of the construction of television programmes and films is designed to make them appear as natural and as realistic as possible. Continuity editing, for example, creates the illusion that programmes have a natural flow, that they are put together without seams. With television's technical ability to produce slow-motion action replays and use multiple camera angles, a sporting event viewed on TV has a reality beyond that of

continued

spectating at a live event. In a sense, the television experience becomes 'more real than real'. Inherent in this are obvious consequences for the individual. The postmodernist commentator Jean Baudrillard talks of distinctions between the real and the unreal collapsing, so that TV no longer *represents* the world, it *is* the world. We are overloaded with information and images to such an extent that we no longer differentiate between the real world and media constructions of the world: a condition which Baudrillard describes as hyperreality.

Mediation as a process

When a medium (such as radio or film) carries a message, it is mediating it, simply carrying it from one place to another. Mediation is the act of 'going between', in this case between 'an audience' and 'the world', but this simple process has some very complex implications. Inevitably, the relationship between the world and the audience is changed by the process of mediation. When you sit down and think about it you might come to the conclusion that most of what you know and most of your experiences are 'merely' mediated, since the encounters have been second- rather than firsthand. Think of what you really know about Africa or GM foods, let alone the war in Iraq or al-Qaeda, then subtract all you received on the subjects from 'mediators'. What is left? At best, perhaps, your holiday in Tunisia or the Gambia.

ACTIVITY

Think of some of the ways in which mediation could be described as an 'interested activity'. Bear in mind that mediation does not necessarily imply deliberate distortion or cynical manipulation of audiences (though both of these can occur). Try this 'investigation':

Figure 3.1 Barack Obama

Barack Obama is a regular 'character' featuring in news coverage and beyond on all media platforms, but who is he 'really' (i.e. to you)? Make two lists.

- *List one:* What I know about Obama (if your answer is 'nothing' at least respond to the following prompts: his politics, his age, his ethnicity, his social background, his family).
- *List two:* What I was able to find out about Obama in 30 minutes with internet access (if your answer is 'everything', prioritise).
- *Supplementary:* Does this exercise prove that (1) we know very little about Obama, *or* (2) we don't need to know about Obama as long as we know where to look? And for Obama you might substitute anyone or anything.

The media rarely 'see' by accident and never without interest, although it is often at pains to 'cover its tracks' by allowing reportage and 'realism' to be casually confused with reality. Writing specifically about television realism, Abercrombie (1996, p. 27) identified three aspects of realism (which affects a particular kind of mediation).

- Realism offers a 'window on the world'; an apparently unmediated experience.
- Realism employs a narrative which has rationally ordered connections between events and characters.
- Realism attempts to conceal the production process.

The paradox here is that so much that appears natural, from the live outside broadcast to the painstakingly researched film drama, is in fact the result of a complex industrial process. What is 'real' is defined in terms of what is realistic. Neil Postman (1985) has claimed that 'TV reality is *the* reality', suggesting that the mediated world has become a blueprint for the unmediated version. This is the hyperreality, this world of simulations, that the postmodernists see as central to the way we live now. Baudrillard argues that we now live in economies based on the production of images and information where once we produced 'things' (material products). The danger is that we lose a sense of context, particularly in a historical sense, that the endless mash-up of 'contemporary' and 'vintage' means that nothing is truly over or securely real. In this context, Baudrillard argues, we are open to a

continued

sentimentalised version of the past: "When the real is no longer what it used to be, nostalgia assumes its full meaning." In simple terms in the age of the trans-media narrative the interplay of media representations becomes more important than the relationship between those representations and their subject reality.

ACTIVITY

A major television event of 2010 was the Spielberg/Hanks production *The Pacific*, the latest offshoot of the *Private Ryan/Band of Brothers* family. Watch the trails for this series along with the introduction to any of the first-person shooter WW2 computer games (preferably *Medal of Honor* or *Call of Duty* with *Medal of Honor: Pacific Assault* offering the clearest comparison). What similarities do you notice between the two sets of representations? Given that both consciously offer 'realism', how do you respond to them in the light of the aspects of this process offered by Abercrombie:

- That realism offers a 'window on the world'.
- That realism employs a narrative which has rationally ordered connections between events and characters.
- That realism attempts to conceal the production process.

Stereotypes and minorities

Reality TV offers us 'real people' in 'real situations'. Magazines help us to deal with 'real problems' and the popular press deals with the 'real lives' of 'ordinary people' (as well as celebrities, of course). Soap operas give us an opportunity to share the lives of 'realistic characters' in lifelike settings. But is any of this reality-obsessed entertainment actually real? Of course not. As we have already seen, these fictional and non-fictional texts have no alternative but to provide mediated versions of the world. Some commentators have argued, though, that we as audience members may be organising and understanding our own lives in the terms provided by this mediated version of reality. In other words, there is a link between media representations and the identities of audience members. Representations of 'people like us' suggest to us who we are, what we can become and how we should evaluate ourselves. As Woodward puts it:

> **Discourses and systems of representation construct places from which individuals can position themselves and from which they can speak. . . . The media can be seen as providing us with the information which tells us what it feels like to occupy a particular subject-position – the streetwise teenager, the upwardly mobile worker or the caring parent.**
>
> (Woodward, 1997, p. 14)

Logically, the impact on identity is felt particularly strongly by members of groups which are negatively represented in the mainstream media. In a study of black minority television viewers, Karen Ross found that most of her respondents were critical of British television's representations of ethnic groups and the relations between them. In the following extract, Ross makes it clear that the representation of places as well as groups can have an important impact on feelings about identity and self-worth.

> **The lack of positive role models and the way in which black minority characters are routinely stereotyped contribute to feelings of low self-esteem and failure, especially among black minority children. . . . Because most black minority children in Britain were born in the country, their knowledge of 'home' is very limited, gleaned from what their relatives tell them and, of course, from television. Viewers reported sadness at the reactions of their children to their homelands of Africa, India or Pakistan which, because the media's slant on the developing world tends to be negative, is one of shame at the 'backwardness' of their country of origin.**
>
> (Ross, 2000, p. 145)

continued

ACTIVITY

What are the significant details that define the following as 'real-istic':

- *EastEnders*
- *Britain's Got Talent*
- *Twilight*
- *Family Guy*
- *The Hills*

Representation, namely the construction of versions of reality to stand in for reality, does indeed take place at all levels of the (technical and creative) media process: in the writing, direction, camerawork and action. However, as Abercrombie points out, it is one of the abiding characteristics of realism that "the illusion of transparency is preserved". He goes on to clarify this when he writes, "The form conspires to convince us that we are not viewing something that has been constructed."

The representation, for example, of minority groups often founders at a simple level. We fall for the one about the neutrality of the media, the plausibility of 'the camera never lies', and we confuse 'resembles' with 'represents'. The former is an implication, the latter an active process. If we wish to represent a multicultural society or one in which women are challenging the traditional roles allocated to them, we must do so. It is disingenuous of media professionals to act as if the ideological meanings of a text are a mystery, unknown even to its makers and even beyond its makers' influence. Although it may be true that ideology operates at the level of the unconscious, this is not to say that ideological issues are invisible.

ACTIVITY

Imagine that the next two days of your life are being filmed as an innovative 'total drama' project, with the working title *Yet Another 48 Hours*. For 48 hours cameras will unobtrusively track your every move and interactive viewers will be able to monitor your 'actions'.

You are called in at the end of the project to discuss the production of an edited 90-minute version. You are asked for your opinion on two issues.

1. What would be the differences between a film of your life for two days and a conventional film or television 'drama'?
2. What principles would you suggest on which to model a 90-minute version of the recording?

The representation of minority groups often amounts to a failure to be proactive, as any amount of content research will prove. People with disabilities, for example, seem to have dropped 'beyond the frame' of the mediated world as if they were always just out of shot. This is what Barthes (1977) called 'absent presence', the fact that the very invisibility of some groups becomes an almost palpable issue. If we consider the representation of minority ethnic groups in the British media, the world of television situation comedy or game shows will furnish fruitful examples of absent presence. Conversely, a consideration of human interest stories and accompanying photographs in local or national newspapers might be relevant.

It would be easy to see 'absent presence' in mainstream soap operas like *Coronation Street* and even *EastEnders* as a pressure that has progressively prompted programme-makers to address this issue. However, we must not succumb to a crude oversimplification of the issue and merely see the problem in terms of a journey from 'none of them' to 'more of them', whomsoever 'they' may be. This is not a numbers but a meanings game: it is not about quotas but about questions.

Stereotypes are moulds into which reality can be poured, or at least part of it. A stereotype is a shorthand form and as such a reduction of the complexity of the reality represented. Stereotypes do not normally try to open debates about, for example, gender representations; they actually paper over them or 'skirt' around them.

The idea of stereotyping is often used with negative connotations, as if the removal of all stereotypes would make media representations fair and unbiased. However, a brief examination of the concept reveals that stereotypes are a necessary component of all mediated communication. There is never the time or space to do justice to the complexity of human beings. The variety of our environments and the sheer diversity of individuals make

continued

it inevitable that short cuts are taken in the telling of stories and the reporting of events. Furthermore, in an influential essay on stereotypes, Tessa Perkins (1997) made the point that we tend to make assumptions about stereotypes which can in themselves be misleading. For example, we sometimes assume that stereotypes are always wrong and always negative; but this is not necessarily the case. Nor is it necessarily true that stereotypes always concern minority or oppressed groups, or that they are simple and unchanging. On the other hand, it is possible for contradictory stereotypes to be held of the same group (see Perkins, 1997, p. 75).

Perkins goes on to reinforce the point that stereotypes are essentially *ideological* because they are predominantly evaluative beliefs expressed about groups and by groups. As with any ideological effect, the repetition of stereotypes and the absence of plausible alternatives means that the values wrapped up in the stereotype come to appear as 'common sense'. The stereotype does more than simply *describe* characteristics assigned to a particular group; it also carries value judgements. Andy Medhurst illustrates this principle in relation to stereotypes of gay men:

> **❝ [T]he image of the screaming queen does not just mean 'all gay men are like that', it means 'all gay men are like that and aren't they awful', which in turn means 'and they are awful because they are not like us'. ❞**

(Medhurst, 1998, p. 285)

In terms of the representations of minority groups stereotyping is often a double handicap, as even the range of stereotypes is often limited.

ACTIVITY

Consider the following groups. Bearing in mind Tessa Perkins' points, examine the prevalent stereotypes and explain how they are delivered either in the popular press or on television:

- fathers
- the police

- terrorists
- the French
- bankers

What are the particular issues for us as Media Studies students in each case?

Stereotypes are clearly useful in the sense that any shorthand is: they allow us to take a quick look and know what we're being given since we only need the 'gist' – that he's French, she's a bimbo and he's Irish, for example. However, what we're also doing is undermining the integrity of the world we are 'viewing', unless we are also given the chance to address or challenge these crude assumptions.

Alternative representations

As noted above, the ideological effect of stereotyping is most pronounced when stereotypes are reinforced by repetition and an absence of alternatives. However, it would be a mistake to see all media representation working in this way. There are many justifiable concerns about negativity and bias in media representation, but it is worth bearing in mind some of the following.

- There are alternatives to the mainstream media.
- The mainstream media often provides space for alternative representations.
- Many groups have intervened successfully to take more control over representation.
- 'Dominant' representations can change with great speed.
- The media provide many positive role models.
- Campaigns against biased and negative stereotypes have succeeded in changing industry practices, voluntary codes of conduct and statutory controls (laws).
- Media-literate audiences have a sophisticated understanding of the techniques and devices used to 're-present' reality.

An excellent case study for the alternative take on representation is provided by Matt Groening's *The Simpsons* which has been inhabiting its own heightened reality since 1989 in the most conservative TV environment

continued

in the world. Here the cartoon form is used to animate all kinds of debates about how the world is and how it can be. The show targets cant and hypocrisy wherever it finds it, from the exploitative manipulation of mass advertising to the crusading mock respect of political correctness. In one episode, Apu, the Hindu manager of the 'Kwik-e-Mart' (a large corner shop!), reveals to Homer his shrine to Ganesha, the elephant-headed god. Homer is certainly challenging in his response: 'Wow. You must have been out having a wazz when they were giving out the gods.'

On the other hand, if you want a summary of dominant stereotypes of gender, ethnicity or social class, where better to go than to the films of the Farrelly Brothers or that dubious British classic 'brand', the *Carry On . . .* series of films? Here the stereotypes are so crudely humorous that they unconsciously provide a platform for their discussion or at least an exposure of their limitations. The same may be true of *Footballers' Wives* or *Sunday Sport* or rap music videos, or even *Hello* magazine.

Types of realism

Ideology is about the relationship between representation and power, which is why representations of the powerless are always more significant than representations of the powerful. We are surely right to be more concerned with negative representations of ethnic minorities and women than those of middle-aged white men merely because the dominant ideology is, according to Fiske (1989), 'white, patriarchal capitalism'.

INFORMATION BOX i

Ideology is forever raising the stakes and leading us into the temptation of ready-made ideas: stereotypes which draw the personal always in the direction of the general and, with a little luck, the universal.

In a society bombarded with images of women in high heels and lingerie or both, we are constantly challenged by the assumption, 'this is what women are like'. We are also provided with a set of reasons why this should be so, which at their most persuasive are described as 'common sense' (perhaps the most powerful form of ideological communication). This is the battleground of what

Gramsci calls hegemony, the aggressive negotiation of meaning in which the dominant ideology must engage to keep itself 'healthy' and perpetuate itself. In simple terms ideology has become an active ingredient in society, embedding itself within social institutions like education and the media. We find social values everywhere, disguised yet actively persuading us in every aspect of our lives (work and leisure) that society's dominant opinions are indisputable.

Take a look at the picture of Graham Norton in Figure 3.2 and see how easy it is to employ the anchor 'this is what gays are like' and how it is almost impossible to imagine that 'this is what men are like'. In fact Norton's preferred word would probably be 'queer', a classic piece of appropriation by the gay community of a favourite form of homophobic abuse. The TV drama *Queer as Folk* took this to the limits and still stands as a byword for courageous and controversial programming. It is deliberately provocative to the 'straight' community which may have settled for the rather more coy representations of 'gay'. In the same way that rap group NWA helped to reclaim the word 'nigger' to the discomfort of liberal whites in particular, so 'queer' is a mite more powerful than the limp-wrist 'salute'. Graham Norton is a flamboyant role model and pioneer, but he is also 'professionally gay'. What we see is a persona, performance and a good deal of staging: something constructed inside and outside the terms of his sexuality.

Figure 3.2 Graham Norton

continued

ACTIVITY

Identify the elements that make up the Graham Norton 'phenom-enon' as presented in Figure 3.2. Which of these elements are also components of his perceived sexuality?

Introduction to case studies

The case studies that follow investigate some of the issues which are involved in our creation of and participation in a mediated reality. At the same time they hope to remind all of us that representation is the broadest and most significant media issue. In considering the representation of 'place' we are trying to dispel the impression that something as multidimensional and organic as a site of human settlement, a village, a town, even a country, might be semantically neutral. The fact that we don't think too much about the meaning of our towns, cities, even country, is an issue in itself. Places are significantly represented across the media in both casual and detailed ways, from the offhand things that people write and say to the fully fledged 're-creations' that are modern British soap operas.

Case study

'SLUGS AND SNAILS AND PUPPY DOGS' TAILS': THE MEANINGS OF MEN

'Straightforward' and 'unproblematic' are not words used often to address issues of gender representation. Gender is an issue embodied by most representations of the human form in any context. Gender is usually to some degree expressed as a binary opposition where being male (for example) is partly understood in terms of not being female.

In her 1990 book *Gender Trouble*, Judith Butler argued that certain cultural configurations of gender have gained a 'hegemonic' hold. These are those that stress gender as a binary opposition: one thing or the other. This necessarily disallows views of gender which are more fluid. This division, which tends to leave men powerful, has ironically only been confirmed by feminism, which has unwittingly reinforced the dichotomy. In other words, the issues of gender are never reached because we are too concerned with the particular problems of inequality. Butler claims that the whole issue of gender and sexuality is ideologically manipulated in a context where sex (male, female) is seen to cause gender (masculine, feminine) which is seen to cause desire (heterosexuality). In other words, the assumption of much of what we receive from the media is that gender is somehow fixed. Thus boys will endlessly be stereotypically boys and girls girls, and masculine men will forever consort with feminine women.

This would appear to be the agenda for the new generation of so-called lads' mags which began by claiming that they were underlining the progress gender equality had made by being ironically retro about it. Suddenly 'dolly birds' were back, albeit in the context of Austin Powers movies and the popular 1990s programme *TFI Friday*, and 1960s chic became the trend. Men took their lead from *The Italian Job* (1969) and Andy Williams re-released 'Music to Watch Girls By'. Even those magazines that appeal more directly to the new willingness of men to take themselves seriously as (though always rugged) 'things of beauty' like *Men's Health* and *Men's Fitness* rely on the old dispensation. For fear they might descend into a perilous self-love/vanity/anxiety, these magazines regularly provide a plausible reason for all this posing.

ACTIVITY

Consider the roles of men and women in one or more of the following media contexts:

- MTV or an equivalent music channel
- TV news and current affairs programmes
- a mainstream magazine for men or women.

To what extent are the roles (and meanings) of women predicated upon/related to the roles (and meanings) of men?

continued

In the representation of men in the mass media, the primary question 'Who is he?' tends to amount to 'What does he do?' (What role has he achieved?) If the same process is followed for the representation of women the questions tend to be very different. In this case, 'Who is she?' tends to mean 'Who is she related to?', 'Who is she doing that for?' or even 'Whose is she?' This even happens at a metalingual level, at the level of the media code, where men are still much more likely to be the focuses of media texts, the central characters. As a result females and female characters are much more likely to find their roles ascribed. For example, in the most ideologically regressive medium of all, mainstream Hollywood cinema, it is highly likely that at least one of the functions of any female character is to be the wife, partner, mother, sister or 'love interest' to at least one more significant male character. Try this out next time you visit your local multiplex cinema or watch a film on television at home. Women are more often than not defined by their relationships with men. Even when there is good reason to do so, we do not conventionally read men this way.

ACTIVITY

Figure 3.3 The Royal Family

Figure 3.4 *Gavin and Stacey*

Look at Figures 3.3 and 3.4 and think of the ways in which these publicity photographs present male and female characters. What are the significant paradigms?

This is, of course, central to Laura Mulvey's arguments in her influential essay 'Visual Pleasure and Narrative Cinema' (2003), which reinforce the idea that women understand what it is to be looked at, to be an object of what Mulvey usefully labelled the 'male gaze'. 'Male gaze' is, it seems, the dominant perspective of the mass media: what else could explain the predominance of certain kinds of images of certain kinds of women? Not only is this a patriarchal perspective but it is supported by a hegemonic alliance of common sense and prejudice which suggests that this boys watching girls stuff only works one way. Men look at women in a particular way because of how they're wired, it is argued; women, on the other hand, don't particularly like looking at men in this way.

continued

John Berger perhaps summed this up best in his seminal study *Ways of Seeing* (1972): "[M]en look at women. Women watch themselves being looked at. This determines not only most relations between men and women but also the relation of women to themselves."

In an age of Botox injections and cosmetic surgery this issue is hardly being addressed; 'Because you're worth it' too easily translates for many women into 'because it's all you're worth'. Writing in the *Observer* of 2 May 2004 in a piece with the tagline 'Women who buy into the illusion of youth delude themselves if they think it is an act of emancipation', journalist Yvonne Roberts attacked the ways in which women in particular are persuaded to look younger. She questioned the ways in which women are sold cosmetic improvements as something for themselves. Roberts uncovers the 'social, political and economic inequality' that is the basis of this issue, suggesting that "females have always been strongly conditioned to believe that beauty is a large part of a woman's worth". She is most scathing on the beauty industry, revealing "the most vital of beauty secrets: cash conquers all", but also on what she calls "the female physical elite" who end up with "the face of a child, the body of a boy and the neck of a woman heading towards old age". She also, almost mournfully, quotes sociologist Wendy Chapkis who has pointed out that "we end up robbing each other of authentic reflections". In other words, we've lost our perspective on what it is to age.

A new twist was applied by an article in *Zoo* magazine on Swedish uberbabe Victoria Silvstedt in February 2004 which had the provocative tagline: 'I hope your readers like my boobs'. This is interesting because what the article revealed was that these 'boobs' were, as it were, 'new' (for new read 'enhanced') so there was an even more real sense of their existence as extrapersonal objects. It is as if the process of disempowerment has become even more profound or desperate. Where the traditional pin-up would once say (in effect), 'Look at my lovely boobs which I am lucky enough to have', they are now saying, 'Look at my lovely boobs which I have been clever/wealthy/desperate enough to buy'. Despite the significant increase in the popularity of plastic surgery, there are just no semantic equivalents.

Men remain representationally largely free to be what they are (if not what they want to be) and even at times to be who they are. Our tendency in the representation of men is to allocate meaning specifically, to take them one by one. Women are more readily allocated to predetermined 'role' groups wherein their meanings are long established. Once identified, this is a relatively easy process to challenge and there are plenty of examples in all media forms of work that set out to establish interesting and problematic female characters, who require us to apprehend them as individuals rather than as types. However, it remains true that part of the power of these progressive pieces is an acknowledgement that the norm is still one that offers us endless variations on the mother/virgin/bitch/whore paradigm.

Moreover, it remains overwhelmingly the case that women are largely excluded from whole swathes of media output by the very nature of this limited range of representations. For example, in a media sense women are not funny (the exceptions prove the rule), perhaps because comedy lives on imperfection and an ugliness that women are not really allowed to have. This is an acid test, where the proof of the pudding lies very much in the eating: ask yourself if this is true (not if it should be). Then ask yourself why, despite the plethora of pretty girl exploitation shots in Media Studies text-books, it is also true that representations of men are significantly more interesting than representations of women. The ideology here is multilayered in a world that is flooded with images of a few sorts of women, yet is much more telling in its representation in far fewer images of a more significant range of men. Even when the focus is as narrow as 'fitness'.

Figure 3.5 *Men's Fitness* advert

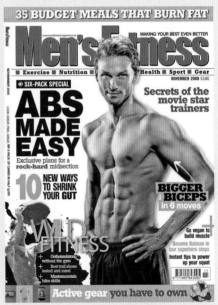

Figure 3.6 The cover of *Men's Fitness Magazine*, November 2009

continued

ACTIVITY

What do we learn about men from these two 'advertisements' (Figures 3.5 and 3.6)? In what ways are the meanings directed by significant anchors?

Interestingly the focus here is rather more impersonal that in the average pretty girl pic. It's the six-pack that offers a dominant focus in both cases, a grid of muscles that can be worked irrespective of the rest of you and to a degree independent of your natural (or God-given) endowment. Although this takes work, it dosen't define you, and anyway everybody knows (in other words it is common to the representations we see of the world) that men of all shapes and sizes get women of the right shape and size.

ACTIVITY

Man sues over lack of 'Lynx effect'

A luckless Indian romeo is suing Lynx after he failed to land a single girlfriend during seven years of using their products.

Vaibhav Bedi, 26, is seeking £26,000 from parent company Unilever for the "depression and psychological damage" caused by the lack of any Lynx effect.

Court officials in New Delhi have agreed to order forensic laboratory tests on dozens of his half-used Lynx body washes, shampoos, anti-perspirants and hair gels.

Lynx – marketed as Axe in India – is famous for its saucy ads showing barely-clothed women throwing themselves at men.

But Bedi says in his court petition: "The company cheated me because in its advertisements, it says women will be attracted to you if you use Axe.

"I used it for seven years but no girl came to me."

When contacted Unilever declined to comment on the case.

But India's leading compensation litigator Ram Jethmalani warned: "There is no data to substantiate the supposition that unattractive and unintelligent men don't attract women.

"In fact some of the best looking women have been known to marry and date absolutely ghoulish guys. I'd suggest that the company settles this issue out of court."

http://web.orange.co.uk/article/quirkies/man_sues_over_lack_of_ly nx_effect?sid=393db7306793

What messages are there in this story about the different ways in which men and women are represented and understood? Are these messages substantially different for male and female readers?

Reality TV: the heights and depths of hyperconsciousness

No exploration of the issues of representation can ignore the impact on a study of realism that has been made by reality TV. For postmodernists the very idea that you would need to use the 'R' word is perfect proof that the whole project of realism, the feasible representation of reality, is in crisis. If 'What Katie Did Next' is 'reality' then what about all the other things Katie does on TV, including promoting what she's doing next? There can be no going back to an old dichotomy of 'reality' and 'representation' once you inhabit a hyperreality which itself comprises versions of versions of reality. Baudrillard called these 'simulacra'.

A more positive take might suggest that 'Reality TV' evidences a more subtle understanding on the part of audiences and producers, who appreciate the ironies involved, who have a hyperconsciousness to greet their hyperreality. One significant television moment was the collision of airliners into the World Trade Center on 11 September 2001. In the midst of countless horrors and widespread disbelief was a double seed of doubt, not only that we might not be being told the truth but also that these pictures were themselves failing to convince. This was a wake-up call. In registering the unpalatable fact that representations (live recordings) of a genuine disaster were unconvincing by the standards we expect from, for example, feature films, we learnt something about representation, and hopefully reality.

continued

Television has always 'employed' reality as a component in its output. We are well used to discriminating between realistic drama, of the sort that *EastEnders* or *Casualty* serves up and the representations which are going on whenever a celebrity appears on TV, 'playing themselves', you might say. In short, television has always shown us 'real' people being themselves, often using their own names. They populate a sliding scale which runs from so-called 'stars' to television journalists and weather girls (or, as they're now called, 'the cast' of *I'm a Celebrity, Get Me Out of Here!*).

From *BB* to *Celebrity Big Brother*: pride comes before a fall

What happened with *Big Brother One*, and the formalising of 'Reality TV' (largely by Endemol) is that this age-old hierarchy was first disrupted and then in time reconfigured. Acting on a hunch that 'ordinary' people were at least more interesting than B list and C list celebrities, Channel 4 unleashed *Big Brother* and suddenly we were all stars or versions of stars. The show had been a massive hit in Holland, demolishing the argument that 'it could only happen here', and it took Britain by storm. *BB1* was presented as a social psychological experiment but there were questions to ask even from the start. While the 'reality' was a focus for marketing the show, ironically the real focus of the show was the contrivance: the house and the 'game' – a prize £70,000 if you can convince us you're a genuine human being.

BB was an extension of the fly-on-the-wall documentary with more cameras and more control over the environment in which the observation would take place. It was a technique common in natural history programming. Where a subject could not be adequately filmed in their own habitat, a faithful reproduction of that habitat would be built, into which camera positions would be mounted.

ACTIVITY

What differences, if any, do you see between:

1. Photographing the yellow-bellied sapsucker in a faithfully reproduced version of its natural habitat?
2. Recording the antics of contestants in the Big Brother House?

Anyway, whatever the differences, for a short period there was a spate of shows that gave ordinary people chances of a number of lifetimes. What were being peddled, and being sought if not engineered by programme-makers, were 'rags-to-riches' narratives. For a while social psychology was replaced by social work as Jamie Oliver offered 'n'er-do-wells' the chance to be chefs in *Jamie's Kitchen* while in the background various manifestations of a talent show massed their melancholy armies. *Jamie's Kitchen* was a fairly standard and effective 'warts-and-all' documentary which offered insights into the problems associated with so-called problem children. It also and probably more compellingly told us a lot more about celebrity chef Jamie Oliver.

The rest of the story is interesting since it represents the almost total transformation of the apparent focus of reality TV from 'ordinary people' to 'celebrities', in representational terms a complete role reversal. This is partly because the first unforeseen implication of shows like *BB* was that it created instant celebrities, even out of those, like the late Jade Goody, who finished fourth. But it was also the fact that, on reflection, the lives of B and C list celebrities proved more interesting, particularly if we the public were allowed to goad them. What many commentators have missed is that reality TV was driven not by humankind's desire for more reality but rather by technology, by conditions being right for a new kind of interactivity and transmedia experience. The involvement offered was not with reality but with the shows and an experiment in a limited form of management of programme outcomes by audience vote.

continued

One 'platform' that has embraced the public vote is our ailing popular press
and a raft of rudely healthy celebrity magazines. As ordinary people have
given way to celebrities (or become them) so the 'character' of the 'franchise' has changed. Led by the hugely successful Ant-and-Dec-fronted *I'm
A Celebrity, Get Me Out of Here!* this new wave delights not in exploring
'reality' but rather by giving vaguely undeserving celebrities a taste of it. It
is interesting to speculate whether this 'Celebrities Uncovered' theme is
part of a long-term reconfiguration of the popular press in particular following the fallout from the accusations of intrusive reporting which resulted
from Princess Diana's death in 1997. At the time the public seemed to
feel that things had gone too far. In the celebrity-behind-the-scenes gig
our intrusiveness is endorsed. There are many issues here, since aren't
celebrities by definition those people we are prepared to pay to see appear
as themselves?

At the end of the day our narratives of the everyday have become celebrity
narratives (and transmedia narratives at that), and reality TV has folded
itself back into the 'play of illusions and phantasms' that is 'celebrity'.
'Celebrity' may, in fact, be even more than Disneyland, in the postmodernist

Baudrillard's terms "the perfect model of all the entangled orders of simulation". Queen of the 'Reality TV' side of things is Katie Price (aka Jordan) whose stock rises and falls on a-series-by-series basis. She has lately been undermined by the failure of her marriage to the hapless hunk Peter Andre and subsequent quickie remarriage to an orange-faced, transvestite cage fighter.

ACTIVITY

Strangers in a fight

On the celebrity hustings words fly thick and fast and nothing remains unlabelled. What are your initial impressions (today) of these characters who will feature in our next story:

- Katie Price
- Peter Andre
- Alex the cage fighter
- Cheryl Cole
- Ashley Cole

On what are these impressions based?

Like an old tale still . . . the myths of modern celebrity

Baudrillard famously wrote that "when the real is no longer what it used to be, nostalgia assumes its full meaning" and much of what is done representationally to celebrities seems to be harking back to days of clearer values. The stories we are told of Katie and Peter and Cheryl and Ashley are no more or less than contemporary myths, stories particular to our 'tribe' which allow us to articulate our concerns about our culture.

Ellis Cashmore's extensive work on David Beckham's celebrity proposes Becks as a blueprint for modern celebrity. Beckham has been turned into a product in an unprecedented way but can seemingly do no wrong, escaping infidelity and pink nail varnish with comparative ease. Cashmore suggests that central to this identity is having a good story, which is a traditional one: "The Beckham fairy tale – which like all fairy tales embodies ideas about ourselves." The 'ourselves' here is as much collective and cultural as it is personal and psychological.

continued

The contemporary celebrity fairy tale is very much a traditional structure with tabloid and magazine editors and cable TV producers vying to unfold the developing narrative from love at first sight to taking sides in the messy divorce. One theme that seems to reassure us is that despite their money, talent, looks and status these celebrities can't find happiness. If this can be rubbed in with a bit of moralising about good, old-fashioned family values, all the better. If you're prepared to prostitute your marriage to the highest bidder as a spectator sport, what can you expect? Remember, however, that this is a popular media who brought us the reality show *Jodie Marsh: Who'll Take Her Up The Aisle?*

When 'Dosh and Pecs' (aka Peter and Katie) hooked up on a reality TV show it seemed a marriage made in TV tabloid heaven. As Britain's most famous glamour model and Australia's most famous six-pack, their 'affair' seemed both expedient and doomed. Six years, and one marriage and one divorce later, they are still inextricably linked. Moreover, they have become properly established within the frames of reference of even those who take little interest in celebrity gossip. As well, people will take sides in their affairs on the basis of strongly formed opinions of their characters as human beings. This phenomenon was created out of an extended reality TV franchise which directed our attention to the similarities between their stories and the essential lives we all lead as boys and girls, husbands and wives, sons and daughters, mums and dads, with a bit of glamour and sexual electricity thrown in for good measure.

The relationship as media narrative was officially launched in March 2004 with a WORLD EXCLUSIVE (was the world listening?) in *OK* magazine.

Figure 3.7 Jordan and Peter Andre on the cover of *OK!* Magazine, March 2004

ACTIVITY

Looking back at 'where it all began', what strikes you about this cover? Who has fared best since this shot was taken in terms of enhancement of their meanings? The evocation of 'Posh and Becks' is interesting: how do 'Dosh and Pecs' compare?

The journey from then to now can be told in a set of titles, including one abortive foray into the late-night chat-show format:

When Jordan Met Peter
Jordan & Peter: Laid Bare
Jordan & Peter: Marriage and Mayhem
Jordan & Peter: The Baby Diaries
Katie & Peter: The Next Chapter
Katie & Peter: Unleashed (chatshow)
Katie & Peter: Stateside
What Katie Did Next
Peter Andre: The Next Chapter

ACTIVITY

What do you have to say about this grand narrative built by Katie, Peter and Jordan?

This journey has made Katie and Peter two of the most recognisable celebrities in Britain, and has generated millions of column inches across not only newspapers and magazines but also celebrity comment on TV and radio. In the serious end of this have been concerns about both the corroding influence of 'pure' celebrity (defined in terms of people who are famous for being famous) and the poor role models which are being offered to their young fans. Katie, as ever, has attracted the most criticism, particularly among some feminists, who fear that she is taken as some sort of post-feminist icon by young women. Caitlin Moran in *The Times* spells it out.

continued

"All over the world, humans are fizzing and buzzing and thinking. They are knocking off the entries on humanity's billion-year-long To Do list – which has slowly raised us from protozoa and germs into two-legs with iPhones and trilbies.

And, in the midst of all this, like some impossibly contrarian parlour game, there are people who will argue that Katie Price is a feminist role model for young women. 'She's strong, she's clever, she's Celebrity Mum of The Year, she's making it in a man's world,' they say. 'She's a modern businesswoman.'

OK – I want to go through these. Following what seems to be a media obligation, this week *Hello!* refers yet again to Price's intelligence – calling her 'as smart as paint'. Aside from noting that, as yet, not a single country in the world has yet to employ a 2-litre tin of Dulux Non-Drip Emulsion as Chancellor of the Exchequer, over the years I have devised a very simple IQ test for public figures. It is to ask: 'Who around here has been forced to eat a kangaroo's anus by Ant & Dec in the last two weeks?' If you raise your hand, you're probably not leaving through the door marked Mensa. Stephen Hawking has never chowed down on roo-bum.

'She's strong.' No, she's not strong. She's incredibly weak. At the tail end of 10,000 years of patriarchy, there's nothing strong about being a woman with gigantic silicone tits and a face full of filler, who's into ponies and the colour pink, and goes on about blow jobs a lot. She's scarcely a black lesbian physicist wearing slacks in Alabama in 1932.

Also, strong people tend not to go quacking to the press every week about how they're 'feeling' and how unfairly everyone's treating them, and what an arse their ex-husband's been. As Blanche in *Corrie* said: 'In my day, when something bad happened, you'd stay at home, get drunk and bite on a shoe.' Price could learn much from this. This idea that Price is 'strong' has come solely from the fact that she keeps saying 'I'm strong', while doing really weak things. There's a similar bit of neurolinguistic programming going on with her being a 'great parent', and being voted Celebrity Mum of The Year.

'I take care of my kids,' she says. Well, to quote the comedian Chris Rock: 'You're SUPPOSED to look after your kids! What do you want – a cookie?'

Thing is, I don't really mind anyone misguidedly thinking that Price is like some cross between Einstein, Nelson Mandela and Ma Walton. It's a busy, mixed-up world and we've all got to pick our fights.

But what I find absolutely intolerable is people who claim that she's a feminist role model – simply because she has earned a lot of money.

The reasoning is this: men still have all the power and money. But men have a weak spot – sexy women. So if what it takes to become rich and powerful is to sex-up the blokes, then so be it. That's business, baby. You might be on all fours with your arse hanging out in 'glamour' calendars – but at least you're making the rent on your enormous pink mansion.

Well, there's a phrase for that kind of behaviour. It is, to quote Jamie, the spin doctor in *The Thick of It*, being a 'mimsy bastard quisling f***'.

Women who, in a sexist world, pander to sexism to make their fortune are Vichy France with tits. Are you 32GG, waxed to within an inch of your life and faking orgasm? You're doing business with a decadent and corrupt regime. Calling that a feminist icon is like giving an arms dealer the Nobel Peace Prize.

I once spent a week with Price for a feature. Do you know the worst thing? She couldn't hold a conversation to save her life. As she has to turn out an 'exclusive' about her life pretty much every week, it means everything she thinks or says has a price. Even politely asking 'What did you do last night?' involved her calculating whether what had happened was an anecdote she could 'give' to me, as part of 'the package' – or sell to another magazine for a bit more.

I dunno. Maybe I've got my priorities wrong. But if I were worth £30 million, yet were getting my management to ring a journalist the morning after an interview to say: 'Could you not print Katie's bra size? I know she mentioned it to you – but we want to sell it to *OK!*',

continued

I would think my life was going a bit wrong. I think I'd get on my pink pony and gallop away for a couple of years."

(http://www.timesonline.co.uk/tol/comment/columnists/caitlin_moran/article6944843.ece)

What is the substance of Caitlin Moran's argument? Imagine you have been charged with briefing Katie Price for a 'right to reply'. What are the counter-arguments?

While the upmarket rags pick around the absurdity of super-inflated people being interesting to us, and worry about a world that is obsessed with surfaces, the popular media sticks with the traditional stories of the 'natural' relationships between perhaps men and women. If on the one hand it's difficult to be a feminist if your cup size is larger than a D, it's also impossible to be a 'real' woman if you are seen, repeatedly, to hold the whip hand in your relationship (particularly a relationship with a patently 'real' man like Peter Andre). In the trial by television Peter proved (convinced us) that he was a 'good father', but, without cynicism, you must admit that the standards for fathers and children are hardly stratospheric. Any father who finds 'quality time' with his brood on a regular basis has by these standards climbed into the top half of the parenting 'markscheme'. Mothers on the other hand must always put their children first and no career will trump this 'natural' responsibility.

These issues were further highlighted in the last years of the Noughties by the juxtaposition of 'Dosh and Pecs' with [C]ashley and Cheryl Cole following news of their (seemingly inevitable) breakup. Again the extent to which traditional representational models were dominant is of some concern. Despite the attempts of our football-obsessed culture to suggest that footballers are not 'empty' celebrities because they have 'talent' it is clear that both Cheryl Tweedy and Ashley Cole are products of fame academies and that objectively such relationships are likely to come under particular strain. However, without the kind of 'permission' that might have been implied by *Jordan & Peter: Marriage and Mayhem*, the Cole marriage too has become a site on which the popular media has reworked some well-worn themes. In this narrative Cheryl is Superwoman: managing an immaculate appearance, looking after her old mum and representing timeless working-class Geordie 'lassishness'. Ashley, on the other hand, is a feckless, libidinous, immature and arrogant 'arsewipe' who prefers phonesex with unspecified slappers to love with "the world's most eligible lady". Here is a set of representations which are carrying an awful lot of value and values.

What do the stories of Cheryl and Ashley Cole tell us about attitudes towards:

- Social class?
- Regionality?
- Ethnicity?
- Gender?
- Marriage?
- Material success?

The article from *Heat* magazine may provide some prompts.

DIGNIFIED CHERYL:

"I NEED TO BE ALONE"

SHE KNEW IT WAS OVER AS EARLY AS LAST JUNE   HE BRAGS: 'SHE'LL BE BACK'

A RELIEVED NATION PUNCHED the air last week when Cheryl Cole finally announced that she was leaving her cheating husband Ashley. But *heat* can now reveal that the dignified silence she is keeping masks her secret heartache – their marriage was over some months ago, with pals close to the couple claiming they haven't had sex for months.

While Cheryl put every ounce of her energy into saving their relationship, cocky Ashley repeatedly refused to accept that his infidelity was the cause, instead blaming those she loved most – including her mum Joan Callaghan

continued

(who has shared their marital home for two years), Girls Aloud bandmates, rapper will.i.am and even her dogs. The love rat is still bragging to friends, "She'll be back."

Now, as she finally walks away with her head held high, *heat* gives you the truth proud Cheryl hid from the world about her ruined marriage.

THEY STOPPED HAVING SEX

The passion in their marriage dwindled to virtually nothing over recent months. In the evenings, Cheryl and her mum would stay up watching television together while Ashley either played video games with friends, including fellow Chelsea sex-cheat John Terry, in six-hour stints, or went to bed.

"Their relationship took a hammering two years ago after Aimee Walton went into great detail about their alleged night together," a source close to the star tells *heat*. "Things couldn't just go back to the way they were after something like that and in a way, Ashley should have to pay for his crimes. It's hard to go back to the way things were when you know he has been with someone else. As hard as Cheryl tried to make it work, in the bedroom was a different situation all together." Ashley refuses to take any responsibility for the breakdown of this important part of their relationship, instead blaming everyone but himself, including her mum and her dogs. He once complained that the latter – two Chihuahuas named Coco and Buster that she allowed to sleep in the bedroom – "got in the way of marital intimacy". Asked recently if she was pregnant, Cheryl replied, "No. Chance would be a fine thing."

THREE PEOPLE IN THE RELATIONSHIP

Cheryl's mum Joan has lived with the couple for almost the entire length of their marriage and in both of their marital homes, not just since Ashley's infidelity as has been reported. Joan doesn't trust Ashley and he insists her living there is the reason for his and Cheryl's sex life almost vanishing.

"He blames a lot of their problems on Joan being there all the time and killing the passion," our sources says. If Ashley was doing his favourite thing, playing his PlayStation, Joan would simply walk in and unplug it, saying it was immature and that he should be making more effort with his wife.

A pal of the footballer told us, "It's no secret that Cheryl's mum living with them didn't go down very well with Ashley and he often felt as though he was living at her house rather than the other way around. He would moan to Cheryl that he couldn't do what he wanted to in his own house and that Joan was cramping his style, but Cheryl was insistent that her mum should be there – she wanted her there. He tried telling her that he wasn't happy with the living arrangements, and it was the source of a few rows. He felt they couldn't be spontaneous with their relationship with the mother-in-law there all the time. It was suffocating." Rather than join his wife in trying to save their marriage, Ashley chose to have sex with other women, resulting in the revelations that would ultimately see her ditch him.

SHE TRIED TO SAVE THEIR MARRIAGE

Despite suffering the humiliation of seeing Ashley's affairs revealed so publicly, Cheryl masked her private heartache and tried to rebuild the marriage. Ashley, driven to jealousy by the massive increase in the public's admiration for her and seeing his own reputation was left in tatters, made little effort to help.

"Cheryl did her best to make that marriage work. Ashley complained about not being involved and that he felt left out because her career took over and she was away a lot, but she would always invite him down to *The X Factor*. Often he couldn't make it because of games, but that's not her fault and when he did come

down he'd be backstage in the dressing room. Cheryl wanted to involve him and unlike a lot of the judges after the show would return home rather than going out until late. She took her marriage seriously. She always made sure that Ashley was a part of the party and if you look at pictures of them on nights out, she is always with him holding his hand in a very public display of affection. Particularly since the allegations of an affair with Aimee Walton – she wanted people to see that she was putting the past behind her and that other people should too. Of course, there was a lot of repairing that had to be done – but it needed to be both sides that were working on it. It's easy to say the word sorry, but his actions, she has since found out, clearly indicate that he didn't mean a word of it."

SHE IS LOSING WEIGHT AND BECOMING DEPRESSED

Though Cheryl appears as glamorous as she always has to the outside world, her friends fear that she is going to collapse from not eating and that she could end up depressed. She has accepted visits from best pals Nicola and Kimberley, but has even told them that she needs some space. Her friend told us, "Cheryl isn't eating at all. She seems so utterly miserable all she can do is mope around the place, which is

continued

understandable. She isn't taking care of her diet and we are all so worried that she is going to overdo this and get ill. She needs to keep up her energy, but it seems she just doesn't have the will or desire to eat or do anything at the moment."After Ashley's first affair, Cheryl dropped to 6st. Now she has lost five pounds in the last three weeks alone, the anguish she feels over his betrayal allowing her to stomach little more than peppermint tea.

DESPITE EVERYTHING SHE REMAINS PROUD AND DIGNIFIED

Cheryl was further rocked by claims she had entered into a relationship with dancer Derek Hough when she escaped to LA after the latest round of revelations about Ashley emerged.

Despite all that her cheating husband has done to her, she's still doing his best to respect his feelings.

"Her relationship with Derek was purely professional," her friend told us. "She was upset that she was accused of seeing him and being close to him and she thought it cheapened what she had with Ashley, suggesting she would go off with the first bloke she clapped eyes on."

HAPPY ENDING

Now that Cheryl has ditched the dead weight of Ashley, she is finally free to focus entirely on her career. We hope she also eventually finds a decent man who will give her the love and respect she deserves. One thing's for sure, she won't be short of offers.

Figure 3.8 Page spread from *Heat* Magazine, 6–12 March 2010

This article tells the whole story through subheadings. Think about how this might be illustrated as a display or podcast:

They stopped having sex

Three people in the relationship

She tried to save their marriage

She is losing weight and becoming depressed but despite everything she remains proud and dignified

Happy ending

Meanwhile, as Cheryl's bright star rises, so Katie, now Jordan, glowers in the penumbra, playing the 'bully' to Cheryl's dignified spouse, Tramp to her

Lady. And so we return to the simplest issues of representation; what is there between THE LADY and THE TRAMP?

Figure 3.9 The Lady and the Tramp: cover of *Heat* Magazine, 6–12 March 2010

ACTIVITY

Make a detailed list of the components of these two images of young women. What do they share? How is such a difference in meaning achieved?

Case study
THE REPRESENTATION OF PLACES

Places are represented to us in the same way as people and ideas, with various degrees of approval, malice and indifference. In doing their work these representations create for us a sort of semiotic map of both Britain and the World that for most of us resembles those maps made by early cartographers and explorers. The general shape is there, but the detail is largely provided by accident: either you've been there or it was featured in that series on the telly. You may have only really heard of 'West Bromwich' for its 'Albion', Sale for its 'Sharks' or Hamilton for its 'Academicals'. If asked for an opinion on places such as these you will instinctively reach for any associations which have tended to surround them as a result of others' representations which may be equally uninformed. If there are enough of these you may even have a stereotype to draw on.

ACTIVITY

Land down under

Your task is to illustrate/support the word AUSTRALIA by selecting *five* images and *five* words or phrases. You should try and express what this area of the world means to you as straightforwardly as you can.

You may or may not have chosen boomerangs and kangaroos but it is very unlikely that either failed to skim/hop across your mind. Equally a set of more specifically media images may have reared their heads, perhaps *Neighbours* or one of those Minogue girls (perhaps your parents would mention Rolf Harris). For the blunter of you the words may have included 'convicts', for others 'cricket' or 'Aborigines'. The very fact that some of you will have been relatively careful about what you chose for fear you might be being given some kind of test of your values or might reveal something about yourself tells us that these matters are interesting, even with a fairly remote idea like 'Australia'.

What you have made is a crude map of meaning which may be read as such and will likely tell us something about how we see Australia. You will likely be nodding along with this but read that last sentence back slowly.

Perhaps a more pertinent question for most of us is 'In what sense do you see Australia?', since most of us will never have been there. To some degree we are sharing in a collective process of meaning-making and for most of us this collective significantly includes a range of media sources from *Crocodile Dundee* to *Skippy the Bush Kangaroo*. Our Australia is a set of myths, though it may feel more substantial.

It is hardly profound to say so but the world we think we know is prompted by the partial coverage provided by our national media. Even with multiple news sources you would need tireless energy to sight some versions on the Western news agenda.

INFORMATION BOX – MAP OF THE WORLD ACCORDING TO BRITISH MEDIA COVERAGE

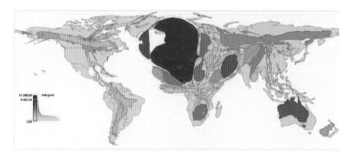

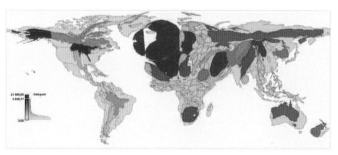

Figure 3.10 The world according to the *Daily Mail* and the *Guardian*

Much of this is perfectly understandable: we would expect Portuguese affairs to feature massively on Portuguese news, though on our map Portugal is barely an unpicked spot (called Cristiano Ronaldo). More interesting are our own semiotic maps of Britain's hot-spots and not-spots. As suggested before, to many of us we're talking about the Mappa Mundi.

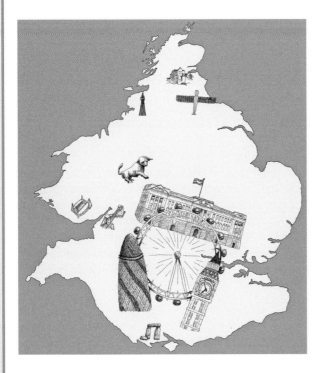

Figure 3.11
Distorted Mappa Mundi-style map of perceptions of Britain

ACTIVITY

Explore the map of Great Britain (Figure 3.11) and discuss the different codes of representation that are operating as you travel around the map. Add your own significant locations. You may wish to consider, for example, the following:

continued

- Regionality (Why is North versus South stronger than East versus West?)
- Nationality
- History
- Social class
- Culture
- Personality/character of inhabitants

You may also wish to consider where you would most/least like to live, as well as the extent to which your meanings will or will not accompany real experience of the places you are 'understanding'. Which is the best British town you have visited? And the worst? What are your reasons?

When Middlesborough, a town on the river Tees on the North East, was voted the worst town in Britain, Sky Sports anchorman Jeff Stelling, himself from nearby Hartlepool, blew a fuse on live television. Stelling leapt into a now famous rant against the nature of these polls which adds much to our ongoing discussion in an entertaining fashion. You can assess "Jeff Stelling loses it" (the rant crosses a commercial break and is only interrupted by Everton scoring a goal) on YouTube at http://www.youtube.com/watch?v=XxrJqtf0RJI.

ACTIVITY

North versus South: Jeff's telling

"The people who compile this tosh, no disrespect, are the type who only go north of Rickmansworth when they're going to the Edinburgh festival and think that people in the North live in Coronation Street-style terraces."

Stelling's broadside is both tongue-in-cheek and genuinely felt. What oppositions does he set up between North and South, to what extent are these representations identifiable and what useful purpose, if any, do they serve?

Obviously for some to come from Britain's worst town would be a veritable badge of honour. A durable media narrative is the 'girl/boy from nowhere' story and if nobody's heard of Tanworth-in-Arden or Little Rock or even Althorp before you came on the scene the better 'somewhere' seems. It seems that humdrum towns are often the spur to creative types, if only to leave them. John Cleese regularly gives Weston-super-Mare and his desire never to return as a reason for his success. When Ricky Gervais decided it was time to do something with his life, his father apparently replied, "But you haven't seen all of Reading yet." Perhaps our own places always seem lesser, more mundane because more situated American names have far greater force, romance, scope. The writer Julie Burchill makes this point about the epithet 'American' in a review of Charles R. Cross's Kurt Cobain biography *Heavier than Heaven*:

> **American downfalls always seem bigger and sadder than other types – attain instant gravitas – because we seem to hear the lonesome wind of the American dream, the settling and the savagery and the submission of all else, howling through one simple life. (That's why, say, American Beauty and American Gigolo sound like such profound titles compared with Belgian Beauty and German Gigolo).**

It is often said that If Shakespeare were alive today he'd be writing *The Sopranos*/working in Hollywood. Shakespeare's place names are chosen to add drama and intrigue and are most often Italian due to that region's hot (and dirty) reputation. Julie Burchill is arguing that for the modern European imagination America does a similar job so that *The Merchant of Manhattan* is infinitely better than *The Merchant of Mansfield* and *Timon of Alabama* trumps *Timon of Aldershot*.

The American city with its spectacular play of light and shade is a model for both modern and futuristic metropolises everywhere: comic, computer games, feature films (though these often blur).

continued

ACTIVITY

Vice City. Liberty stories?

Consider the meanings of the locations of one of the following:

- The Vice City locations of the GTA franchise
- The significant locations of a major Hollywood film with a fictional setting
- The imaginary world created by an American-produced comic
- The significant locations from a fictional US TV series
- The significant locations of an American-style theme park.

Subsidiary 1

Baudrillard said that "everywhere in Disneyland the objective profile of America . . . is drawn". To what extent is this true of your locations?

Subsidiary 2

Imagine a computer game whose Vice City was based on photofit British cities. How would it differ?

Subsidiary 3

To what extent is there a historical dimension to these representations?

ACTIVITY

Five formats in search of a setting

Suggest interesting and predictable British settings for the following:

- Drama about clever successful types
- Soap set in a close-knit community
- Film about teenage hopelessness
- Gentle comedy about generation differences
- Docu-drama following a minority ethnic family.

You get the picture. Representation is an interested activity which matters to people, since beyond all else it is a personal way in which we make sense of the world.

New and digital media

For some, the first casualty of new media is the singular concept of 'the media' itself. This is not to say that media industries have ceased to exist but rather to suggest that a significant shift has occurred. Models of media manipulation just don't hold water any more in a world where 'savvy' audience members are scheduling media outputs to their own convenience, or sharing reviews or even alternative endings with other 'readers'. This is a difficult environment for media institutions since so many of the technical innovations are steps way from the old models of media consumption and are therefore trickier places to make money.

The industrial models which imply a relatively stable relationship between producers, products and consumers are looking progressively more inappropriate. Having spent many years pursuing pirates (largely unsuccessfully) and trying to put the frighteners on all of us, the larger media institutions have at last begun to consider the new world rather than dreaming of the old one. Things were easier when texts were things you could carry, before 'records' became music and before 'the media' became media. We are leaving an era where 'the media' was the message for one where media are, once again, messages.

continued

ACTIVITY

In what ways do you see records as being different from music? What are the implications of this important shift? Do you think life might have been easier when media products had a physical or analogue quality?

What is the significance of media as opposed to the media? What do you think are the implications for A2 Media Studies students?

Of course media dynasties and moguls such as the Murdochs and Berlusconis of the post-digital media world are still powerful but the power to make sense of the world on our behalf is no longer available. Murdoch's *Sun* no longer wins elections, *The X Factor* no longer picks the Christmas number one and Manchester United fans no longer wear red and white. And the media institutions continue to try and find ways to charge for that which we all have ways of getting for free.

Ten years ago Anthony Giddens could write that "television, and the other media, tend to destroy the very public space of dialogue they open up, through relentless trivializing, and personalizing of political issues" (Giddens, 1999, n.p.). In those days television, in particular, was seen as a positive menace since it appeared to some to be both degrading social life and at the same time undermining it. Families, for example, were seen to be under threat as televisions and their allies video and DVD players invaded every room. Actually the explosion of new forms of social communication, particularly blogging and social networking, has left "TV and the other media" decidedly out of step and trying desperately to get back on-message. The media is suddenly significantly less important to many people who can take them or leave them, and they're finding it hard to get used to it.

One issue, made significantly more critical by the worldwide financial crisis, is the economics of new media. Emily Bell, the *Guardian*'s Digital Director in 2008, predicted the loss of up to five national newspapers and "the regional press heading for complete market failure". She also predicted hard times for broadcasters with foreign ownership being the only feasible option for all but the BBC. She spoke about the online revolution as "hurricane of knowledge and publishing" to which no institution was sure how to respond.

ACTIVITY

The BBC has come under fire because of the amount of content it generates and gives away for free. For example, it is argued that the BBC's publicly funded website with a vast amount of free content serves to undermine attempts by commercial media producers to charge a fair price for their output. They argue, for example, that quality journalism can only be produced if people are prepared to pay a fair price for online content in both quality and popular titles.

Do you think there are good arguments for reducing funding to the BBC and perhaps subsidising commercial media producers such as independent TV companies to enable them to compete more fairly?

What about media and democracy?

The recent British General Election campaign (spring 2010) provides a useful case study on the impact of new media on our democracy. The campaign that was meant to be the first of the digital age became dominated by three television debates billed as 'American-style' but in fact progressively more like old-fashioned political mud-slinging: the public meeting rather than the presidential debate. At the same time the attempts of the party machines to mobilise support via social networking formats proved once and for all that things had moved on.

Figure 3.12
The 2010 election debate on the BBC

continued

This was the American-style election which proved that neither political parties nor the collection of organisations formerly known as 'the media' could decide what kind of election it was. The theory was that lessons should be learnt from Obama's apparent mobilisation of new channels of communication in the US election of 2008. The leaders' debates had been coming for a while and once again the theory was that this was a step towards 'appearance' politics. In this context it was assumed that the younger, better presented Tory leader, David Cameron, would take full advantage.

In fact the set of three staged encounters was far from the contrived electronic showcase that was envisaged. Rather, it was a little 'back to the future' in character, having something of the feeling of the original hustings. It also unwittingly dramatised the inanities of the British electoral system and, partly as a result, Lib Dem leader Nick Clegg jumped 11 points in the polls. Clegg's line was simply: "do you want these two (Labour and Conservatives) scoring points off one another or do you want a real change?"

Clegg's rise to potential power-broker raised the old guard to anger and he was personally attacked in the following week's tabloids. This sparked a further demonstration that things had genuinely changed. The debates had proved also a focus for each party's feeble attempts to 'use' social networking as a set of broadcast media (doh!). This took the form, for example, of Tory Party chairman Eric Pickles using Twitter to tweet "I think David Cameron was very effective in this week's debate" or some such like. The power and character of Twitter was then better demonstrated by an 'Iblamenick' campaign which off the back of the tabloid's ludicrous rubbishing of Clegg simply invited tweeters to blame him for any particular grievances they had (from losing their keys to the Gulf War). The result? Well, no bad thing for Clegg but rubbing it in for the so-called party machines and conclusive proof of Cameron's law: "Too many twits make a twat."

ACTIVITY

How far do you agree that technological innovations such as social networking sites, blogs and Twitter have encouraged a positive exchange of views in terms of our social, political and cultural lives? To what extent do you think they are irrelevant to any or all of these? Do you feel empowered by technology?

What about the changing role of the producer?

Certainly for *Guardian* Digital Director Emily Bell, the change is clear and explicit. In a piece in which she reflects on the unwillingness of most MPs to genuinely engage with the new 'connectivity' (77 per cent not on Facebook), she offers the following reading of where we are:

> **One could argue that a collective misjudgment about what it means to shift from an age of representation to an age of participation is what has pushed both the mass media and politics to the brink of crisis.**

This is a big deal because in Media Studies it changes everything. We are moving from "an age of representation", where media organisations offered what they thought readers should know to "an age of participation" where conversation replaces imposition. This hits all 'producers' of media content even before the 'prosumers' and 'mash-up' men arrive. If people can predict the imminent demise of the prolific MTV in the face of the release of a nine-minute video to promote Lady Gaga's single 'Telephone' on YouTube which promoted 20 million hits, nothing will be safe. Ironically MTV 'arrived' on the back of such a scoop with Michael Jackson's *Thriller* video premiere.

Aside: Impact on music industry

There can be few areas of media output that have been more greatly effected by new media technologies than music. Traditional patterns of distribution of recorded music via singles and albums available on CD formats have been supplemented, although not, interestingly, replaced, by the opportunity for consumers to download music direct to their own personal recording devices. This situation is further complicated by the fact that a significant number of downloads by consumers take place through peer-to-peer sites and are consequently free, and so generate no revenue for the music industry or the bands it has signed.

Debate rages at the heart of the issue of 'piracy' with record companies on the one hand arguing that such downloading is equivalent to theft while the downloaders themselves argue that a commodity like music should be common property and that it is the record companies that are exploiting both fans and the bands themselves. Clearly there is an argument for both

continued

sides, but the issue of copyright and intellectual property has been thrown very much to the fore by the way in which the web makes it so easy to acquire media output without payment.

ACTIVITY

I fought the Law and the Law lost: piracy and pop

Music companies need to stop resisting and accept that illegal downloading is a fact of twenty-first-century life, according to a new study by music rights holders. Researchers analysed the downloading of Radiohead's 'In Rainbows' – which was made freely available through an official website – and found that a majority of fans still pirated the music.

Not only did many more fans illegally download the album than those who bought it in shops, they downloaded it from illegal P2P and torrent sites like Pirate Bay than from the official Radiohead site.

"Even when the price approaches zero," reads the report, "people are more likely to act habitually (say, using Pirate Bay) than to break their habit (say, visiting www.InRainbows.com)." While Radiohead are a beloved band, an illegal website like Pirate Bay may still be "a powerful brand with a sterling reputation in the minds of millions of young music fans".

Researchers pointed out that despite the illegal downloads, 'In Rainbows' was a success – CD versions were bestsellers and Radiohead tours continue to sell out. Garland described the 'In Rainbows' release as "stunt marketing at its best".

The authors of the study argue that music rights-holders need to find "new ways" and "new places" to generate income from their music, rather than chasing illegal downloads – for example, licensing agreements with YouTube or legal peer-to-peer websites. In other words, they ought to do the musical equivalent of giving away free ice-cream and selling advertising on the cones.

(Sean Michaels, guardian.co.uk, Monday, 4 August 2008)

- What is the message of this research as far as illegal downloading is concerned?
- What is your attitude to sites like Pirate Bay, which are clearly not disguising their intentions?
- What do you feel about Radiohead making the album freely available?
- Is it possible to legislate against illegal downloads and file-sharing? Are the downloaders and sharees equally culpable?

This is, interestingly, just one example of bands and artists giving their music away for free. The music industry reacted angrily at a decision in 2007 to give away the new album 'Planet Earth' by US artist Prince with a tabloid newspaper. The album was offered as a "covermount", where newspapers attempt to lure readers with DVDs and CDs. As an industry spokesman said, "It is yet another example of the damaging covermount culture which is destroying any perception of value around recorded music." Prince was keen to promote a series of O2 shows later that year.

For many music fans, in the music industry, record producers are leeches exploiting the talent of young hopefuls, making or breaking careers by choosing which to promote and which not to promote. This is further compounded by talent shows, such as *The X Factor*, where record companies like Simon Cowell's Syco label use the publicity engendered by the shows to promoted artists who have already received massive attention from the public through primetime television exposure. This has led to a situation where many bands, artists and musicians have chosen to cut out the middleman, the record producer, and gain direct access to their fans. Sites such as YouTube as well as individual sites developed by bands provide a platform through which music fans can gain direct access to the work of new and up-and-coming bands who might only have been seen by a privileged few at local gigs.

The web also encourages new and established artists to speak directly to their fans, a facility that significantly eroded the importance of the music press, perhaps symbolised by the demise of the seemingly evergreen *Smash Hits* in 2006. The web also allows for a two-way interaction between fans and the bands they support. On the one hand this has provided an afterlife for those who have passed beyond their major label life while at the same time presenting an ever more viable alternative to getting involved in what

continued

Morrissey described as the world of "A List! Play List! Please them, please them, please them."

Lily Allen, who recently walked away "for a while" (she started a two-year sabbatical in early 2010), is one for whom the DIY route has proved successful. She created an account on MySpace and began posting demos in November 2005 (http://en.wikipedia.org/wiki/Lily_Allen#cite_note-pitchfork-21) which attracted thousands of listeners. She then produced two mixtapes, artfully entitled *My First Mixtape* and *My Second Mixtape*, by which time she had accumulated tens of thousands of MySpace friends. In March 2006, the *Observer Music Magazine* included an article about Allen's success through MySpace. She was offering her 'friends' access to new material as it was being developed including songs that would ultimately become mainstream commercial hits, like 'The Fear', her first number one (which originally appeared as 'I Don't Know'). The social networking site was the focus for her musical journey and it is estimated that Allen's songs have been downloaded from her MySpace page 19 million times. (http://en.wikipedia.org/wiki/Lily_ Allen#cite_note-autogenerated1-24)

As of 9 February 2009, Allen had 448,000 MySpace friends.

ACTIVITY

You're just the same as I am: meeting your idols in cyberspace

Most bands, big and small, have websites and engage in all manner of other 'reach-out' activities (those activities formerly known as merchandising). Choose both an established band and a local or barely known one and compare their offers. Focus on:

- Features (history, discography, etc.)
- Benefits (downloads, discounts, etc.)
- Interactivity (do U2 really read all of your messages?)

How do these 'official' sites compare with fansites and with sites catering for other media like film and TV?

What about the changing role of the audience and the consumer- and user-generated content?

For theorists of the active audience (and more) like De Certeau and Fiske new and digital media technology is merely continuing what audiences have always been engaged in. This is not just actively constructing meanings but is being positively subversive. In their view, the products of mainstream media culture can be appropriated by the audience to use as ammunition in ideological battles with the dominant value system. In the field of music, as we have seen, this argument would point to home recording, illicit downloading, pirate radio, sampling and mixing as examples of resistance which use the technology and products of the mass media.

In support of this view, John Fiske has suggested that ordinary people frequently resist and evade the preferred readings of what he calls 'white patriarchal bourgeois capitalism'. Fiske acknowledges that there is a 'top-down' force which attempts to impose a value system on media audiences, but he sees popular culture as a means of counteracting that power. Now that audiences are better armed with the weapons of semiotic resistance, he predicts the emergence of a 'semiotic democracy'. Whether or not you are convinced by this optimistic view of 'people power' depends to some extent on your view of the supporting evidence. Certainly hijacking *The X Factor*'s Christmas single, immediately doctoring every party election poster as they hit the streets and providing better cuts of *Blade Runner* than the director could offer power to Fiske's argument. He takes a positive view of audience members using media products for fantasy or escapism. These strategies show that audiences are aware of their material situation: "Dismissing escapism as 'mere fantasy' avoids the vital question of *what* is escaped from, *why* escape is necessary, and *what* is escaped to" (Fiske, 1987, p. 317).

ACTIVITY

Biting back

How do people use the technology and content of the mass media to resist or subvert dominant ideology? Find examples from:

- Video production
- Blockbuster films
- TV advertising
- The internet.

continued

The same arguments about the audience's power, activity and capacity to resist have also appeared in recent theory and research in the area of internet usage. On one side of the debate stand the optimists, who see the internet user as savvy, well informed and creative, and distinctions between production and reception blurred to the point of irrelevance. Optimists point to online and virtual communities in which members may interact not only with each other but also with the producers of mainstream texts such as films and television programmes. Websites encourage discussion and involvement rather than passive reception by users, and the web puts a phenomenal amount of information at the disposal of anyone with a PC and a modem. Politicians expect and receive a great deal of comment and response via emails and feedback to their personal or government websites. This explosion of interactive communication has led some commentators to suggest that the internet points the way towards a new democracy. The late Robin Cook MP stated that: "The new technologies can strengthen our democracy by giving us greater opportunities than ever before for better transparency and a more responsive relationship between government and electors" (Coleman, n.d.).

Ross and Nightingale see the internet as a radical development for audiences and the study of audiences:

> **The diverse character of contemporary audience net-work demonstrates the ways the information age is changing what it means to be an audience. Audiences are no longer passive receivers of media texts. They have outgrown the models proposed in 'active reception'. Audiences are learning how to *be* the media, how to net-*work*.**
>
> (Ross and Nightingale, 2003, p. 161)

It may be unfair to describe those on the other side of the debate about internet audiences as pessimists, but they are certainly more dubious about the liberating and empowering aspects of this medium. Many of the more critical perspectives on the internet point to the differential levels of access and use. Studies of internet users have shown a very unequal distribution in terms of gender, age, ethnicity, region and social class. Another cause for concern has been the increasing levels of corporate domination of the internet as big companies exploit the potential for making money from users. As we have already noted, the apparent independence and trustworthiness of the web can also be exploited by 'viral' campaigns. There are also concerns that levels of control and surveillance are inhibiting the spirit of freedom, autonomy and creativity once associated with the net.

Jenkins suggests a path somewhere between the two sides of the debate outlined above. He argues that:

> **It would be naïve to assume that powerful conglomerates will not protect their interest as they enter this new media market place, but at the same time, audiences are gaining greater power and autonomy as they enter into the new knowledge culture. The interactive audience is more than a marketing concept and less than 'semiotic democracy'.**

(Jenkins, 2003, p. 280)

However, we must also remember the relatively short time in which 'interactivity' has been a significant feature of our media experience and the significant innovation that this has been (and continues to be). We are a very long way beyond the 'phone-in' and 'Right to Reply', though both of these are still viable (consider the success of Radio 5 Live's 6:06). Now, in whole swathes of television we expect to have our say: to, as it were, shape the content. It was perhaps a lasting frustration of the leaders' debates that although we had an opportunity to suggest questions we weren't allowed to vote one off each week. We were left with the far less dramatic and convincing 'format' of British democracy on 6 May 2010.

Reality TV

The way in which television is consumed has been changed quite fundamentally by the development of interactivity. By no stretch of the imagination can audiences be seen as passive receptors of televisual messages. A generation has now grown up with the ability to influence what takes place on the screen and this has a profound impact on the relationship between producer and audience. Nowhere is this seeming ability to impact directly upon the programme itself more manifest than in reality television productions. Indeed, some would argue that the way in which we vote in general elections has itself been affected by the impact that reality television has had upon the public. One of the proofs of this 'convergence' is the shock

continued

and horror which was registered when a clutch of broadcasters were fined for dodgy practices surrounding telephone vote-ins (which for a time became a dominant force on both daytime and late-night TV). ITV was fined a record £5.6 million by Ofcom for abusing premium rate phone services in viewer competitions featured in TV shows *Ant and Dec's Saturday Night Takeaway, Gameshow Marathon* and *Soapstar Superstar*. Voting scandals seem particularly painful in a liberal democracy.

Reality TV has also used the internet as an extension of its formats. *Big Brother* has been functioning as a 24-7 experience for a while now. The internet is an aspect of communications technology that has had an important influence on the way in which we consume television. The internet is essentially a voyeuristic medium. Not only can the audience remain anonymous; they can disguise their true identities in order to interact with other people's lives. The reverse side of voyeurism is, of course, exhibitionism. The web encourages people to behave in an exhibitionist way that they might not consider in public. The webcam allows web users to give worldwide access to the intimate details of their daily lives. Here is an opportunity for people to celebrate the ordinariness of their daily lives by allowing all of it to be transmitted across the internet.

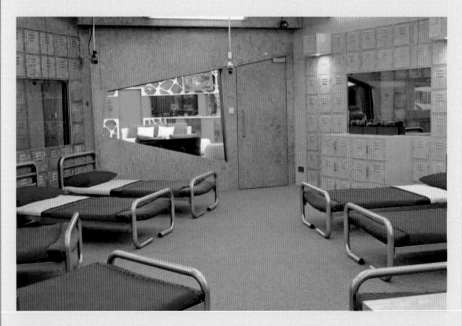

Figure 3.13 *Big Brother*: one of the many cameras viewers can choose to watch through

Another important dimension the internet has brought to television viewing is that of interactivity. When using the web, audiences have an important degree of control over what appears on screen. They are also able to change what is on screen by the click of a mouse. The ability to do this is inevitably going to make viewers dissatisfied with any passive role of simply receiving whatever television broadcasters choose to send them. Email, telephone lines, the red button and text messaging are all methods by which an audience can influence what is on screen, primarily by voting for characters and personalities they do or do not like. By voting for an unpopular or abrasive personality to remain on the show they can add to the narrative conflict and increase the level of excitement in a programme. Potentially the most telling technological innovation is the capacity of digital satellite receivers to respond directly to televisual output by direct interaction through the remote control. This technology allows such direct engagement that, as the technology becomes more widely available in homes, it is likely to mean the development of more and more interactive opportunities in broadcasting, not least through advertising and sponsorship.

This technology enables people to achieve fame and notoriety for no reason other than their willingness to allow other people access to their lives. In a similar way, the participants in reality television shows achieve celebrity status and attempt to build successful media careers on the strength of their involvement with the show. Disturbingly, this often extends the 'freak-show' element lower down the reality TV ladder with people being willing to put their whole lives on the line, even to share their wedding not so much with the world as with the audience of Living TV. The voyeurism and exhibition that we now see as central to much of our culture has its origins in and is a reflection of our society's fixation with surveillance. Postmodern culture has taken surveillance and turned it into fun, although it is potentially a serious threat to all our civil liberties. Programmes such as BBC's *Traffic Cops*, which employ footage shot by traffic police during car pursuits, for example, have done much to popularise a genre of programme which relies on real-life surveillance. Rather than a threat to our liberty, the existence of surveillance cameras has become an opportunity for people to star in their own films, often for ridiculous or even antisocial behaviour. Reality TV becomes an inevitable extension of the idea of playing with surveillance, welcoming cameras to witness our most intimate and often embarrassing exploits.

Media and identity

This section will include:

- Definitions of identity
- The role of the media in constructing identity
- The representation of identities in the media
- The use of representations by the audience to construct identity
- The changing theoretical approaches to the analysis of media and identity.

Defining identity

The concept of **identity** refers to the way in which different groups (family, friends, state, media, etc.) in society see us and the way in which we see ourselves; often in comparison and contrast to others. The factors affecting our identity include gender, race, religion, class, sexuality and nationality which are also inter-linked. Our identities have become more complex as the list of identity categories has increased. Identity is further complicated by political considerations around how we identify ourselves; some people may wish to identify themselves as gay; for others to do so may suggest discrimination or prejudice.

In Media Studies the term identity is used to refer to cultural identity (belonging to a particular group or culture) and personal identity (age, gender, race, etc.), and the overlaps between the two.

ACTIVITY

In considering different definitions of identity, a key question may be posed:

Is identity innate or constructed? Fixed or fluid?

Identity and the media

The study of identity is important in Media Studies for two main reasons:

- How do media texts interpret different identities?
- What is the relationship between audience identity and these representations?

These questions around identity illustrate some of the ongoing – often con-troversial – debates about the role and influence of the media, i.e.:

- What influence does the media have on identity?
- Is the influence positive or negative?
- How is identity affected by repeated ideas about gender, sexuality etc. in media texts?
- Do audiences use the media to select and construct an identity in an active way?
- How does the ability to self-represent in the media affect identity?

These questions may sound rather abstract but the following examples suggest the way in which they have social and political implications.

THE SIZE ZERO DEBATE

Fashion magazines from *Vogue* to *Cosmopolitan* to *Grazia* use fashion models who conform to a specific definition of feminine beauty; one that privileges being thin, white, with large eyes and full lips. The editor of *Vogue* – Alexandra Shulman – has been concerned about the effect these representations have on an audience of young women, suggesting that it creates unrealistic expectations about what 'real' women should look like. This in turn, she argues, affects individual women's identity – particularly around issues of body image and sexual attractiveness. Shulman has accused designers of forcing magazines to hire models with "jutting bones and no breasts or hips" by supplying them (magazines) with "minuscule" garments for their photo shoots and stated that *Vogue* is now frequently "retouching" photographs to make models look larger.

This example illustrates one position within the continuing debate over whether the audience is active or passive. Do the readers of these magazines accept the images as presented and therefore feel inadequate by comparison? Or do readers interpret the images through their understanding of the conventions of magazine publishing and the demands of the fashion industry? How do the different responses to the fashion magazine images affect an individual's understanding of their identity?

The following very different responses to these questions indicate how difficult it is to draw certain conclusions.

AUDIENCE HAS THE POWER

The first response (below) is the dominant one in Media Studies. This approach sees the audience as intelligent and active, using the media in a way which suits them in thinking about themselves and their role in the world (in this case in the context of gender). Gauntlett (2008) summarises this position:

> **Women's magazines – like men's magazines – suggest ways of thinking about the self and propose certain**

> **kinds of lifestyle, which are then actively processed by readers as they establish their personal biography, (and) sense of identity.** 🙶

It is important to recognise that even this position which characterises the relationship between the magazine and audience as interactive (the uses and gratifications model) accepts that the range of options offered by magazines for 'thinking about the self' and 'kinds of lifestyle' are fairly limited and don't challenge traditional definitions of femininity which is always sexy, glamorous and heterosexual.

TEXT HAS THE POWER

The second response is much more concerned about the power of the media in dictating how people (in this case young women) see themselves – in other words, that women's magazines are part of an industry which positions women as passive, sexualised objects. In the context of analysis of women's magazines this approach is usually a feminist one but may also be from censorship, right-wing or religious perspectives. Angela McRobbie (2005) has summed up the concern of many feminist academics in stating: "such publications trap their readers into cycles of anxiety, self loathing and misery that have become a standard mark of modern womanhood." She goes on to illustrate how this is related to identity: "'normative discontent' about body image, about never being beautiful enough, about success and fear of failure . . . become all encompassing, invading the space of other interests and other activities."

This illustration of the conflicting debates around identity in the media demonstrates the importance attached to this area – this can be further seen in a recent report commissioned by the Home Office into *Sexualisation of Young People Review* (2010). This research, carried out by a psychologist, was in response to concerns about the effect on young people of – what was assumed to be – the increased sexualisation of society. The main focus of the report is the media – specifically teen magazines and social networking sites. The conclusions of the report echo McRobbie's view with the argument that:

- there is a connection between the media and identity;
- young people are particularly vulnerable in believing media images without question;
- the media does damage to young people's sense of identity which may have lasting effects;
- opportunities for self-representation – such as on social network sites – are actually just another example of conforming to norms of beauty and sexualisation.

The report defines the process of sexualisation as occurring when:

- a person's value comes only from his or her sexual appeal or behaviour, to the exclusion of other characteristics;
- a person is held to a standard that equates physical attractiveness with being sexy;
- a person is sexually objectified – that is, made into a thing for others' sexual use, rather than seen as a person with the capacity for independent action and decision making;
- sexuality is inappropriately imposed upon a person.

The concerns of the report are summed up in the following quote:

> For adolescents, untrammelled access to sexualised images at a time when they are forming their own identity and coming to terms with their emerging sexuality makes for a potent mix. For any child, the pressure is huge. But what about those children who don't fit the 'norm'? Those who're gay? Those who are disabled or come from a minority ethnic background? The ideal for female beauty is not only narrow and unrealistic, it is also racially biased.

In addition, the report makes recommendations for ways in which these effects can be countered – such as through education – suggesting that primary schools should make specific reference to the influence of the media on body image and personal identity within a new programme of study on 'Understanding Physical Development'.

Identity as construction

Despite the different viewpoints evident in these approaches, both evaluations of the relationship between the media and identity share the view that identity can be constructed and that it can change – rather than being fixed. The disagreement comes over who is in control of this construction – the audience or the media.

ACTIVITY

How many identities?

- How do you define yourself?
- How do you describe yourself? This might be to yourself or to others. If you have a social network page how have you described yourself on it?
- Do you refer to your age, sex, gender, race, religion (or lack of), nationality, regionalism, class, education, political allegiance, taste in music, in food, in fashion?

Of these characteristics and attributes, which would you define as fixed and which are fluid? Are some of these fixed by birth while others might change over time?

How do you think that your current list of identifying features would compare to a list written five years ago – or even ten years ago? Which identities would the different lists share?

Do you think some of these identities are more important in defining who you are than others? Of these, how many do you think will change over time?

The idea that any identity is innate and fixed is one that has been challenged – particularly by feminist theorists.

JUDITH BUTLER AND DEFINITIONS OF SEX AND GENDER

Butler (1990) contends that not only is gender culturally constructed, so is our way of understanding biological difference. It has become accepted to define gender as a constructed identity based on the expectations of a particular society at a particular time. Butler argues that this understanding of gender has affected the way in which a society divides people by biological difference as male and female. Butler isn't denying that there aren't biological differences but points out that society has chosen to categorise individuals along those differences rather than any other. To provide evidence for this she demonstrates how historically this was not always so and problematises the definition by pointing to the existence of a third category – hermaphrodite. Butler's analysis forces us to question the validity of some of the most fundamental categories – male and female – which we recognise in society.

Looking again at your list of characteristics, how many of the identities are based on an opposition? Theories of cultural and personal identity suggest that when we identify ourselves we are by implication positioning that identity in opposition to – not being – something else, for example:

- Female (not male)
- English (not Scottish, Welsh, French, etc.)
- Young (not old)
- Heterosexual (not gay)
- White (not black, Asian, etc.).

Is this list merely an objective description of a series of characteristics or are there connotations attached which suggest that one particular form of identity is superior to another? If we accept the argument that all categories of cultural identity – even sex – are constructed then it is likely that this is the case.

The construction of oppositions can lead to an acceptance of the idea of 'us' and 'them' in society. The 'us' is familiar, reassuring, normal; the 'them' is strange, unnatural, unsettling.

When the lines – or borders – between these identities begin to break down or are not clearly separated it seems to provoke anxiety.

Lady Gaga and cultural identity

The following are two – typical – stories about Lady Gaga's biological sex (both from the *Sun*'s gossip column, Bizarre):

Gaga got a poker?

THE Bizarre squad have been debating whether or not LADY GAGA should in fact be known as LORD GAGA.

Gaga: I am a lady

SINGER Lady Gaga has blasted rumours that she's a hermaphrodite as "ridiculous".

Quizzed on an Aussie radio show, she said: "It's too low brow for me to even discuss."

The US pop star, real name Stefani Germanotta, was responding to internet speculation about a controversial concert video.

But Gaga, 23, told Oz's *Matt and Jo* show: "I've made fun of it before but to talk about it is ridiculous."

ACTIVITY

An analysis of the persona of Lady Gaga might suggest why such rumours developed around her. What provoked the rumours that she was an hermaphrodite?

What does this reaction suggest about society's expectations about how female pop stars should look and behave?

ACTIVITY

Image analysis

Figure 3.14 Images of Lady Gaga

Collect a range of images of Lady Gaga from different contexts: CD covers, fashion shoots, public appearances, stage shows, music videos, paparazzi shots, etc.

Analyse the range of images of Lady Gaga with reference to costume, make-up, hairstyle, figure movement, etc. What connotations do these elements have for the audience? How might these ideas link with areas of identity?

Some approaches to deconstructing the Lady Gaga cultural identity:

- The platinum blonde wig, false eyelashes, exaggerated sexual characteristics (breasts emphasised by low necklines, the hourglass figure) signify Hollywood glamour of the 1950s – particularly stars such as Marilyn Monroe and Lana Turner.
- The exaggerated nature of these elements makes it impossible to look at her in the same way as these previous stars, since her appearance is clearly signalled as manufactured and false. This foregrounding might raise questions about traditional representations of women as objects of the male gaze.
- Lady Gaga's eyes are usually heavily lidded with false eyelashes or covered by sunglasses or futuristic eye wear – again disrupting the conventional relationship to the male gaze.
- On album covers and in videos Lady Gaga makes explicit reference to Hollywood genres, particularly science fiction, which allows her to appear robotic, almost non-human.
- These parts of her persona refer to gender identity – playing with stereotypical convention of female attractiveness – but also national identity; these are specifically American signifiers of beauty.
- In addition to mainstream signifiers she also references a more alternative, experimental culture through, for example, wearing her hair styled as a telephone or appearing in a lobster hat (both references to surrealism in general and to the artist Salvador Dali in particular). In the video for *Telephone* she wears a large eye mask made out of burning cigarettes – which is closer to conceptual art than conventional music video. These signifiers shift her persona to a more European tradition of the avant-garde, away from the mainstream.

To develop this analysis further you could compare these images with those of other female pop stars such as Beyonce, Rhianna or Cheryl Cole.

A useful tool to analyse images/personas which play with gender characteristics is that of camp. Simply put, camp is a style – whether in film, fashion, comedy, behaviour – which relies on the exaggeration of gender characteristics. Camp representations may reverse gender expectations (the 'butch' woman or the 'effeminate' man) or take them to extremes: the diva and the macho man. This explains why action stars such as Arnold Schwarzenegger and Sylvester Stallone are camp. Camp is a way of seeing the world as an aesthetic phenomenon, of being aware of the artifice and construction. Camp emphasises style over content.

Some conclusions about Lady Gaga and representations of cultural identity:

▥ Lady Gaga seems to provoke anxiety among certain parts of the media – whether expressed humorously or with anger – because she doesn't conform to the conventions of female beauty in the pop world.
▥ It is worth remembering that this world is still a very conservative area when it comes to reinforcing gender roles – with clear lines between what is 'natural' or 'unnatural' in a woman's appearance.
▥ Questioning the naturalness of these traditional representations of female beauty has led to the rumours about her physiology – suggesting that to reject conventional femininity is to put your right to identify yourself as female in doubt ('she isn't a real woman').
▥ It is unclear whether Lady Gaga herself started this gossip as part of developing a brand, but the important point is that people could believe it – something about the persona cast doubt on her sex.
▥ That Lady Gaga is also a huge mainstream star suggests that these ideas about gender – that it is fluid, constructed – which were once controversial, are now much more readily accepted.
▥ To identify as a Lady Gaga fan is to signify a challenge to the conventional ways of thinking about gender identity.
▥ That all this can be discussed without reference to her music – beyond its genre – is also indicative of the contemporary music and media landscape.

Lady Gaga provides an illustrative case study for two key critical approaches in analysing identity: post-feminism and postmodernism. In feminist theory of the 1970s the dominant approach to identity was to understand female identity in opposition to masculinity – with clear borders between the two. One of the criticisms of this analysis of gender was that it seemed to assume that gender was biologically determined rather than a result of society's expectations. This is most clearly seen in the formulation that the male is active and the female passive. In the 1980s and 1990s post-feminist and postmodern theorists argued that gender characteristics should be seen as a construction or performance – a form of clothing and props which are put on to mean either masculine and feminine. If this is the case then there is no longer the concept of naturally feminine and masculine – everything is an act.

The concept of identity is not new but its meaning has changed in the last 100 years. In early modernity cultural identity was based on a binary opposition between modern, metropolitan life and a traditional and primitive culture. To be modern was to be free from a cultural identity – such a description applied to a specific place and people: those stuck in the past, living a primitive, traditional life outside of the cities. Cultural identity was about being fixed (stuck); to be modern was to be in a process of change and development.

INFORMATION BOX – MODERNITY AND MODERNISM

The word *modern* is often used simply to describe something up to date and contemporary but *modernity* refers to a specific historical period (early to mid-twentieth century) and ideas of scientific progress, new technology and a move away from religious, pre-industrial cultures. Modernism refers to the particular literary and artistic movements associated with modernity which are experimental in form (abstract painting, stream of consciousness in literature, etc.).

The dominant ideologies of this period, Marxism and Liberalism, saw cultural identity as nostalgic and sentimental, something which held people back. In modernity cultural identity would be superseded by universal values and identities based on rationality and progress. It is clear now that this didn't happen – the effects of globalisation have instead brought about a rethinking of cultural identity.

INFORMATION BOX – GLOBALISATION

Globalisation is a political, economic and cultural phenomenon which has developed rapidly in the past 40 years from a beginning that can be dated to the first developments in telecommunications in the nineteenth century. Globalisation can be defined as the reduction of barriers between nations and territories through a range of means: air travel, telecommunications, broadcast of mass media and the transportation of people, goods and services. For some, globalisation is a positive

continued

Rethinking cultural identity

Ideas about cultural identity have moved on from the conception of identity in terms of binary oppositions. One way to consider this is to trace the way in which particular critical approaches have developed an analysis of identity.

Context: identity and the self

If possible identities and an individual's sense of their identity have changed then it raises the question of how and why this occurred. The various explanations for this change agree that the shift from a traditional to a modern and postmodern society has had a fundamental effect on our sense of identity. What is contentious is exactly how this has happened.

IDENTITY IN TRADITIONAL SOCIETY

When a society is shaped by adherence to tradition and convention, people do things (get married, have children, work, don't work, etc.) because there is a precedent to do so – you follow the actions of the previous generation. In post-traditional societies where traditions are less important these actions become a matter of choice, not predetermined roles to be followed. If there are no longer clearly defined roles based on tradition, then each individual has to make their own decisions about their role. Making these decisions has been compared to telling a story about your life, constructing a narrative to explain who you are.

If this shift from predetermined roles within traditional societies to free choice in modernity is true, then an immediate question is likely to be – How did this happen? When did one generation choose not to take up their traditional roles and why?

The reason for this change in roles and identity (and of course it is worth considering how much of a change it actually is) is keenly debated across different critical approaches. One model which developed in Sociology but has been influential in Media Studies analysed the way in which individual choice (micro aspects of society) and society's structures (the macro elements of state, corporations, globalisation, etc.) continually influence each other and don't exist in isolation. In this analysis, the relationship between the micro and macro elements of society may help to explain the relationship between the media and identity.

Gauntlett (2008) uses the example of the way in which the media might influence an individual's perception of their relationships. He does this by referring back to the concept of narrative: "Whether in serious drama, or celebrity gossip, the need for 'good stories' would always support an emphasis on change in relationships." These fictional representations are then reinforced by factual media which report on lifestyle trends and actual changes in family life. In this illustration knowledge from factual and fictional genres is used by people in various ways – perhaps to validate their own non-traditional choice of roles. This analysis of the interactive relationship between media and audience has been controversial because it suggests the ability of the media to 'not merely *reflect* the social world . . . but contribute to its shape'.

What do vampires tell us about identity?

An investigation into the recent popularity of films and TV series which feature vampires illustrates some of the different approaches to discussing the relationship between the media and cultural identity. This type of analysis can be structured in the following ways:

- The representation of different identities: vampire texts are a rich source here because they tend to focus on themes around the family, nationality, gender and sexuality.
- The way in which identity is constructed through opposition to the 'other' (them); vampires are 'other' because they are non-human but are often used symbolically as a stand-in for other fears in a society at a particular time.
- They also show how the reaction to the 'other' has changed over time. Many vampire stories emphasise the possibility of moving between human and vampire, suggesting that the line between the two isn't that hard to cross.
- An audience study – examining fan culture and audience demographics. How are fans using these texts to construct an identity? (For more analysis on audience response to the *Twilight* series see p. 170.)

A renewed interest in vampires in popular culture has been evident in recent years. These new entries have been notable in their subversion of some of the most familiar and apparently rigid rules of the genre; the shift in identification and sympathy to the non-human; the setting which is contemporary or future societies not the past, and the more explicit treatment of vampire/human love affairs.

Recent examples include:

True Blood (US, HBO, 2008–)
The Vampire Diaries (US, CBS, 2009–)
Being Human (UK, BBC, 2009–)
Cirque du Freak: The Vampire's Assistant (US, Paul Weitz, 2009)
Twilight (US, Catherine Hardwicke, 2008) (and sequels)
Let the Right One In (Sweden, Tomas Alfredson, 2008)
Daybreakers (US, Michael Spierig, Peter Spierig, 2010)

VAMPIRES IN THE MEDIA: THE SECOND WAVE (1980S AND 1990S)

Clearly the current interest in vampire in popular culture exists within a context; they are close relations to the development in gothic horror – aimed primarily at a youth audience – in the late twentieth century. Films such as *The Lost Boys* (US, Joel Schumacher, 1987) and *Near Dark* (US, Kathryn Bigelow, 1987), the TV series *Buffy the Vampire Slayer* (US, 1997–2003) (based on a less successful film from 1992) established some of the themes, style and characteristics evident in the more recent examples. These include the reinvention of genre rules, a con-

Figure 3.15 Vampire films of the 1980s: *The Lost Boys* and *Near Dark*

temporary, small town setting, concern with issues around the family, gender and sexuality. (In both *The Lost Boys* and *Near Dark* the male hero is attracted to a female vampire who has to be rescued and made human before they can be together. Buffy's love interest is Angel, a vampire, but one who has a soul and a conscience, making him at least part human.)

The themes of identity evident in these examples are structured around a system of oppositions:

▩ Law and order against criminality and anarchy
▩ Nature and deviance.

These themes are then addressed through a narrative which centres on the family and teenage sexuality, using these as concepts to explore what is acceptable to society and what needs to be rejected. The fun and attraction of vampire films is that the border between the acceptable and unacceptable is constantly broken down – the vampires seeming to move between the two sides of the divide. The hero's family in these films is non-traditional in some way and vulnerable to attack from the vampire. The vampire 'family' is a secure and stable unit demonstrating traditional gender roles, such as the patriarch and the maternal woman. In contrast the vampires also represent chaos and anarchy, a threat to the civilised, law-abiding society, but this is part of their glamour and excitement, providing the temptation for the hero to turn into a vampire.

These seeming contradictions – where the 'other' is more attractive than the recognisable and reassuring – are usually resolved at the end of the film. The narrative is structured around the battle between human and vampire for the love of the female vampire; the human hero wins, the vampires are vanquished and the narrative conforms to the conventional heterosexual resolution. Therefore, despite the fact that the vampires are attractive and charismatic they are ultimately unacceptable to society (and to the audience).

COUNT DRACULA: THE FIRST WAVE (1890S)

The genre conventions we now recognise in vampire texts were established (drawing on myths and legends) in *Dracula* (1897), the gothic horror novel by Bram Stoker:

▩ The character of Dracula is 'foreign' and doesn't belong to a specific country – he is able to travel freely across borders
▩ Dracula inspires terror and desire in his victims
▩ Dracula attacks both male and female victims
▩ He is 'undead'
▩ He can only be killed by daylight or by a stake through the heart
▩ Garlic and crucifixes are effective weapons against him
▩ He has no reflection
▩ Dracula must be 'invited in'.

The character of Dracula has been the focus of many attempts to explain the audience's fascination with this genre. Much of this work has examined the way in which he operates as a symbol for discussing various taboos and anxieties in society – these have tended to focus on issues of identity such as nationality and sexuality, with the vampire challenging accepted definitions and boundaries. In *Reading the Vampire* (1994) Ken Gelder describes this: "A vampire's function is to cross back and forth over boundaries which should otherwise be secure – between humans and animals, humans and God, man and woman." This analysis suggests that we like vampires so much because it allows us to explore different identities – perhaps even ones we feel uneasy about – but we can still come back to our conventional selves by the end of the film. The recognition of the boundaries between humans and vampires (us and them) is evident in the taglines for *Daybreakers*:

> *In 2019, The Most Precious Natural Resource. . . Is Us.*
> *The battle between immortality and humanity is on.*
> *The face of humanity has changed forever*

And in the final line of the film: *We can change you back*.

All of this suggests a clear dividing line – if it is crossed then you must cross back to being human. In contrast *Twilight* suggests a much less rigid divide between the two groups, emphasising instead the romantic possibilities of the two groups coming together.

> *When you can live forever what do you live for?*
> *Forever.Begins.Now.   Nothing will be the same*

Figure 3.16 Human/non-human relationships: *True Blood* and *Twilight*

A2 MEDIA STUDIES: THE ESSENTIAL INTRODUCTION

While the vampire is most commonly discussed in terms of sexuality, the idea that Dracula is a metaphor for issues of national identity is also common. The original novel uses the fear of an attack on national identity to create the horror of Dracula – he is a diverse figure, made up of many races, something which was seen as undesirable. Dracula's diversity signified confusion and instability, something which national identity seeks to overcome to create a powerful and stable society. Dracula's move to England from Eastern Europe had connotations of invasion and contamination.

ACTIVITY

Identity analysis

Take a contemporary vampire text and consider how it explores themes of identity. Does it fit into any of the categories discussed above?

To help in constructing an analysis make notes on the following:

- Who is the audience intended to identify with – vampire or human? Both?
- Which rules of the genre are adhered to and which are broken?
- What examples of a family unit are there? Biological or constructed, vampire or human – what values do these different families represent?
- How are the vampires signified as 'other' than human? Twinkling? Sucking blood? What is the vampire's own response to these non-human characteristics?
- What examples are there of national or ethnic identity in the text? Is there any link between being non-human and these identities?
- Are there a range of representations of sexuality and sexual relationships? List the different examples in your text.

Case study

CONSTRUCTION OF IDENTITY IN VAMPIRE TEXTS

Gender identity

Twilight questions the conventional gender roles in vampire texts (with the exception of Buffy) by featuring a female central character that is drawn to the male vampire rather than the other way around. Bella Swan, despite her feminine name, is a tomboy who wears casual clothes which hide her body, is bookish and drives a truck (some viewers might recognise this character as very similar to the 'Final Girl' of the horror genre). While this representation of gender identity challenges the dominant feminine stereotype in some ways, Bella is still rescued by the male characters and is driven by love and emotion. There are other characters in the film that seem to cross the traditional borders of gender conventions, such as Eric whose love of gossip and fashion is more usually coded as female.

National and ethnic identity

In *Twilight* the town of Forks is a symbol for the US and as such it draws on a range of cultural signifiers, traditional and contemporary. Forks does exist but its representation on screen is not about realism. Forks on screen draws on a romanticised view of small-town America which seems to refer back to the past (or at least to films of the past), emphasising the community structure of home, high school, the diner, independent shops and the local sheriff. The town has an ethnic mix with American Asians and African Americans playing prominent roles. The town is divided however in some ways across ethnic lines with the Quielete reservation remaining a separate community. The conservative, nostalgic view of national identity symbolised by Forks is undercut by the ethnic diversity of the characters and of course by the two groups of vampires who are foreign to the town.

Sexuality and the other

Gay and straight sexuality is represented in *Twilight* and Eric conforms to the popular Hollywood character of the gay best friend – a sympathetic character familiar from rom-com and sit-com. In keeping with the conventions of this type of character, Eric doesn't have any on-screen relationships. Bella's female friends at school are all in different stages of heterosexual relationships. The experience of Bella's own parents who have separated works as a contrast to the 'true' vampire love which will last 'forever'. Bella and Edwards' relationship is in many ways coded as heterosexual and the narrative stages are very similar to a conventional romantic plot line: the initial apparent dislike which changes following a dramatic event (he saves her from being crushed by a car), the happy interlude of a romantic dinner, confession of his secret, declaration of love, meeting the family, the union disrupted when happiness is almost snatched away, but she is saved and they are united in an embrace at the high school prom. The normalising of the human non-human affair has been read in different (sometimes contradictory) ways:

- It appeals to a young teen audience who want the emotion and drama of a fantasy romance but not the physical engagement.
- It's a signal that diverse cultures, sexualities, ethnicities are now integrated into the mainstream.
- The human/non-human love affair is a stand-in for other 'taboo' representations (at least in mainstream media), such as homosexuality.
- The character of Edward is coded to be read as 'queer' to some sections of the audience; that he has to lie to fit in, go against his natural urges to be accepted in society, that he 'comes out' to Bella, have all been used to read the vampire as a symbol of those individuals and groups who are not accepted by society.

Queer theory

Queer was used as a term of abuse for gay men, but has now been 'reclaimed' by groups as a form of positive identification (it should be noted though that it is still a controversial term). Queer is not synonymous with gay but instead questions such narrow definitions of sexuality and gender. Queer refers to people who identify as gay, lesbian, bisexual, transgender, intersex, but also has a wider meaning in referring to anyone who doesn't feel part of the mainstream heterosexual ('heteronormative') society. Queer theory developed out of a frustration with the narrowness of traditional feminist and gender approaches. Queer is anti-essentialist, arguing that as identity is constructed, all attempts at definition are unhelpful and restrictive. Within queer was also a rejection of the use of positive images to promote acceptance in society – to be queer is to reject the mainstream and not to try to conform to its conventions. This approach is apparent in queer cultural products – particularly cinema – but also in fan-produced forms such as 'slash fiction' (for more discussion on queer theory and its application to media texts, see p. 92).

Identity: a summary

- In Media Studies the concept of identity intersects with representation, audience and ideology
- Representations of identity can subvert the concept of positive and negative images
- The concept of identity has evolved from being innate and fixed to constructed and fluid
- In a post-traditional society we have the choice of a range of identities; in choosing identities we construct a story of our life
- The media can play a role in constructing an identity – but whether it is something 'done to us' or something we choose is fiercely debated
- Popular culture represents an increasing range of identities but there are still dominant identities (heteronormative).

4 PASSING MEST3: CRITICAL PERSPECTIVES

MEST3 comprises 50 per cent of your A2 course.

The exam is made up of two sections. In Section A you answer questions on unseen texts and in Section B you answer an essay question using one of your individual case studies.

MEST3 is based on the study of two pre-set topics; the first two are:

■ Representations in the media
■ The impact of new/digital media.

The pre-set topics will change, but you will be told well in advance so that you have time to plan and prepare.

The AQA specification (http://store.aqa.org.uk/qual/gce/pdf/AQA-2570-W-SP-10.PDF) tells you what the MEST3 unit and the exam are all about.

To do well you are expected to meet certain assessment objectives. These are:

AO1 Demonstrate knowledge and understanding of media concepts, contexts and critical debates
A02 Apply knowledge and understanding when analysing media products and processes to show how meanings and responses are created.

This means you are being tested on your ability to evaluate media texts using:

■ media concepts – forms, including media language, genre and narrative and representations, institutions, audiences or values;
■ the media issues and debates that are raised by the texts and applying relevant theories to help your evaluation;
■ the relevant wider contexts.

Individual case study

You will complete two individual case studies, one on each of the pre-set topics.

You need an individual case study on each of the pre-set topics because the three questions in Section A will be based on the pre-set topics. For some of the questions you will be rewarded for supporting your answers with your own examples, beyond the unseen exam texts.

You will only need Section B essay practice on one of the pre-set topics, because you only have to answer one essay question in Section B.

You will be rewarded in the exam for individual and independent case studies. With the guidance of your teacher, you can follow your own interests and passions and do your own analysis and research.

Whatever case study you choose, you need to be confident you can answer Section B questions on the following topics.

Representations in the media

How and why a social group or place is represented across a range of media platforms and products, and the relevant media issues, debates and theories and wider contexts.

- dominant representations
- possible alternative representations
- stereotyping
- representation and audience
- representation and genre
- cross cultural factors
- effect of globalisation
- values and ideology.

Or

The impact of new/digital media

The impact of new/digital media across a range of media platforms and products (including the effect on competing traditional media) and the relevant media issues, debates and theories and wider contexts.

- media institutions
- media and democracy
- the changing role of the producer
- the changing role of the audience and the consumer and user generated content
- the effect of globalisation

- the attempts of traditional media to survive/compete
- cross-cultural factors
- values and ideology.

You could start off with a class overview of the topic and then conduct a mini-class case study. You will then need to choose your own individual case study. Think about issues, genres and texts you are interested in and what will allow you to answer any of the exam question areas listed above.

It will be useful to have:

1. A plan with a general overall title to focus your case study. In addition, a list of the core texts you will study in detail, although it is useful to make brief references to others, and some possible media issues, debates and wider contexts that you think will be relevant; you will obviously add to these as you complete your case study.
2. Collect your texts, and include a variety, for example, different genres, made by different kinds of institutions, with different representations and values and that cover a range of platforms. Analyse the texts using the media concepts.
3. Complete lots of secondary research that is relevant to your case study. For example, is there a chapter in a textbook about the representation of men in the media that you could apply to your case study? Is there an article on an industry website about the impact of new and digital media on the music industry?
4. Research and apply media issues, debates and theories and wider contexts. Most importantly apply them to your case study and texts.
5. When you are completing your case study you can present it in different ways, for example, as a formal essay, an illustrated essay, a portfolio, or a presentation to a small group or your whole class.

Exam

You are assessed by a two-hour written examination paper, made up of two sections.

SECTION A

One hour (including 15 minutes' reading/viewing and planning time) 32 marks (40 per cent)

There are *three compulsory questions* based on unseen media products. The questions will be based on three areas:

1. **Media concepts**   (*8 marks*)

    Use the unseen products to answer a question on forms, representations, institutions, audiences or values.

2. **Media issues and debates**   (*12 marks*)

Use the unseen products to answer a question on media issues and debates. You may move beyond the texts, referring to other media products to support your answer.

3. **Wider contexts**   (*12 marks*)

Use the unseen products to answer a question on wider contexts. You should move beyond the texts, referring to other media products to support your answer.

One hour   **48 marks (60 per cent)**

Answer *one question* from a choice of four questions, two on each pre-set topic.

You should use evidence and examples from your own individual case study to answer the essay question. You will be rewarded for using your own case study to produce an individual and autonomous response.

You will be rewarded for showing breadth in your answers, for example, a variety of texts, different genres and a range of platforms.

Questions will be open-ended, so candidates can respond to the question using any of the media products that they have studied.

The emphasis will be on questions that are relevant to up-to-date media issues and debates.

Mark scheme

The mark scheme describes Level 4, the top level, as follows.

SECTION A

Question 1

A sophisticated and detailed analysis and evaluation of both texts, showing very good critical autonomy.

Demonstrates sophisticated knowledge and understanding of the media concept within both texts.

Detailed and sophisticated application of media concepts.

The answer is well structured, articulate and engaged.

A sophisticated and detailed analysis and evaluation of both texts, showing very good critical autonomy.

Detailed and sophisticated application of media concepts.

Detailed and sophisticated application of a wide range of critical debates, issues and theories.

Supports answer with a wide range of examples from other texts.

The answer is well structured, articulate and engaged.

A sophisticated and detailed analysis and evaluation of both texts, showing very good critical autonomy.

Detailed and sophisticated application of media concepts.

Detailed and sophisticated application of a wide range of critical debates, issues and theories and wider contexts.

Supports this with a wide range of examples from other texts.

The answer is well structured, articulate and engaged.

SECTION B

A sophisticated and comprehensive discussion and evaluation, showing very good critical autonomy.

Sophisticated and detailed application of critical debates and current issues about media representations or new/digital media. A clear focus on the question.

Answer is supported by a wide range of examples. The use of the candidate's own case study shows detailed evidence of independent study.

The answer is well structured, articulate and engaged.

MEST3 Specimen Paper

> You're advised to spend one hour, which includes 15 minutes' reading/
> viewing and planning time on Section A. Section A is worth 32 marks, which
> is 40 per cent of your MEST3 marks.
>
> The exam paper will include a short introduction to the unseen texts. Read
> this carefully and think about how the information can help you answer the
> three questions. For example: What audience are the products aimed at?
> What genre are they? What kind of institution produces them and how does
> this shape the products? What related media products are there and what
> does this tell you? What are the relevant media issues and debates and
> wider contexts?

Figure 4.1 Cheryl Cole in *Heat* Magazine, 19–25 September 2009

Heat magazine is published by Bauer Media, a multi-platform media group.
The Heat brand was launched in 2000 as a magazine and is now available
over a number of platforms: heat magazine, www.heatworld.com, heat radio
and heat mobile. It markets the brand by claiming, "a heat moment is always
an Oh.My.God! moment." Its audience is ABC1 women, aged 16–35, who are
"obsessed with celebrity gossip . . . entertainment literate: avid cinema-goers,
DVD-renters, internet-users, music-lovers, TV-addicts . . . smart and prolific
shoppers".

Cheryl Cole became a member of the all-girl pop group Girls Aloud after winning
ITV's reality television programme *Popstars: The Rivals*. Girls Aloud have achieved

commercial success with consecutive UK top-ten singles, including four number ones. In 2008, Cole became a judge on ITV's reality television programme *The X Factor*. Her first solo single, 'Fight for This Love', was the fastest selling single of 2009 when it entered the UK singles chart. It used an extensive online marketing campaign, including a live webchat on MySpace and an exclusive video on MSN Messenger.

Figure 4.2 Homepage of www.miauk.com, M.I.A.'s official website

Mathangi Arulpragasam, better known as M.I.A., is an English hip hop/dance artist of Tamil Sri Lankan origin. M.I.A. and her family had to stay in London as refugees because of the political group her father belonged to in Sri Lanka. She became well known in 2004 through the file sharing of her single 'Sunshowers'. Her debut album *Arular* was released in 2005 and was nominated for the Mercury Prize. She achieved mainstream success with her second album and the single, 'Paper Aeroplanes', which was used in the film *Slumdog Millionaire*. In 2008 she started the record label N.E.E.T.

This extract is the home and video page of her official website, which also includes news, a blog and links to MySpace and YouTube. The Internet Marketing Bureau says, "the internet music revolution . . . goes straight to the very heart of the decades-old reliance on record companies to discover, launch and market new artists".

1. Evaluate how the two media products represent women.
2. What pleasures and appeals do official band or artist pages have for audiences?
   You may also refer to other media texts to support your answer.
3. What opportunities and threats does the internet offer the music industry?
   You should refer to other media texts to support your answer.

Possible answers to Section A

The following bullet points are only possible points that you could make. No candidate would be expected to make them all and there are lots of other valid points you could make.

1. Evaluate how the two media products represent women.

> In Question 1 you need to produce a detailed evaluation and analysis that focuses on one of the media concepts. Your main focus is on the two exam products, but you can include brief examples and points beyond them to support your analysis.
>
> How are the women represented? How is each representation a positive and/or negative representation of women? How is it stereotypical or not? How is it a dominant and/or alternative representation of women in the music industry and media? How does who is producing the texts and the audiences they are targeting shape the representation? What similarities and differences are there in the ways the two products represent women? Include lots of detailed examples from the two products to illustrate the points you make.

Heat is a dominant representation of women in the music industry and the media. It is a mainstream celebrity magazine.

▓ Cole is constructed for Mulvey's male gaze, as *an object* to be looked at by men. It positions women to put themselves in her place to be looked at and presents her as an *aspirational* character for the mostly female audience of ABC1 women aged 16–35. *Heat* shows a contradictory representation of women, offering Cole here as an aspirational character but filling their pages with detailed criticisms of women's bodies for being, for example, either too thin or too fat. The message of women's magazines to their readers is that women need to be improved. The advertising that the magazines rely on for their profit depends on women feeling dissatisfied with themselves as they are. John Berger in *Ways of Seeing* (1972) described the way advertising images work as stealing her love of herself as she is and offering it back to her for the price of the product (*e.g. short, tight clothes, "SEXY! YES YES YES"*).

▓ The representation of women is dominated by their *physical appearance*, and Cole is judged almost completely by what she looks like. It asks the female audience to judge themselves and other women by their appearance, not, for example, by their character or intelligence. The marketing campaign for her new album sells it on her appearance and sex appeal, not on the music or any talent she may have. It also shows a very narrow definition of beauty as white, very thin and heavily made up. In *Media and Values* (1990) Jean Kilbourne argues that many women judge themselves by the media's unrealistic ideal of beauty. As a celebrity she avoids what Kilbourne argues is the dismemberment of women's bodies into legs, breasts or thighs, which reinforces the message that women are not whole and complete individuals (*e.g. the image-led pages are dominated by photos of Cole in different outfits, "CHERYL'S RAUNCHY NEW LOOK", six photos with the headline, "FROM EEK TO CHIC", "AN EDGY NEW IMAGE"*).

▓ When it does mention her creative talents, it focuses on the personal meaning of her lyrics, defining women by their relationship to men and showing that women are and should be led by their *emotions*. This has dominated the representation of Cole in the media, with huge amounts of coverage in the tabloids, celebrity magazines and gossip websites devoted to her on-off relationship with Ashley Cole and her fragile emotional state. Dyer argues that the media creates a star image which may not be anything like the person in real life and that it uses this star image to sell products. The star image carries values, for example, in Cole's image that women should be judged by their relationship to a man, are vulnerable and emotionally fragile, and must be conventionally beautiful to be successful (*e.g. "Please Don't Talk About This Love is particularly personal – it's clearly about her relationship with Ashley"*).

In contrast, the representation of M.I.A. is more alternative at times.

▓ M.I.A. is not only represented by her *physical appearance*. Not all the images are in sexual poses (*e.g. less revealing costume, close-ups of her singing.*

The bright, colourful, busy design puts less emphasis on her physical appearance. The home page text includes the titles of her songs 'Boyz', 'Bird flu', etc.).

Some of the facial expressions and gestures do present her as sexually available – her appearance is still used to sell her music; this is seen as essential by the music industry. She is still young, slim and made up, although her Tamil background widens media definitions of success and beauty. She has set up her own record label N.E.E.T., so does this suggest she has more power and control in the media, so more control and choice over her own representation?

▪ The website photos focus on *M.I.A. performing*; she is active not passive and judged by what she does, not just by what she looks like (*e.g. five different videos on the video link page*).

▪ The two pages suggest that there is a range of roles that women can play (*e.g. the range of costumes, settings, body language, the contrast between the Bucky Done Gun and Jimmy photos*).

▪ The website also suggests a wider range of topics and issues than conventional pop songs about love and relationships with men. It suggests that her music and part of the media image which sells her music is *political*. This is a different star image that carries different values, for example, that women have political views, we live in a society with political problems. Her record label is called N.E.E.T., which is the government term for young people not in employment, education or training. She has had some mainstream success but does the political content of some of her music make her less attractive to the music industry than the mainstream pop songs about love and dominant representation of Cole (*e.g. the list of song titles on the video page; the map of Africa; The photos of male leaders*)?

▪ The *men* play *supporting roles* to M.I.A., an alternative representation. She isn't defined by her relationship to men or by her emotions. She is a woman in the male-dominated genre of hip hop (*e.g. the secondary photos are of men and they are often cropped so that we can't see all the faces or bodies, which emphasises their secondary role*).

2. **What pleasures and appeals do official band or artist pages have for audiences?**

   You may also refer to other media texts to support your answer.

In Question 2 most of your answer will still focus on the two media products, but Question 2 is about media issues and debates, so you can move beyond the two exam products and think about what they show about the music industry and the media in general. For example, what trends do they show in the music industry? Here you can use the final quote in the introduction to the two products to help support your answer.

Think about what pleasures audiences could get from this official artist's website and music websites in general. Include a range of pleasures; don't base your answer on just one, and look carefully at the whole website home page and the links. How is the audience positioned in relation to the artist? What pleasures can a website offer in particular that other platforms can't? What is the aim or purpose of an official website? It is part of marketing so how does it sell the artists and their products? What can official websites offer that unofficial ones can't and vice versa? What theories could you apply that explain how audiences use the media? Include lots of examples from the two exam products and other media products to support your points.

▧ The M.I.A. website and other band websites offer *intimate access* to bands and artists. They appear to be *unmediated*, suggesting a direct relationship between the artist and the audience, and offering Dyer's utopian pleasures of intimacy instead of fragmentation and alienation. Audiences can be active and find out about music themselves or through social networking sites and music streaming sites (*e.g. M.I.A.'s blog, artists' Facebook sites*).

▧ They can *cut out the record company* and *empower the audience*. Some smaller artists' websites and social networking pages are created by the artists themselves.

▧ However, they are usually carefully constructed *marketing tools*. Many bands have used the internet as a marketing tool, for example, The Arctic Monkeys and Lily Allen, although they will often be backed by a powerful record company as well.

▧ They are *fast, free and easy to use* for audiences.

▧ The 'official website' *promises the audience 'the truth'* about the artist or band. However, audiences can be active in the way they use the official website and other websites of the same artist. They could have Morley's negotiated reading of the official website of a big mainstream artist and find other less official information from, for example, unofficial websites, gossip sites or social networking sites.

▧ They promise more *up-to-date and exclusive* information, adding value to other marketing techniques (*e.g. "NEWS/TOUR" link, "M.I.A. ART" link, pre-release downloads used by other bands that are only available on the official website*).

▧ They have a *commercial* element with, for example, a shop with merchandise, ticket sales and exclusive, free or pre-release downloads of tracks (*e.g. 'STORE'*).

▧ They often have *forums* that offer a chance to speak to other fans, and audiences can send links, images and information from the website and the links to friends offering Bulmer and Katz's uses and gratifications of personal relationships.

3. **What opportunities and threats does the internet offer the music industry?**

   You should refer to other media texts to support your answer.

> In Question 3 your starting point is still the two unseen media products, but you need to move beyond them and think about what wider contexts they raise. For example, what trends do they show in the music industry? Here you can use the second paragraphs in each of the introductions to the two products to help. There may be some possible overlap with Question 2 but aim to make new points in Question 3.
>
> How is the internet good for the music industry? Think in particular of economic reasons. How is it a threat? Again think in particular about economic reasons. How has the music industry reacted to the internet in the past, what affect has this had, and has it changed its tactics?
>
> Think of specific examples from the two exam products and other media products to support your points.

- The music industry has been *slow to react* to developments in new and digital media. Many of the ways of making money from music through the internet have not been created by existing record companies (*e.g. iTunes, Spotify*).
- The profits of record companies have been severely damaged by *illegal downloads and file sharing*. The Digital Economy Bill plans to address this problem by cutting off the internet connection of people who repeatedly infringe copyright by, for example, illegally downloading a film or track. This has been criticised as a threat to freedom of expression, consumer rights and privacy (*e.g. the film industry has also been fighting against this, such as battles between cinemas and film companies about cutting the time from the cinema to DVD release*).
- The internet is a *new place to sell and market music* for record companies and individual acts. It offers an instant global market. Bands can give their songs away for free to start with, but use this to get themselves known and create a loyal fan base (*e.g. Cheryl Cole used a range of online marketing techniques. Many artists offer exclusive or advanced release of tracks on their websites.*).
- It can *cut out the large record companies* because bands and *artists can communicate with and sell directly to their audience* online. It has been argued that the music industry is thriving; it is only record companies that are struggling (*e.g. artist and band social networking site pages, YouTube live performances*).
- The internet has *viral power*. For example, users on social networking sites can quickly communicate and share tracks and links about new acts or new releases.

- Sales of singles are increasing and album sales are falling. Audiences can buy the singles they want rather than a whole album with tracks they don't like. There are also increasing profits in sponsorship, live shows and merchandising. Record companies and the music industry now need to *make money from all the different parts of the music*, not just traditional single and album sales (*e.g. the comebacks of older artists and bands like Take That*).
- News music streaming services like Spotify are still struggling to make *profits (e.g. Spotify aims to make money by getting people who use the free subscription service to become paying subscribers)*.

SECTION B

You should answer one question in Section B from a choice of four questions, two on each pre-set topic. You are advised to spend one hour on Section B. It's worth 48 marks, which is 60 per cent of your MEST3 marks.

In Section B you are rewarded for producing your own answer to a question using your individual case study.

Be careful not just to write everything you know about your case study or to just describe it; instead evaluate and analyse. Focus on the question and use your case study to support and illustrate your answer. The examiners are looking for critical autonomy, the ability to think for yourself and apply your understanding to a particular question.

Include lots of detailed examples from your texts to illustrate the points you make.

Include a wide range of relevant media issues and debates and wider contexts. Apply theory to help you explain and support the points that you make.

The examiners are looking for an engaged answer, which means that you show them you are interested in the topic and have your own ideas and opinions.

Remember that in Section B you are writing an essay, so you need to take time and care over the structure of your answer. The best way to do this is to spend a few minutes preparing a plan. For example:

1. Read the question and underline the keywords.
2. Complete a short spider diagram on all the points you could make in the essay.
3. Check you have got examples, media issues, debates and theories and wider contexts, and add a note on any of these you have missed.

---

4. Divide the diagram into about three sections, by, for example, joining up two points that could be answered together.
5. Add an introduction and conclusion.
6. Number your sections (e.g. 1–5).

Then write your essay using the plan. This will make the best use of your time; for example, you can work out roughly how long you should spend on each section. It will give your essay a clear structure. It will also stop you running out of what to say or panicking half-way through about what to write next, as you will simply look at the next numbered section in your plan.

4. a) **"The newspaper or a very close electronic cousin will always be around. It may not be thrown onto your front doorstep the way it is today. But the thud it makes as it lands will continue to echo around society and the world."**

Rupert Murdoch on Australian radio in 2008.
How and with what success have media platforms threatened by new and digital media attempted to survive?

b) **Developments in new and digital media have made the media more democratic, with more equal participation by more people. Discuss the arguments for and against this view.**

c) **Media representations reflect the values that are in the interests of those in power. Why and to what extent is this true for the representation of the group or place you have studied?**

d) **Whether a representation is seen as positive or negative, accurate or inaccurate, fair or unfair is subjective; it depends on the values and opinions of the audience. Discuss this statement with reference to the group or place you have studied.**

What makes an active MEST3 student?

Are you an active or passive student?

AS Media Studies: The Essential Revision Guide describes what active and passive students are. To get the most out of your Media Studies course and to achieve the best grade possible you need to be an active student.

■ Stay up to date with issues, trends and events in the media. Impress the examiners with your own class and individual up-to-date knowledge of the media.

For example, use www.mediaguardian.co.uk or www.digitalspy.co.uk to produce a weekly class quiz that is organised by individuals or as a group league.

- Watch, read and listen to a wide range of media, not just what you would choose yourself.

  For example:

  - A class display board of examples of controversial or innovative media products.
  - YouTube end-of-lesson reward clips of favourite media products.
  - Keep your own e-portfolio or hard copies of interesting media products. Make notes on them so you can use the relevant ones to illustrate points you make in the exam.

- Develop your own ideas and opinions and be able to explain and justify them.

  For example:

  - Class debates on media issues and arguments.
  - Pair presentations on media issues and debates in small groups.
  - A class display board of reviews of new films, websites, ad campaigns, etc.

Preparing for the exam and revision

Look back at your AS MEST1 exam to see what you can learn from it.

ACTIVITY

What mark and grade did you get in MEST1?

What section do you think you did best on – Section A with the unseen media product and questions, or the essay in Section B?

Why did you feel confident in the section you did well on?

Why did you find the other section harder?

What could you do to improve the mark you get for the section you found hardest? For example, many students find the Section B essays harder, so do you need to do lots of essay plans or practise timed essays? Do you need to revise your individual case study more, so you can use it more confidently in your exam?

Are there any straightforward mistakes you need to avoid this time? For example, answer all the questions, and stick to the suggested time to spend on each section.

How did you prepare for your MEST1 exam?

What parts of this were useful that you could use again in MEST3?

- Practise past papers as a class, in groups, in pairs and on your own.
- Create your own Section A exam papers, with chosen texts and the questions.
- Create Section B essay plans on all the main possible essay topics that include analysis and detailed examples, relevant media issues and debates, applied theories and wider contexts.
- Learn media terminology with class and group match-up exercises.
- Learn media theory with class and group match-up exercises and individual theory mind maps. Remember: it's not enough to just learn theories; you get your marks in the exam by using them to answer the questions, and by applying them to media products.
- Summarise your individual case study on a grid or mind map. Include analysis and detailed examples, relevant media issues and debates, applied theories and wider contexts. Make your summary as visual as possible, for example, by colour coding different sections, using boxes and arrows, using pictures to stand for different sections or points.

THE EXAM

Media Studies examiners are interested less in all the knowledge you have and more about how you can apply it to particular media products and questions.

Include lots of detailed examples to support the points you make. These will obviously be examples from the unseen MEST3 texts and your own case study. However, also include your own individual examples that you have collected and researched yourself throughout your Media Studies course.

Make your answer individual and autonomous. Show the examiner you can think for yourself and that you can explain and justify your own opinions.

The key words in the mark scheme that describer a top-level answer are:

For Section A

- Sophisticated and detailed
- Analysis and evaluation
- Articulate and engaged
- A wide range of examples.

For Section B

- Sophisticated, detailed and comprehensive
- Discussion, evaluation and application
- Critical autonomy
- A clear focus on the question
- A wide range of examples
- Individual case study shows independent study.

Both ask you

■ To be articulate and engaged.

MEST3 – representation

This section includes:

■ **An introduction to representation**, with sections on mediation, meanings and values, audience, dominant representations, alternative representations, stereotyping, representation and power, and ideology and values.
■ **A case study**, the representation of Manchester, with sections on dominant representations, possible alternative representations, stereotyping, representation and audience, representation and genre, the effect of globalisation, and values and ideology.

Whatever case study you choose, you need to study how and why a social group or place is represented across a range of media platforms, genres and products and the relevant media issues, debates and theories and wider contexts. You should be confident you can answer questions on:

■ dominant representations
■ possible alternative representations
■ stereotyping
■ representation and audience
■ representation and genre
■ cross-cultural factors
■ effect of globalisation
■ values and ideology.

You can organise your study of pre-set topics by:

1. **Overview of topic**
2. **Class case study** – media concepts, issues, debates and theories and wider contexts
3. **Individual case study** – your own detailed analysis using media concepts, issues, debates and theories and wider contexts.

Introduction to representation

Representation is the way people, groups, places, issues and events are shown by the media. The media constructs versions of these subjects and transmits them through media texts to an audience. Age, gender, class, ethnicity, nationality, sexuality, disability and place are particularly important in how representations are constructed.

Mediation

A media product and the representations it contains is not the real thing. The media takes something that is real (for example, an anti-war demonstration) and changes it into a media product (for example, a news website report on the demonstration). No representation is real, but is only one version of the real. The media comes between the audience and the original source; it mediates. The media selects, it chooses what to include and constructs, it puts together the elements in a particular way. This selection and shaping *represent* the world. We don't see reality, but only one version of it.

When you analyse a media text think about how it is mediated.

Mediation is more obvious for fictional media (for example, a soap or an advert). However, media texts that are presented as 'real' or the 'truth' (for example, the news or reality television) are just as constructed.

ACTIVITY

How is a reality TV programme, such as *I'm a Celebrity, Get Me Out of Here!*, constructed? How does the media construct representations of particular contestants, encouraging us to like some and dislike others? Think about what happens when the programme is being planned, filmed and edited into a TV programme and what happens outside the programme in other parts of the media.

Any representation is made up of:

■ the constructed *media product*
■ the *people making* the representation and the *institution* it is produced by
■ the *audience* that read the representation
■ the *context of the society* in which the representation is made and consumed.

Audiences get used to consuming media products and become familiar with the codes and conventions that are used to construct them. This can mean that the construction may seem natural and invisible. It can also mean that the representations also appear natural and not constructed. They are not questioned and are accepted as normal and natural.

Meanings and values

Representations carry meanings with judgements and values about people, places, issues, etc. Representations help the audience to make sense of the world and tell us how to view and value things. The representations contribute to the way we think about ourselves and others. Representations reflect the opinions and values of the people, institutions and society that produce and consume them.

However, remember that the media is only one influence on our opinions and values. We are also influenced, for example, by family, friends, education, the law, politicians. The media is sometimes used as a scapegoat; it carries all the blame for a problem in society. It is easier to blame the media than the whole social, economic and political system, particularly for those in power.

ACTIVITY

1. On your own or in groups, think about bands or artists who have been blamed for negative issues in society (for example, gun crime, suicide). Think of examples of their media products that have done this (e.g. lyrics, CD covers, adverts, interviews, live appearances).
2. Then on your own or as a class think about the possible social and economic reasons for the issues in society.

However, also remember that record companies and other media can create and exploit a negative media image to sell an artist's music. Some record companies have been accused of contributing to a negative representation of young British Afro Caribbean and African American men in the way they market hip hop music, sometimes to a white audience.

There is a good study of this at www.mediaed.org/assets/products/226/studyguide_226.pdf.

What is not represented is as important as what is. If a group of people are rarely or never seen in the media it suggests that they are unimportant and not normal. For example, Gross describes the representation of gay men and lesbians in the media as "symbolic annihilation" (1989); annihilation means the complete destruction of something. They argue that gay men and lesbians are either not represented at all or are negatively stereotyped (for example, as unstable, colourful or over-the-top characters).

Representations change over time, reflecting the social, political and economic contexts in which they are produced and consumed. In recent years the representation of gay men has improved to some extent. This reflects their increasing social, economic and political power, the growing number of out gay men working in powerful positions in the media and changing social attitudes. However, it is still limited and often stereotypical, and there are still very few representations of lesbians in the media.

ACTIVITY

There are very few representations of young gay characters in the media as a whole. How might this make young gay men and lesbians feel? What does it suggest are society's values?

However, there are exceptions and some improving representations, for example, in TV drama.

1. On your own or in pairs choose a gay or lesbian character in a TV drama (for example, *Shameless*, *Skins*, *Torchwood*, *Glee*). How is the gay or lesbian character represented? Which media institution has produced the representation, and how has this influenced the representation? Is the representation shown on a mainstream channel and at peak viewing time or not, and how might this affect the representation? Does the audience the programme is targeted at influence the representation?
2. Create a list of all of your characters and work out the similarities and differences in how they are represented, by what channels and for what audiences.

Figure 4.3
Characters Christian and Lee kiss on *EastEnders*

Representation and audience

The selection and construction encourage the audience to read the media product in a particular way. However, whether a representation is seen as positive or negative, fair or unfair, accurate or inaccurate is subjective; it is based on opinion. The text does have a preferred reading, the reading the producers encourage the audience to have. However, audiences are not necessarily passive victims of negative representations. Reception analysis theory argues that different audiences can read texts in different ways and can reject the preferred reading.

David Morley in *The Nationwide Audience* (1980) argued that audiences are active. This reception analysis theory argues that audiences make sense of media texts according to their social position, for example, their age, gender, class, ethnicity.

ACTIVITY

As a class, look at a range of different magazine front covers. Include some controversial ones, like *Nuts* or *Zoo* magazine.

1. First, for each example write down what you as an individual think of the person on the front of the magazine.
2. Then split into mixed gender groups and compare your readings.

The media product stays the same but audiences can have different readings.

However, these reception analysis theories can ignore the influence of powerful media institutions. For example, a straight young woman might not see the model on the front of *Nuts* magazine as attractive; her reading may be different, but the magazine cover is encouraging her to put herself in that position, telling her she must look and behave in a certain way to be attractive to men and should judge herself on how she looks, rather than on her intelligence or personality.

Developments in new and digital media mean that audiences now have more opportunity for self-representation, to represent themselves in, for example, blogs and social networking sites.

New technology allows individuals to create their own media products cheaply and
distribute them to a potentially large audience. This can mean that there are a
wider range of representations in the media and that people can use their own
voice to tell their own story. Audiences can see self-representations as more 'real'
and authentic than mainstream media representations. However, you shouldn't
consume them uncritically as if they are the truth; self-representations are still
mediated and are still only one version. Further, a positive and alternative representation may only be consumed by a tiny audience and sometimes only by people
who already agree with the representations and values, thereby reducing its
impact.

Audiences can also subvert existing texts, poking fun at or changing the representations and values. For example, the Game blog at www.guardian.co.uk described
how game players and hackers are subverting existing games or creating new
ones that satirise existing games. For example,

> *Noor the Pacificist*, an online gamer, decided to play
> through to the highest levels of World of Warcraft
> without intentionally killing anything. Also, The Sims 3
> is set up as a game of middle-class aspirations: get a
> job, find a home, make money, work hard, find a partner

and have a family. But in the blog narrative *Alice and Kev*, games design student Robin Burkinshaw created homeless characters. The moving narrative followed the paranoid and delusional Kev and his daughter Alice as they attempted – mostly unsuccessfully – to find jobs and love in a conformist world. **„**

Figure 4.4 Banner from the Alice and Kev blog http://aliceandkev.wordpress.com

Dominant representations

By being repeated within one media, throughout the media and over a period of time, one dominant representation is built up. What is represented is only one view, but by being repeated it becomes accepted as the right view, and as normal and natural. It isn't questioned and it shuts out other views. The representations are repeated and so are the values they carry. The cultivation theory argues that audiences are gradually affected by media representation over time by repeatedly seeing the same representation.

ACTIVITY

What is the dominant representation of war in gaming?

"Many video games are based on the theme of war, a theme that has been a part of the video games industry from the beginning – and part of traditional games for much longer. However, in a post 9/11 world and in a time when the United States is still engaged in the 'War on Terrorism', it is important to think critically about the messages sent by these games."

(www.mediaed.org)

continued

1. Go to a war games website.

    Read the description of the game, watch the trailer and study the screen shots. How does it represent war? For example:

    ■ What aspects of war are shown and what aspects of war are ignored? Is war represented in a positive or negative way?
    ■ Who is the game player positioned to be with and to be against? Who are the heroes and villains?
    ■ What is the narrative of the game? For example, what is the player's aim, what does the player need to do to 'win' and get narrative resolution? What values does this communicate about, for example, how to solve problems?

    Use the following quote to help you:

    "The concern is that with such attention to the technology of war, again what room does that leave for thinking about a lot of the other aspects of war? Yes, the casualties of war – the immediate casualties of both our side and the enemy side and of course the innocent civilians side. What are the implications after the war? What will happen to this country we may be invading – or that you may be battling in the video game – after the action is over?"
    (From Militarism and Video Games:
    an interview with Professor Nina Huntemann from
    www.mediaed.org/news/articles/militarism)

2. From www.mediaed.org: video games, and other forms of entertainment like films and comics that play at war, glorify and glamorise the idea of fighting and combat. They condition us to accept war. If we are engaged in this type of media on a regular basis, we will be less likely to ask questions and expect our country to seek out alternative responses when a real war comes along.

    Consider this statement on your own or discuss in groups. Do you agree or disagree with the statement?

Alternative representations

However, there are alternative representations in the media that represent people, groups and places differently from the dominant representation. They usually have different values from the dominant ideology and are often made by non-mainstream media companies.

ACTIVITY

1. Watch a range of adverts and videos from the Dove beauty brand website (www.dove.co.uk).

    Adverts –
    www.dove.co.uk/#/products/sawitinanad/

    Other videos –
    www.dove.co.uk/#/features/videos/

    How do the adverts and videos represent women in an alternative way?

    It is rare for a media product to be a completely dominant or alternative or positive or negative representation. What is the main way in which the adverts still represent women, and what do they tell audiences is the main criterion by which a woman should be judged and defined?

2. The Dove brand is owned by Unilever, who also own the Lynx brand aimed at young men. Watch some Lynx adverts; how do they represent women?

    For example, www.youtube.com/watch?v=bw0nMQxqL6s.

    Lynx adverts have been accused of being offensive to women, representing them as sex objects, with the message that they are sexually available for the price of the product.

    As a class, vote on whether you think some of the Lynx adverts are offensive in the way they represent women.

    Then look at the decisions the Advertising Standards Authority made following complaints about Lynx adverts at www.asa.org.uk/Complaints-and-ASA-action/Adjudications.aspx?SearchTerms=lynx#results.

    Discuss the reasons why the complaints were not upheld.

3. Do the Lynx adverts suggest that Unilever is interested in producing alternative representations of women in advertising, or are the Dove adverts and the accompanying Campaign for Real Beauty just a cynical marketing technique?

continued

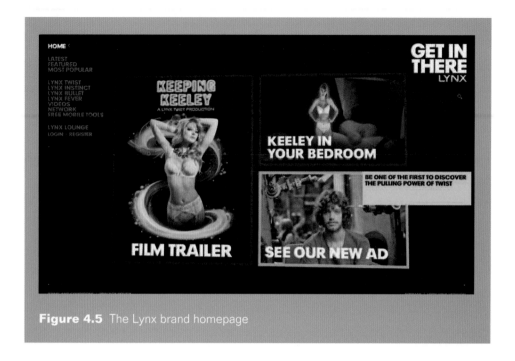

Figure 4.5 The Lynx brand homepage

Developments in new and digital media means there are now a wider range of representations. Audiences can seek out a wider range of representations that offer an alternative to the mainstream media, such as, through the internet or digital TV channels. For example, Zee TV broadcasts programmes to Indian and British Indian people in the UK. On its website it describes itself since its launch as offering "programming for South Asian viewers, who up until then, had never been witness to such a wide variety of dramas, comedies, news bulletins, documentaries or Bollywood blockbuster movies." In March 2010 it broadcast matches from the Men's Hockey World Cup featuring India, an event which wasn't available on the mainstream UK TV channels.

Stereotyping

A stereotype is a simple, generalised and exaggerated representation. A few characteristics, usually negative, are presumed to belong to the whole group. Stereotypes are over-generalised, people are not seen as complex individuals and they don't show the range of experiences of one group. Stuart Hall in *Representation* (1997) argued that stereotyping reduces people to a few simple characteristics, which are shown as natural or fixed by nature. He said stereotypes are, "essentialising, reductionist, naturalising". Richard Dyer (1993) argued that audiences make stereotypical judgements to help us create order out of everyday life and provide us with a sense of group identity. Stereotyping of enemies or oppressors can provide social cohesion.

The media often simplify people and events when they construct a representation. It may be argued that the media inevitably use some degree of generalisation and categorisation of people; they can't show everything and everybody. Stereotypes provide a short cut for media workers, a quick and simple way of drawing a character and making them easily and quickly recognisable. Limits of time or space can mean that stereotypical representations are constructed rather than rounded, complex individual characters. Stereotypes are representational shorthand, communicating a relatively complex message simply and quickly. They bring well-established, known messages and meanings already pre-packaged in a character, for example, the male action hero.

ACTIVITY

1. Go to a website where you can create your own superhero characters (e.g. www.heromachine2). Create your own superhero that is an alternative representation of women. Give her a name, a special power, a mission and some enemies.
2. When you have completed your creation, copy and paste it into a DTP document and make notes next to the image about how it is an alternative representation of women. Comment in detail on, for example, pose, hair, costume, facial expression.

Tessa Perkins (1997) argued that stereotypes have some of truth in them; they can't be too far from the real world or they won't work. There are economic reasons for stereotypes: they can be commercial and popular and seem less of a risk than something new. Audiences can enjoy stereotypes, getting pleasure from familiar and predictable characters, appealing to existing beliefs and prejudices. Stereotypes allow stories to concentrate on aspects other than character development. For example, action films often have stereotypical characters, so that the film can concentrate on the action that sells it and that audiences enjoy. Stereotypes are not always necessarily bad in themselves; there are some positive stereotypes.

However, on balance, stereotyping is seen as negative, particularly for groups that have little power in the media or society.

Representation and power

How a group or place is represented is influenced by their social, economic and political power. It is also influenced by their position in the media, whether they are adequately represented as workers within media organisations, particularly in positions of power. Groups with little power in society and the media are less likely to have their voice heard or to tell their own story. They are more likely to be under-represented in the media or represented in a negative and stereotypical way.

When representations of groups begin to improve they can sometimes be only tokenistic. Tokenism is where more, or more positive representations might give the appearance of an improved representation but really there is no significant change. For example, there are some improved representations of people with disabilities on TV, but they are often only one token character, a minor character or only in the programme for a short time.

Stuart Hall (1997) argued that media representations divide 'normal' from 'abnormal': "Representations define what is 'normal', who belongs and therefore who is excluded."

It excludes everything which does not fit, which is different, dividing media representations into us and them, normal and deviant, belonging and excluded. It constructs the excluded people as 'other'. He argued that this tends to happen when there are inequalities of power. Minority groups or those with little social, economic or political power are stereotyped.

Ideology and values

Ideology is a set of values, beliefs and ideas held in common by a group of people or society. It organises the way in which people see the world. Ideology is present in all media products; a set of ideas and values decides the way in which the media represents the world. The dominant ideology is a set of values that reflects and reinforces the values of those in power. The dominant ideology is often reproduced in mainstream media texts. It is argued that the media and its representations play an important part in communicating the dominant ideology. This view comes originally from Karl Marx, who argued that the dominant ideology works in the interests of the ruling class to keep them in power. Those who own the means of production also control the means of producing ideas, including the media.

Gramsci's hegemony theory (1971) argues that those in power govern by consensus, where people are encouraged to agree with the dominant ideology. To do this the dominant ideology is portrayed and becomes accepted as 'natural' or 'common sense'; this is hegemony. Because they are shown as common sense, audiences don't question the ideas and values, and people develop a set of values without thinking about it. The media and the representations it shows play an important role in communicating hegemonic values.

Create a film poster that communicates an alternative ideology. For example, a rom-com about a gay couple, an action adventure film with a female protagonist, a crime thriller where the protagonist is a British Afro Caribbean detective, a comedy about three elderly women friends.

Include a key image, title graphics, a tagline, actors' and actresses' names, and a credit block.

Noam Chomsky (1988) argued that the media plays an important part in maintaining the position of those in power. He argues that the media's role is the "manufacture of consent". The media ensures that the top 20 per cent in society keep their position of power and the other 80 per cent are kept happy with escapist media such as celebrity magazines, reality TV and soaps, which divert people's attention from the real issues and their real position in society.

These dominant ideology models have been criticised for assuming that audiences are too passive and that all areas of the media are communicating the same values. The Pluralist position argues that the media offers a wide range of choices to audiences, with a variety of different representations and values. Advances in new media enable audiences to achieve what Fiske (1989) called "semiotic resistance", which means that audiences can create and disseminate their own meanings, irrespective of media organisations.

In addition, the very fact that we are accessing more of our information and entertainment online means that well-tried media business models are becoming obsolete. Late in 2008 the *Guardian*'s Digital Director, Emily Bell, spoke of the need to bring to an end the "age of representation" and the need to embrace the "age of participation".

All of this was demonstrated in Christmas 2009 when Jon and Tracy Morder decided to launch a Facebook campaign to get the appropriately titled American Nu-metal band Rage Against the Machine to the Christmas number one. This started as a bit of fun, with Tracy pointing out: "It was one of those little silly ideas that make you laugh in your own house." When 'Killing in the Name' reached number one the couple received a congratulatory call from Simon Cowell; was he happy that the whole event and the accompanying publicity only helped to further market his X Factor brand?

1. Why might the undermining of 'old' media like newspapers and terrestrial television weaken the 'dominant ideology' model of media?
2. How might the 'age of participation' differ from the 'age of representation'?
3. What other examples of audience resistance to the plans of media organisations can you find?

MEDIATION the media comes between the audience and the original source; it mediates.

DOMINANT REPRESENTATION the representation that comes to dominate the media; it is repeated in the media over time.

ALTERNATIVE REPRESENTATIONS a representation that is different from the dominant representation, usually with different values from the dominant ideology and often made by non-mainstream media companies.

DOMINANT IDEOLOGY a set of values that reflects and reinforces the values of those in power.

STEREOTYPE a simple, generalised and exaggerated representation. A few characteristics, usually negative, are presumed to belong to the whole group.

SELF-REPRESENTATION when a group represent themselves in the media.

Case study
THE REPRESENTATION OF MANCHESTER

You can study representation in lots of different ways, using a place or a social group. The case study below is the representation of Manchester. You can use the headings, the suggested questions and the Manchester answers and examples to help you complete your own individual case study.

You need to have an overview of the topic that covers representation of your social group or place in the media, looking at media concepts, issues, debates and theories and wider contexts. It may be worth starting this using a Media Studies textbook or Media Studies website (e.g., www.mediaedu.co.uk, www.mediaawareness.com, www.mediaknowall.com, www.theory.org.uk, www.englishandmedia.co.uk/mm).

DOMINANT REPRESENTATIONS

ACTIVITY

- What is the dominant representation of your social group or place and which representation is repeated in the media over time? In particular consider the influence of age, gender, class and ethnicity.
- How does this dominant representation represent your group or place? Does it result in a mostly positive or negative representation?
- How fair and accurate is the representation? Research wider contexts to support this. Is it possible for the media to produce fair or accurate representations?
- What wider contexts influence the representation? For example, how does the ownership and control of the media and those who work in the media, particularly in positions of power, influence the representations?

The dominant representation of Manchester in the media is of a white, working-class city, with social and economic problems, but with strong

continued

women and strong family and community values. See, for example, TV dramas such as *Shameless* and *Coronation Street*, or films like *Raining Stones* (1994) and *Looking for Eric* (2009).

Figure 4.6 *Shameless* and *Coronation Street* offer representations of Manchester

This dominant representation can lead to a negative and stereotypical representation of Manchester. The city is shown to be almost all white, and overall, Manchester dramas do not accurately reflect Manchester as the multicultural city it is and always has been. Seventy-three per cent of Manchester's population are white and 26.2 per cent belong to a non-white ethnic group, including 5.7 per cent Pakistani and 3.9 per cent black African. Manchester's 3.6 per cent Chinese population is virtually invisible in media representations (www.manchester.gov.uk). Manchester has a long history of immigration, from Eastern European Jews in the 1880s, to West Indians in the 1950s and 1960s, Indians, Pakistanis and Bangladeshis in the 1960s and Hong Kong Chinese from the 1970s onwards. This is not reflected in the dominant representation of Manchester.

The dominant representation shows Manchester to have a lot of social and economic problems. This does reflect reality to some extent; Manchester has a higher crime rate than the national average and higher unemployment figures. However, it does result in a negative representation of Manchester and is sometimes used for economic reasons, to attract an audience with shock and humour, and to generate dramatic storylines.

However, there are positive representations of Manchester in the dominant representation. It represents Manchester as having strong community and family values. Manchester dramas often offer the nostalgic pleasure of community. Richard Dyer's Utopian Pleasures theory (2002) argued that audiences use the media for a kind of fantasy escape from reality, looking to the media for things which they lack in their own lives. He would argue that we live in an increasingly fragmented society; people no longer live in the same place or do the same job all their lives, so they look to the media for the Utopian pleasure of a close-knit community.

Media issues, debates, theories and wider contexts

How does ownership and control of the media affect the representation of places? The ownership and control of UK media is concentrated in England, the South East and London. This could negatively affect the representation of Manchester. However, there is an increasing number of media companies in Manchester and some national companies have Manchester bases. According to The North West Development Agency in 2008, the North West's digital and creative industries generated £15.8 billion, 16 per cent of the region's output, and is the second largest creative cluster in the UK. The cluster is estimated to employ 320,500 people in 31,000 businesses, 10.6 per cent of the region's workforce. As a national public service broadcaster the BBC has a policy of moving some of its production out of London.

continued

In 2011 it will relocate sport, children's TV and Radio 5 Live to Salford's Media City. How will this affect the representation of Manchester? Is the media becoming more or less centralised? The Guardian Media Group, which has a long history in Manchester with the *Manchester Guardian*, sold the majority of its regional interests, including the *Manchester Evening News*, to Trinity Mirror in March 2010.

POSSIBLE ALTERNATIVE REPRESENTATIONS

ACTIVITY

- What alternative representations are there of your social group or place?
- How does this alternative representation represent your group or place? Does it result in a mostly positive or negative representation? How is it different to the dominant one?
- Is it a fairer and more accurate representation on its own or put together with the dominant representation?
- Who is producing the alternative representations and how does this influence the representations?
- What audiences do the alternative representations target and reach? How does this affect the power of the representations?
- What wider contexts influence the representation? For example, have developments in new and digital media led to a wider range and more alternative representations?

However, there are exceptions. Some media products have begun to reflect the social and economic changes in Manchester and shifting social values. For example, following the regeneration of Manchester city centre after the IRA bombed it in 1996, media representations saw in a younger set of characters, some middle-class, urban professionals, that reflected the regeneration of the city centre with thriving clubs, bars and upmarket shops, for example, the TV drama *Cold Feet*.

Some media products have begun to show Manchester as a multicultural city, for example, the changing ethnic mix of the characters in *Coronation Street*, which now has British Indian and British Afro Caribbean characters, although some of these representations have been stereotypical.

In addition, representations sometimes reflect Manchester's large gay community and its increasing economic, social and political power, and changing attitudes in audiences and the media towards gay men. This was first seen in Channel 4's 2002 drama *Queer as Folk*, about the lives of three young gay men. The local newspaper, the *Manchester Evening News'* listings website (www.citylife.co.uk) has gay and lesbian news and features sections every week.

Figure 4.7 Page from www.citylife.co.uk

Media issues, debates, theories and wider contexts

Developments in new and digital media mean that there are a larger number of representations. Has this greater number of representations led to a wider range and more alternative representations? For example, although many areas of traditional media have been threatened by new and digital media, radio has been offered new opportunities. There are now many more radio stations available through DAB radio, the internet, mobile phones and via social networking sites. Manchester has always had lots of pirate, student and temporary Restricted Service License stations. Asian Sound Radio broadcasts, "a blend of news, interviews, competitions, music and information in English, Urdu, Punjabi, Bengali and Gujarati" across the North West to the Asian community. Unity Radio describes itself as "Manchester's

continued

newest and freshest urban radio station". Its changes mirror developments in radio over recent years. It started off as a pirate radio station in Moss Side, developed into an internet station and has now been granted an FM license to launch in summer 2010.

STEREOTYPING

ACTIVITY

- What stereotypes are there of your social group or place?
- Are they mostly positive or negative representations?
- Is there some truth in the representations? What characteristics do they emphasise? What is ignored?
- What wider contexts influence the stereotypes? For example, how does the power or lack of power of your group or place in society and the media influence the stereotypes?

Stereotyping is more likely for groups that are in a minority or lack power in society and the media. *Coronation Street* has been criticised for having some stereotypical representations; for example, its first British Indian family owned a cornershop and one of the first female characters was escaping an arranged marriage.

However, there are some positive stereotypes in the representation of women; for example, the strong northern woman who suffers, but keeps her family together, although her power is in the domestic sphere, a dominant representation of women.

Media issues, debates, theories and wider contexts

Channel 4's 2007 *Race, Representation and the Media Report* said, "Ethnic minorities accused mainstream broadcasters of tokenism and stereotyping, screening exaggerated and extreme representations of minority communities and failing to reflect modern ethnic minority culture."

Tessa Perkins argued that stereotypes sometimes reflect a social reality. When Indian people came to the UK they encountered racism when they were looking for work, so some set up their own businesses, such as shops. However, because the family was the first and at the time the only British Indian family in *Coronation Street*, they carried the burden of representation for that group, which meant they had to represent all British Indian people. The soap didn't show the range of different experiences of one group or portray individual characters as complex. The Channel 4 report found that black and ethnic minority audiences felt that "a single ethnic minority character (say, in a soap) cannot begin to represent the richness of an entire community".

REPRESENTATION AND AUDIENCE

ACTIVITY

- How do the representations position the audience in relation to your group or place?
- What different audience readings could there be? In particular think about how audience members from your group or place might read the representations differently.
- What self-representations are there? How and why are they similar or different to other representations?
- What wider contexts influence audiences? For example, who owns your local area's media? Is local media expanding or is media ownership becoming more centralised?

David Morley (1980) argues that different audience members can read the same text in different ways. Is this true for representations of particular places? How does a local audience read media products differently? We are more likely to challenge media representations of things we have direct experience of, but does that mean we accept biased and inaccurate media representations of places we don't know? For example, Moss Side in Manchester is often represented by the media in a negative and stereotypical way, based especially on negative and stereotypical representations of young British Afro Caribbean men. How would people in different areas of Manchester and the UK respond to a negative story about Moss Side? In 2009 the then Shadow Home Secretary visited Moss Side and said, "What was going on there at the time was nothing short of an urban war" and "*The Wire* has become a part of real life in our country." Khan Moghal of the Manchester Council for Community Relations said, "We wish the national media in London would come up to Manchester, spend some time here and understand the people and places." (www.manchesterevening news.co.uk).

continued

Developments in new and digital media have meant that it can be cheaper and easier for people to create their own media products and representations of the places in which they live. The media institution that creates a media product will shape the representations within it, so is it important that more representations of Manchester are produced by people who live and work there?

Media issues, debates, theories and wider contexts

How does local media represent a place differently? Will it be more accurate or fair, or not? For example, www.manchestermule.co.uk has a news website and produces a quarterly newspaper. It argues that, "Traditional local media is facing hard times. Budget cuts and the turn away from serious reporting means there's an information vacuum waiting to be filled in our communities . . . the commercial media system is dominated by a small number of huge corporations and wealthy individuals. MULE aims to cover the burning issues that the mainstream media neglect." The *Salford Star* is "written and produced by people in Salford for people in Salford. And it's totally independent." It aims to "give the community a voice . . . to inform, campaign and entertain".

Figure 4.8 Banner from the *Salford Star* website www.salfordstar.co.uk

However, are these local alternative representations only seen by a small niche audience and does this mean they can't really challenge the power of the dominant representations produced by mainstream media? Or is new and digital media changing this?

ACTIVITY

- Is the representation of your group or place different in different genres or not? Why?
- What wider contexts influence this representation? For example, is there a history of a particular genre in your place?

Do representations vary across different genres? The dominant representation of Manchester comes from a tradition of social realism in northern film and TV drama. Social realism tells stories of working-class life and explores social and economic problems, often set in the North. For example, the BBC1 drama series *The Street* is set in a fictitious terraced street in the North West and has explored issues such as racism, poverty and domestic violence. Screenonline argues that "better than any other genre, social realism has shown us ourselves" and has put "the experiences of real Britons on the screen" (www.screenonline.org). The generic conventions of location shooting, naturalistic *mise-en-scène* and unknown actors claim authenticity.

Media issues, debates, theories and wider contexts

Social realist texts are now influenced by the British New Wave films of the 1960s. *A Taste of Honey* (1961) was set in Manchester and told the story of Jo, a young girl who becomes pregnant by Jimmy, a black sailor. It reflects the time it was made, for example, in the lack of social and economic power of the female characters and the sometimes negative reactions Jo receives when she is expecting a baby with mixed parentage.

Manchester music has been dominated by the indie genre, with most bands made up of white, working-class men. Why have the many Manchester British Afro Caribbean bands and artists not had the same commercial success?

continued

ACTIVITY

- How has globalisation influenced the representation of your place or group?
- Has it led to an increased merging of cultures and is this a good or bad thing?
- Has it brought people closer together or divided them up into smaller niche audiences?
- What wider contexts influence this representation? For example, does globalisation lead to more shared experiences?

Media issues, debates, theories and wider contexts

Globalisation argues that there is a breaking down and merging of different nation's cultures and values. Marshall McLuhan (1964) argued that developments in technology have shrunk the world to a 'global village' where people can share the same information and experiences as if they lived in a small village. Developments in new and digital media, such as digital TV and websites, have meant that people can have access to, for example, TV programmes from across the world. For example, the major British TV companies sell their programmes all over the world. ITV Studios Global Entertainment says it "distributes programmes to over 3,500 broadcasters and home entertainment partners in more than 350 territories worldwide". ITV uses the brand value of programmes such as *Coronation Street* to increase profits from global sales. How does this represent Manchester to the world? *Coronation Street* is culturally specific, with storylines, settings and characters that can only be understood by a UK audience. However, it is based on universal themes, such as family, community and friendship. How might different audiences read the representations differently? Viewers from across the world can also discuss the latest storylines on official and fan websites. Is this a positive effect of globalisation?

ACTIVITY

■ What values does the representations of your group or place communicate?
■ Are they dominant or alternative values?
■ What wider contexts influence the representation? For example, how does the power or lack of power of your group or place in society and the media influence those values?

The dominant representation sometimes leads to a negative representation of working-class Manchester. This representation carries values about the position of the working class in the UK and the reasons for the social and economic problems on which many of the narratives are based. For example, *The Street* explores these social and economic problems from the position of working-class characters. It doesn't simply blame individuals for the problems they have, but looks for wider causes in communities and society. In series three, one episode told the story of a racist character called Kieran. The narrative suggested that he was racist because of the way capitalist society exploited him and the Polish and African economic migrants he hated. His racism wasn't an individual flaw but a result of anger and frustration about his own life in a society that treated him unfairly.

Media issues, debates, theories and wider contexts

Media representations of Manchester reflect many of the moral panics created by the media. Cohen (2002) argued that a moral panic is when the media identifies a problem group and exaggerates the problem through sensationalist stories and stereotypes, leading to panic or anxiety at a supposed threat to society. For example, *Shameless* includes many of the common moral panics associated with youth and the underclass (e.g. underage sex, teenage pregnancy, drugs).

Class and individual case study

Mini-class case study

It will be useful to complete a mini-class case study to show you how to compete your own individual case study. The class case study could be on a different group or place to your individual case study, or it could be on a group that would be relevant to the whole class's individual case studies. Alternatively, it could be a large group; for example, youth and different individual case studies could be on smaller groups within it, such as British Afro Caribbean youth, young women, etc.

Individual case study

Collect examples of the representation of your group or place from a wide range of sources. Include different media products and a range of genres across platforms, for example:

- **Broadcasting**
    - TV
    - Radio

- **Print**
    - Newspapers – popular tabloid, quality press, local and regional, free
    - Magazines – different genres

- **Digital and web-based media**
    - Digital TV channels, including non-British ones if possible
    - Official websites
    - Audience-generated websites (e.g. YouTube, Twitter)
    - Blogs
    - Podcasts

1. Collect examples of products that represent your group or place. You could collect them in an e-portfolio or have hard copies; for example, record your moving image products from TV or use a free online conversion website, print screen and save or print hard copies of website pages and scan or collect print copies.

2. Complete detailed analyses of a range of the products you have collected using the media concepts to evaluate and compare them.
3. What media issues and debates do they raise?
4. Apply theory to support your analysis and explain your texts.
5. Apply lots of relevant wider contexts to explain *why* your group or place is represented in the way it is.
6. You could then split into groups that covered similar groups or places. Compare the media issues and debates, and the wider contexts that your individual studies raised.

Whatever case study you do it would be useful to summarise the results of your analysis and research as a table, including:

1. Products – a list of the products you have collected, with a clear source and date
2. Dominant representations
3. Possible alternative representations
4. Stereotyping
5. Representation and audience
6. Representation and genre
7. The effect of globalisation
8. Values and ideology.

Product				
Dominant				
Alternative				
Stereotypes				
Audience				
Genre				
Globalisation				
Values and ideology				

continued

Storyboard either:

- the film trailer for a new film or
- the title sequence of a new TV drama

about your group or place that mostly shows the dominant representation.

1. First of all decide:

   - Where it is set (e.g. locations, interior settings)?
   - Who are the main characters – ages, class, ethnicity, gender, mix of characters?
   - What will the storylines be about?

2. Use a variety of shots (e.g. distance, angle, framing, *mise-en-scène*).

   The function of a title sequence is to engage the target audience, encourage them to watch, and to create a memorable, recognisable identity for the programme.

   The function of a film trailer is to attract the attention of the target audience and make them want to see the film. Introduce both the main characters and the storyline/s, suggest the genre and set the scene.

3. Make notes on your storyboard to explain how you have represented your group or place.

ACTIVITY

1. Go to http://www.youtube.com/shows and look at the page for one genre of TV shows. Then create your own banner photo and episode summary for a new TV show of that genre that shows mostly an alternative representation of your place.
2. Make notes to explain how you have represented your group or place in an alternative way.

MEST3: the impact of new/digital media

In this section we will look at one of the two MEST3 pre-set topics: the impact of new/digital media. The case study example is news, but you can use the headings, the suggested questions and the news answers and examples to help you complete your own individual case study. This section includes the following:

- **An introduction to news media**.
- **A case study on news**, with sections on media institutions and the changing role of the producer, the changing role of audiences and user-generated content, values and democracy, the effect of globalisation, and the attempts of traditional media to survive.

Whatever case study you choose, you should study the impact of new/digital media across a range of media platforms and products (including the effect on competing traditional media), and the relevant media issues, debates and theories and wider contexts. You should be confident you can answer questions on:

- media institutions
- media and democracy
- the changing role of the producer
- the changing role of the audience and the consumer and user-generated content
- the effect of globalisation
- the attempts of traditional media to survive/compete
- cross-cultural factors
- values and ideology.

You can organise your study of pre-set topics by:

1. **Overview of topic**
2. **Class case study** – media concepts, issues, debates and theories and wider contexts.
3. **Individual case study** – detailed analysis using media concepts, issues, debates and theories and wider contexts.

Case study
THE IMPACT OF NEW/DIGITAL MEDIA ON NEWS MEDIA

You can study the impact of new and digital media in lots of different ways, for example, on a particular genre of music and the music industry, a specific study of social networking sites, film marketing focusing on particular films, or the range of television drama on UK TV. This case study explores the impact of new and digital media on news. You can use the headings, the suggested questions and the news answers and examples to help you complete your own individual case study.

Introduction to news media

You need to have an overview of the topic that covers the impact of new and digital media on your case study, looking at media concepts, issues, debates and theories and wider contexts. It could be worth starting this using a Media Studies textbook or Media Studies website, for example, www.mediaedu.co.uk, www.mediaawareness.com, www.mediaknowall.com, www.theory.org.uk, www.englishandmedia.co.uk/mm.

> **"The content of the Indymedia UK website is created through a system of open publishing: anyone can upload a written, audio and video report or a picture directly to the site through an openly accessible web interface. Through this system of 'Direct Media', Indymedia erodes the dividing line between reporters and reported, between active producers and passive audience: people are enabled to speak for themselves."**
>
> (www.indymedia.org.uk)

New and digital media has had a huge effect on news media. Newspaper sales are falling and all the major newspapers have websites. There is 24-hour news on TV and audiences have access to international news channels through digital TV and the internet. Audiences are now creating the news on sites such as YouTube and Twitter.

How have these developments changed the role of the audience and producer? Have they made the media and society more democratic? Have they provided a wider range of opinions and values?

ACTIVITY

1. As individuals, what is the main media platform and what are the main media products that you get your news from? Why do you choose to use these news sources?
2. Divide your class up into three groups, one for each platform. You all have 20 minutes to find the 'best' news story you can, for example, the juiciest piece of celebrity gossip, the latest sports results or rumours, the most dramatic international news. You can use only the one platform.
    You could divide each group up into smaller groups; for example, the broadcasting group could be split into radio and TV, the digital and web-based group could be split into mobile phones, international websites, digital news channels and user-generated websites.
3. In groups, then as a class, ask: What are the advantages of each platform – broadcast, print and digital and web-based media?

NEWS IS CONSTRUCTED

News is constructed. It is put together into a media product, for example, a TV news programme, that targets a specific audience. The news media mediates; it comes between an actual event and the audience. For example, a football match is constructed into a 30-second TV news report on the game.

continued

ACTIVITY

Even a media product like a live football match on television that seems very close to the real event is changed by the media.

Think of ways in which a live football match on TV is mediated. How is it different from going to watch a live game? Consider, for example, differences in sound, point of view/audience position, what TV claims to add, what the audience can and can't see.

ACTIVITY

Pick one recent big news event.

Search YouTube to find all the clips on the event and compile a list of about five clips with the source and a brief description.

Compare how the clips represent the event:

- What media language does it use that has connotations of realism (e.g. handheld camera, variable lighting)?
- How has it been mediated? For example, what have they included and missed out?
- Who appears?
- What are the most popular results? Why do you think this is the case?

They may appear and be presented as unmediated but even something that seems as real as video on YouTube is constructed and only presents one version of the event.

The media *selects* – it chooses which events to cover – and *constructs* – it puts together a news package, carefully selecting, for example, the images, language and who will be interviewed, which encourages the audience to read it in a particular way.

This selection and construction *represents* the world. We don't see reality, but only one version of it.

ACTIVITY

Imagine that your news editor has asked you to plan a short three-minute piece on why so many British Afro Caribbean boys are being excluded from schools in your local area.

Storyboard a short news report on the story. What will you include? What will the newsreader say to introduce the story? Where will the report come from and what will the reporter say? Who will be interviewed and what questions will they be asked?

Then compare your news reports in small groups. How are they similar and how are they different?

One simple story can be told in lots of different ways. However, later on we will discuss how many news sources often seem to tell the story in the same way.

In your analysis of news media you need to ask yourself: How has the story been constructed?

Different news sources will present the same event in different ways, with their own conventions, house style and also their own values. The messages and meanings the news communicates carry values about people, places and issues, telling us how to view and value ourselves and others.

Each media institution and news source will have its own cultural and political bias. Sometimes this is more obvious; for example, the *Sun* as a British newspaper can be as biased as it wants to be, as can *Fox News* in the USA which is argued to be very right-wing and anti-Barack Obama.

Figure 4.9 Fox TV News
www.thedailyshow.com

continued

However, even news sources that are presented as neutral and trusted (e.g. the BBC News website) are still biased. No news media is completely objective, it will always be biased.

Tony Harcup (in Harcup and O'Neill, 2001) argued that news media have a set of values that influence what is newsworthy, what will appear in the news and what will be shown to be the most important. Harcup updated Gultung and Ruge's news values theory. Refer to www.routledge.com/textbooks/a2mediastudies for a case study on news which covers both of these news values theories (and shows how they can be applied to determine newsworthiness).

ACTIVITY

1. Collect the top three stories from three different news sources. What are the three main stories? For example, the first three stories, the ones given the most space or time.
2. In twos, apply Harcup's news values to your stories. Do the values apply or not?
3. In groups, compare the stories you have collected. Are they similar or different? Is there consensus on what the news media decides is newsworthy or is there diversity and difference?
4. Report your results and conclusions to the class.
5. Compile a class list of the top five stories. Is there consensus on what the news media decides is newsworthy? Should there be more diversity and difference? What do the stories suggest are the values of the news media? What kinds of people, places and issues are included and what is ignored?

NEWS AND THE AUDIENCE

However, the audience are not necessarily passive; they don't just accept the news they are given and believe everything they are told. Particularly with new and digital media, they can actively choose to watch, read and listen to the news they want, when they want it. They also bring their own social position and their own values to their reading of the news.

David Morley in *The Nationwide Audience* (1980) argued that the way audience members read the media is shaped by their social position, for example, their age, gender, class, ethnic background. He also argued that audience members don't always accept the preferred reading, the messages and meanings the producer of a media product may want them to have. They can have dominant reading, where the reader shares the text's values and beliefs and accepts the preferred reading. But they can have an oppositional reading, where the reader does not share the text's values and beliefs and rejects the preferred reading. They can also have a negotiated reading, between the dominant and oppositional reading, where readers partly share the text's values and beliefs, but modify it to reflect their own position.

ACTIVITY

1. Imagine a British soldier has been killed in Afghanistan. Think about how the BBC 10 o'clock news would report his or her death. Have a clear picture in you head. What would the news reader say? What images would be shown? Who would be interviewed?
2. In pairs, work out what the dominant, oppositional and then the negotiated reading would be. Remember: the report stays the same, it's the reading that may be different.

Once you have researched and written up your general overview, complete research and analysis on all the areas in which you could get Section B questions. You can use the headings below.

Remember: for each area consider the relevant media issues, debates, theories and wider contexts.

The news example below includes a very wide range of examples, but it would be a good idea for your own individual case study to focus on a few texts, supported by other, briefer examples. For example, a news topic could focus on one story; this is explained at the end of this chapter. The impact of new and digital media on the music industry could focus on one artist or band, with briefer examples from other acts in that genre and other parts of the music industry.

Make sure you cover a variety of texts, for example, from different genres, made by different kinds of institutions, with different representations and values. Cover a range of platforms.

continued

Developments in new and digital media have changed news production and consumption. Some of the main ways it has done this are given below.

MEDIA INSTITUTIONS AND THE CHANGING ROLE OF THE PRODUCER

ACTIVITY

- How has new and digital media changed the institutions that are producing the media products?
- How has this shaped and changed the products themselves; for example, are they more up to date, are there simply more of them?
- What wider contexts influence the role of the producer; for example, what new technological developments have affected institutions and producers? How are the developments used?

■ **Up to date** – News can be more up to date. Technology such as satellites and broadband means that news organisations can send and audiences can receive news almost instantly (e.g. 24-hour TV news, live streaming of events, posts on social networking sites).

Media issues, debates, theories and wider contexts

The increased competition in news media, and the promise of internet news as being the most up to date and even instant, puts even more pressure on news media to be and to show itself as contemporaneous or up to date. This reflects the famous saying that news is more concerned with being first with the story rather than getting it right. Have developments in new and digital technology made this problem worse?

■ **More news and more news sources** – There is now more news and more news sources. News gathering and reporting can be produced and consumed from a wider range of places, institutions and people (e.g. local news websites, access to international news channels). Some technology also makes it cheaper to produce news, for example, blogs and open access news websites where you can upload news reports. This could support pluralist theories that there is diversity and choice in the media and that if certain views and values are dominant it is because they are popular with audiences. Pluralism argues that the media offers a wide range of choices to audiences. This argument can ignore the power of large media organisations and the often limited range of what audiences are offered.

Just because the technology means something can happen doesn't mean it necessarily will. This can be seen in the ways that wars are reported. Advances in technology mean that audiences can receive instant reports from the battlefield, but it has been argued that in reality reports are now more controlled and censored, with, for example, such developments as embedded journalists. However, technological developments have also allowed, for example, blogs by soldiers on the day-to-day reality of life on the frontline.

In addition, do we really have news reports from a wider range of places or do most audiences still get their news from the mainstream news sources and do these still have a narrow range of people and places that they see as newsworthy?

THE CHANGING ROLE OF AUDIENCES AND USER-GENERATED CONTENT

ACTIVITY

- What new developments have changed the role of audiences and how do audiences use them?
- Is there more audience interaction?
- Has it allowed more user-generated content and how is this consumed by audiences?
- Does it offer audiences more choice?
- Have audiences got more control over what they consume, when and how? What pleasures do the new media products offer their audiences?
- Do the developments really give audiences more power?
- What wider contexts influence the role of audiences, for example, what economic factors influence the role of audiences?

continued

- **Interaction** – There is increased audience interaction with news sources with viewers, readers and listeners being asked to send in photos, videos, phone in and appear; for example, 'have your say' and discussion forum features on newspaper websites.

Figure 4.10 BBC News encourages users to have their say

Media issues, debates, theories and wider contexts

Has interaction really changed the content or only the format of news? Do powerful news organisations still set the agenda or do they need to listen to and respond to their audiences to survive?

- **User-generated content** – Audiences can now create news themselves. Citizen journalism means that ordinary people as well as professional journalists are creating the news. Developments in technology provide audiences with easier and cheaper ways to produce news themselves (e.g. the improved quality of mobile phone cameras). There are also easier and cheaper ways to distribute what they produce (e.g. social networking sites and blogs). For example, mobile phone photos from the London 7/7 bombing were published in tabloid newspapers and news websites, and photos taken by an eyewitness of the plane that crashed on the Hudson River in New York were put on Twitter and then used by the news agency Reuters.

Figure 4.11 The London tube bombing on 7 July 2005

These stories are often picked up by mainstream news sources, but the user-generated content was first. UGC has the promise of authenticity, but not the status of established news sources. Does the mainstream news media still tell us that a story needs the mediation of a traditional news source to validate it? Or do audiences see UGC as less mediated and more authentic and truthful?

- **More choice and control** – Audiences can now choose from a bigger range of news sources, with potentially a wider range of opinions and values. The news can offer audiences Blumer and Katz's *Uses and Gratifications* (1975) of surveillance or information. Audiences can also choose news that offers them the other gratifications of personal identity (e.g. signing up to a particular podcast that reinforces their own opinions and values), or diversion or escapism (e.g. a celebrity gossip website) or personal relationships (e.g. sharing a YouTube clip on a news story with a friend). Audiences can have more control over what they consume and when, to suit their interests, values and lifestyle, from a traditional established mainstream news source such as BBC1's 10 o'clock news, to one person's blog based on their direct experience. They don't have to watch the news they are given at a particular time any longer.

continued

Not all news sources have the same profile, budget or are as accessible. Gramsci's hegemony theory (1971) argued that the media plays an important role in communicating hegemonic values, encouraging people to agree with the dominant ideology, the values that are in the interests of those in power. Gramsci also argued that hegemony is an ongoing process and that the working classes need to develop ideas and values of their own to challenge the values of those in power. Raymond Williams argued that hegemony "has continually to be renewed, recreated, defended, and modified. It is also continually resisted, limited, altered, challenged by pressures not at all its own" (Williams, 1977). What values does the news media communicate? Does the news media that most people get their news from still communicate hegemonic values? Can new and digital media be a challenge to this?

VALUES AND DEMOCRACY

ACTIVITY

- Have developments in new and digital media made the media more democratic? Are more people involved and how do they get involved?
- Does new and digital media provide a wider range of views and values? Does it offer something different to the mainstream and/or more alternative ideas and values?
- Is new and digital media harder to regulate and is this a good or a bad thing?
- Does it provide opportunities for freedom of expression for more people? Can it be used to challenge those in power?
- What wider contexts influence the values? For example have ordinary people got more power or do the big Western media companies still dominate? How do smaller new media companies survive economically and compete?

■ **More people are involved** – More people are now involved in news gathering and production and in online debates and discussions. This could make the media and society more democratic, because more people are involved. For example, during the run-up to the 2010 election a website was set up that spoofed the Conservative Party's billboard poster campaign. It also provided a simple template so that visitors to the site could easily create their own spoofs. The spoof versions received a lot of coverage in the mainstream media and a rival website was set up by Conservative supporters.

www.conservativehome.blogs.com   www.mydavidcameron.com

Figure 4.12 Conservative Party online posters and anti-Conservative spoof online posters

Media issues, debates, theories and wider contexts

However, cultural imperialism argues that the news media is still dominated by wealthy and powerful Western organisations that communicate their news and the values it carries around the world. For example, the US news channel CNN broadcasts in over 200 countries. Rebecca MacKinnon, a Research Fellow at Harvard Law School, argued on her blog (rconversation.blogs.com) that

> **CNN viewed by people around the world today is more American-centric and less objective than the CNN of 10 years ago. The search for profit maximization means that these companies will shape their news to fit the tastes and values of the majority of their most lucrative potential audience.**

continued

Do the large Western news organisations still dominate? They have the budget, infrastructure, easy access and high profile to dominate news production. For example, Sky News is available in 36 countries in Europe, and in Asia, the Middle East and Africa, and it has used new and digital media to extend its reach. It can now be accessed via TV, radio, mobile phones and online.

- **A wider range of views and values** – The increased amount of news sources means that there is potentially a wider range of opinions and values. Alternative news sources print stories that mainstream news sources might not. For example, Wikileaks is a website which publishes secret information that otherwise wouldn't be available to the public. It has published a membership list of the far right British National Party which included teachers and police officers, and information on a video of US soldiers killing Iraqi civilians that the Pentagon claimed it had lost. Emily Butselaar described it as:

> **not just a tool for journalists, it allows ordinary Kenyans to read *a confidential report* detailing the billions their former president allegedly siphoned from the country's coffers. Its repository includes controversial military documents including the US rules of engagement in Iraq and an operating manual issued to army officers in Guantánamo Bay.**

(www.guardian.co.uk, 29 January 2010)

Media issues, debates, theories and wider contexts

Arguments in favour of Wikileaks would say that it makes the media more democratic, by providing a place where whistleblowers can share their stories and allowing ordinary people access to secret information. Arguments against it would say that it is biased and threatens national security. Whatever your opinion, Wikileaks has found it difficult to survive. It says it refuses to accept corporate or government funding so that it doesn't compromise its integrity, but in February 2010 it had to suspend its site to raise funds because of the cost of publishing secret documents. Is democracy and the opportunity to access a wider range of views under threat because alternative news sources find it difficult to survive economically?

- **Regulation** – It's harder to enforce laws and regulations on web-based news sources, such as privacy, contempt of court and libel, especially when the news sources are in different countries; for example, leaks about Michael Jackson's death to the gossip website TMZ and the footballer John Terry's attempt to get a super-injunction to stop newspapers printing stories about his personal life when the story was already covered widely online.

Does this give audiences more access to the truth or does it invade people's privacy and allow false stories to be published? Should the news media be allowed to publish what it wants or should there be regulations or laws? It has been argued that this has affected traditional media organisations as well, because they can now argue that the story is already in the public domain, so they should be allowed to publish it. On *Law in Action* on 23 February 2010 it was suggested that

> **If a mainstream news organisation, for instance, wanted to melt a super-injunction, then surely they could find a way of getting things into the blogosphere and Twittersphere to the extent it becomes in the public domain and the super-injunction is in effect going to melt away because the judge is going to say everyone knows about this.**

Traditional media has also been accused of being in need of more control. In February 2010 a parliamentary report described the Press Complaints Commission, the self-regulatory body that regulates the press, as being "toothless". They used the example of the reporting of the Madeleine McCann story, saying there was an inexcusable lowering of standards. Does self-regulation work?

- **Freedom of expression** – There is a tradition of freedom of expression for the media in the UK, where the news media is able to publish or broadcast what it wants to as long as it doesn't break the law. Some would argue that this is being eroded by recent laws, such as privacy rulings.

Some repressive governments try to control the news media, shutting down TV stations or restricting what can be published or broadcast. Google famously pulled out of an agreement with the Chinese government in March 2010 which originally allowed the Chinese government to restrict the results

continued

of politically sensitive searches on Google in China, such as Tiananmen Square, where many anti-government protesters were killed by the army in 1989. Democratic governments also seek to control what the news media says, by, for example, leaking stories, trying to suppress others or controlling the release of government information. Has new and digital media increased freedom of expression? For example, in 2010 anti-government protestors in Iran managed to get video footage of police violence against them on to the internet, informing the world of the repression. Photos of Neda Soltan, a young Iranian woman, appeared on social networking sites after she had been shot during a protest. It was argued that the image became a powerful symbol of the repression. Further, during the G20 demonstration in London in 2009 amateur video footage was shown on social networking sites and then by traditional news media like TV news and newspapers of Ian Tomlinson, a newspaper seller being hit by police. He later died.

THE EFFECT OF GLOBALISATION

ACTIVITY

- How has new and digital media affected globalisation and the media?
- Has it led to an increased merging of cultures and is this a good or bad thing?
- Has it brought people closer together or divided them into smaller niche audiences?
- What wider contexts affect globalisation; for example, do the large Western media organisations dominate the world's media and what affect could this have? Can the cheap and accessible technology of new media challenge this domination?

- Globalisation argues that there is a breaking down and merging of different nations' cultures and values. Marshall McLuhan (1964) argued that developments in technology have shrunk the world to a 'global village' where people can share the same information and experiences as if they lived in a small village. Developments in new and digital media, such as news websites, mobile phone news updates or internet access and social networking sites, have meant that people can have access to news from across the world and at the same time. Powerful Western news organisations still dominate, but continents such as Africa and India are increasingly coming online, and ordinary people can use cheaper technology like mobile phones to produce and consume news.

It could be argued that new and digital media has led to increasingly fragmented audiences. For example, owing to the huge increase in TV channels available through digital TV there are fewer major media events in the UK that the whole country watches, but rather people are watching channels aimed at small, niche audiences. Coverage of the African Cup of Nations and the World Hockey Championships in 2010 allowed people from Africa and South Asia who lived in other countries or people with a family background from those areas to access coverage of sports events from their home country. Do developments bring audiences together or fragment them?

THE ATTEMPTS OF TRADITIONAL MEDIA TO SURVIVE

ACTIVITY

- How have traditional media companies reacted to developments in new and digital media?
- How has it threatened them?
- How have they adapted their existing products and/or introduced new ones?
- What new opportunities has it offered them?
- How have some organisations attempted to use all platforms and how successful has this been?
- Will they exist in the future?
- What wider contexts influence traditional media's survival? For example how can it continue to make a profit?

- **Decline** – There has been a decline in news consumption from traditional news sources like TV news and newspapers. For example, although the *Sun* announcing that it would not be supporting the Labour Party in the 2010 election was still a blow to Labour, it didn't have as big an impact on the election as the *Sun*'s support for Labour in the last election. Voters are getting their news and opinions from other news sources now, as well as, if not yet instead of, traditional news sources.

continued

Online editions of newspapers aren't as profitable as their print editions. They are expensive to produce and keep up to date and don't attract as much advertising at the moment. Further, do they attract more readers or new readers and create loyalty to the brand, or do they just take readers away from the print edition? Will their attempts to adapt mean that they are only really putting their print edition out of business?

■ **Adapt or die** – Threatened traditional news sources like TV news programmes and newspapers have had to adapt. It has led to big changes in the way they provide and present their news (e.g. newspaper websites with added stories or features, TV news with instant updates through information boxes). For example, in the digital content blog on www.guardian.co.uk James Mbugua, a business writer at Radio Africa, argued

> **Apart from radio, mobile phones are a relevant distribution tool for news. Newspapers only matter in urban areas and with policy makers . . . quite a few of the media houses send out text messages with breaking news, final scores of sport games and stocks.**

It has been argued that this has led to the dumbing down of the news media in an attempt to keep audiences. The news media has been accused of having too much celebrity news and lifestyle features that entertain rather than inform audiences. This could mean that large numbers of people don't know what is happening in their own communities, country and around the world.

In addition, currently most news websites are free to use. As traditional media declines is this still financially possible? Will audiences soon have to pay to access online news content? In March 2010 *The Times* newspaper announced that it would start to charge for access to its online content from June 2010. How will this affect visits to the site? Will it improve its financial viability or lead to its eventual demise? Will other news websites follow?

■ **360-degree content** – Many of the big media institutions aim to provide 360-degree content, producing news across all platforms, including TV, radio, websites, mobile phone/PC updates (e.g. BBC, Sky News).

Figure 4.13 Q&A: charging for *The Times* and *The Sunday Times* websites

Media issues, debates, theories and wider contexts

Does this mean that a few powerful media companies will come to dominate news production? The BBC has been accused of being too dominant in news production in a way that damages other news providers. James Murdoch, Chief Executive of *News Corporation* in Europe and Asia, in his famous speech at the 2009 Edinburgh International Television Festival, was very critical of the power of the BBC in the news media. He argued,

> in this all-media marketplace, the expansion of state-sponsored journalism is a threat to the plurality and independence of news provision, which are so important for our democracy. Dumping free, state-sponsored news on the market makes it incredibly difficult for journalism to flourish on the internet.

continued

Do you agree with him or is he only critical because Sky is in competition with the BBC?

- **New opportunities** – Some traditional media has been given a new lease of life by technological developments. For example, radio is now available on a new range of platforms, through digital TV, DAB radio, mobile phones and the internet.

Media issues, debates, theories and wider contexts

How successful have traditional media organisations been in their attempts to survive? The BBC announced cutbacks in its operations in March 2010, including proposals to cut the digital radio stations 6 Music and Asian Network and parts of the BBC website. Does this suggest that traditional media has to be more selective in the new media into which it extends?

In addition, a number of local newspapers have closed down or made redundancies. Is it the end of local newspapers? Or does the cheaper technology of an online version mean that small, local or alternative news websites can flourish? In the earlier MEST3 section on Representation there are a number of examples of local Manchester news websites like the Salford Star.

Class and individual case study

Mini-class case study

You can complete a mini-class case study by analysing the coverage of one news story over a short period of time, even just one day, over a range of news sources and platforms. Study and analyse the impact of new and digital media on the news, using the headings and examples of some of the relevant issues above.

This could also be applied to other case studies; for example, you could do a mini-class case study on the launch of a new film or album.

Individual case study

You can then choose your individual current news story, anything from an international, economic or political story, to a sport or celebrity story. Choose a big story, so it is covered in lots of different media products. Follow the story and its development over a range of news sources and platforms, to analyse the impact of new and digital media on the news.

This could also be applied to other case studies; for example, you could do an individual case study on a particular genre of music or film focusing on a particular artist/s or film/s.

Collect the coverage of your story from a wide range of sources and platforms; for example:

BROADCASTING

- TV news (e.g. Channel 4, BBC1, ITV)
- Radio (e.g. Radio 1's *Newsbeat*, Radio 5 rolling news and bulletins, commercial radio bulletins).

PRINT

- Newspapers (e.g. popular tabloid, quality press, local and regional, free)
- Magazines (e.g. news, celebrity).

DIGITAL AND WEB-BASED MEDIA

- Digital news channels (e.g. Sky News, BBC News 24, Sky Sports News)
- International news channels accessed in the UK by digital TV (e.g. Fox News, CNN, Aljazeera)
- Newspaper websites (e.g. Guardian Unlimited, www.mirror.co.uk)
- Mainstream news websites (e.g. BBC News)
- Alternative and non-mainstream news websites (e.g. Indymedia, Wikileaks)
- Audience-generated websites (e.g. YouTube, Twitter, IndyMedia)
- RSS feeds (e.g. subscriptions to news alerts to mobile phones or personal computers)
- Blogs with personal accounts of or opinions on events (e.g. from Iran during the anti-government demonstrations in 2009/10)
- Podcasts.

continued

ACTIVITY

1. Collect all the stories. You could collect them in an e-portfolio or have hard copies; for example, record your moving image products from TV or use a free online conversion website, print screen and save or print hard copies of website pages and scan or collect print copies.
2. Complete a detailed analysis of a range of the products you have collected using the media concepts to evaluate and compare them.
3. What media issues and debates do they raise?
4. Apply theory to support your analysis and explain your texts.
5. Apply lots of relevant wider contexts to explain why the stories are presented in the way they are.
6. Split into groups that cover similar news stories; for example, you could have groups based on political, economic, social, international, sport and celebrity stories. Compare the media issues and debates and the wider contexts that your group's stories raised.

Whatever case study you do it would be useful to summarise the results of your analysis and research as a table, including:

1. Products. Prepare a list of the products you have collected, with a clear source and date.
2. Media institutions and the changing role of the producer.
3. The changing role of the audience and user-generated content.
4. Values and democracy.
5. Globalisation.
6. Traditional media: threats and attempts to survive.

Product	Institution + producer	Audience	Values + democracy	Globalisation	Traditional media

ACTIVITY

Organise a short weekly debate on some of the issues above to develop your opinions and be able to explain and justify them.

1. In pairs, take turns to present a brief presentation on an issue. Include examples from your own individual case study to illustrate the issue.
2. As a class, debate the arguments for and against. Organise the debate as a class, with the last speaker choosing the next person to speak. Draw up some debate rules; for example, speak one at a time, speak clearly and to the group, listen carefully, and respect and think about each other's views.
3. Your teacher can write up the best arguments for and against as you are debating and put the list up on an issue and debate display board. Remember: there isn't a right or a wrong answer. You'll be rewarded in your exams for having your own opinions and being able to justify and explain them.

ACTIVITY

1. Research the new Digital Economy Bill. For example, one of its aims is to tackle the problem of online infringement of copyright and performers' rights (e.g. through illegal file sharing). The Bill has been criticised for being a threat to freedom of expression, consumer rights and privacy. One of the most controversial proposals is to cut off the internet connections of people who continue to infringe copyright. The Joint Select Committee on Human Rights argued that

> **The internet is constantly creating new challenges for policy-makers but that cannot justify ill-defined or sweeping legislative responses, especially when there is the possibility of restricting freedom of expression or the privacy of individual users.**

(www.bbc.co.uk, 5 February 2010)

2. As a class, vote on whether you think the Bill should be a law or not.
3. In individual interest groups, produce a list of arguments supporting or criticising the Bill from the point of view of your group's interests. Groups could be new artists or bands, web companies like Facebook and Google, internet service providers, record companies, film companies or websites that sell legal downloads (e.g. iTunes, Play.com, the government).
4. Display the range of arguments from all the groups. Use them to produce your own blogpost that summarises your opinion. You could use a blogger template maker or a DTP package to lay it out.

CITIZEN JOURNALISM means that ordinary people as well as professional journalists are creating the news.

360-DEGREE CONTENT producing news across all platforms.

USER-GENERATED CONTENT media content shown by the mainstream media that is produced by the users or audience.

DEMOCRACY power belongs to all of the people.

FREEDOM OF EXPRESSION everyone has a right to express their own views, but often within certain laws or regulations.

5 RESEARCH AND PRODUCTION SKILLS

In this chapter we will examine:

- The rationale for undertaking production work
- How to build on the skills you developed at AS
- The importance of planning
- The three stages of the production process.

When you undertook your AS production work it may well have been your first opportunity to explore the use of media production technology to create your own media product. What you were expected to produce at AS was supported by a fairly tightly designed framework that offered you a great deal of support as you explored and came to terms with the technology. Working within such a defined context should have made it clear to you what you had to do in order to meet the requirements of the specification. You will, however, find that production work at A2 opens up for you a number of creative opportunities and that it gives you much more of a chance to explore the potential of the medium that you have chosen to work with.

Just as with much of the more academic work required from you at A2, production asks you to move from the 'how' you should recognise from AS to the 'why', which will become familiar territory at A2. Let's look at this assertion for a moment. You will recall at AS spending a lot of time trying to make sure you got things right technically. It may be that you needed a lot of practice before you felt confident using editing software to create a coherent narrative from footage you had shot. Similarly, you may have struggled to get the better of a web design program. At A2 it is assumed that you will have developed at least some technical skills. This, at least in theory, should leave you free to explore the media you are using to a much fuller extent. That exploration should take you in the direction of investigating not just how media products are constructed but why media products are the way they are. Production is a particularly useful way of exploring this issue because most media output is determined by the technology that is used to create it.

With any media work that you do, it is always worth asking the question why you are doing it. Just as you adopt a questioning attitude to theoretical perspectives, so you should be prepared to question the value of undertaking media production. After all, no one would seriously think that A2 Media Studies production work is intended to train you for a job in the industry. So it is well worth asking before you embark on your media production – why am I doing this? Why does someone else (i.e. the exam board) want me to do this? What am I trying to achieve? How is it different from what I did at AS?

ACTIVITY

Before you read any further, it is a good idea to give some thought to these questions. You can then see if the answers you come up with tally with the ones you are about to read below.

Let us try to provide some of the answers and you can see how closely our perception matches yours.

First, remember media production is a discipline. It requires both organisational and technical skills. You will be tested on your ability to work from an initial idea to a finished product dealing with many complex logistical issues along the way. You will also need to demonstrate that you have the technical skill to complete a production. This does not simply mean the ability to use a camera, edit, or use software packages, but also the ability to do such things as write a script, conduct an interview or research background information.

Second, one important trend within the media itself is the blurring of the boundaries that distinguish the producer from the consumer. Access to cheap media production technology combined with a proliferation of potential platforms for showcasing media output has enabled just about anyone with the time and the equipment to make their own media products. Consider, for example, how mobile phones have enabled people to create short films which they can then broadcast on sites such as YouTube. As you are no doubt aware, many of these products are themselves pastiches of mainstream media products. This self-referential nature of media output is a fruitful area of exploration when you consider your production work for A2. Indeed, many commentators would argue that much academic media theory has been made redundant by the media's own relentless critique of itself. If you want to explore the idea further, you might like to start by looking in detail at a programme such as *Charlie Brooker's Screenwipe*, offering as it does a deeply ironic commentary on media products.

Third, and directly related to the second point, is the opportunity production work presents to you to show how well you understand the nature of media products themselves. Just as detailed analysis is intended to reveal the complexity of media products and the issues that surround them, so too can your production work. Of course, this is a complex issue and may well involve you breaking or at least stretching many of the codes and conventions through which media products are constructed. Part of the complexity of what you are doing is the need to demonstrate that you do have a grasp of what these conventions are, and how and why you have chosen to challenge them.

Recap of learning at AS:

Here are four things you may have discovered from your AS production work:

- Production is time-consuming
- Production is equipment-intensive
- Production relies on the cooperation of other people
- If production can go wrong production will go wrong.

So one thing you might think about when doing A2 is that being forewarned is to be forearmed.

Spend a few minutes looking back at your experience of AS production. Based on the results of this contemplation, make a list identifying:

- What went well
- Want went not so well
- What was a total disaster.

Dig out your AS work if you still have it. Don't look just at the product but consider all the research and pre-production that you amassed. Looking through it all, decide:

- What is good
- What is OK
- What is totally embarrassing.

Look back at our list of four things you may have learned about production from your AS work. Is there anything you can add to the list?

So, having looked back at the AS experience, it is a good idea to look forward and think about how you will go about building on this experience.

First, you need to consider the mark value of your production by looking at exactly how marks are allocated to it in relation to A2.

For the AQA the production itself is worth 32 of the 80 marks that are available in this unit. That represents nearly a quarter of the marks you can achieve in your A2 course.

You will see that production is a substantial piece of work that will influence your final grade significantly. Remember that production is work over which you have control, unlike an unseen exam question. In general terms the reward you get for it will be proportional to the work you put into it.

Let us review some of the key elements you will have learned in the production process. A book of this sort is not a good place for us to look in detail at production techniques but does lend itself to an opportunity to tease out the key principles that underpin good production work. If you need help on some more format-specific production skills, your first calling point should be our website which will offer the best and most up-to-date information to help you with your production skills. There you will find some useful advice on the more technical aspects of productions for television and radio, newspapers and magazines, and new media:

www.routledge.com/textbooks/a2mediastudies

In addition, a simple web search will open up to you quite an array of sites that offer help and support on technical issues, such as using Photoshop. There are a number of 'how-to' tutorial videos on YouTube which offer both basic and more sophisticated guidance.

Production skills at AS are likely to have introduced you to at least a couple of production formats. This is a good starting point to consider where to go from there. Logically, you will have built up a level of expertise in handling a technology you are likely to want to stick with and try to develop further. On the other hand, if your review of AS production served only to remind you of what a nightmare it all was, there may be an argument for cutting your losses and trying something new. Remember too that your production skills are by no means limited to class-room learning. If you use production skills in other contexts, for example, taking photos, writing scripts, reviews or features, or even social networking, then use them. The overriding argument that should drive you on is about choosing a technology or technologies appropriate to what you are attempting to do.

What am I trying to achieve? What will the final product look like? What impact do I want it to have on my audience? Imagine best audience reaction.

Planning

The key to effective production work, whether you are a media professional or an A2 student, lies with planning. Time invested in preparing for your production will be time well spent. Production is often a complex logistical operation. This is where your experience of working at AS should really be of benefit. You will have realised that careful planning in the initial stages not only ensures a good outcome, but it can also can save a significant amount of time and energy along the way.

So, before you start, there are three key issues you need to address:

- The medium
- The audience
- The subject matter.

The medium

First, find out which media you are able to work in and what sort of equipment is available to you. Discuss this with your teacher.

- Which media have you had experience of working in before?
- Which did you feel most comfortable and confident with?
- Are you most likely to work on the production *only* in lesson/school time or also outside school/college time?
- How much time do you have available to you?
- What media have you studied previously, and do you feel that you have a working awareness of those media in terms of technique, genre, narrative and so on?

Once you have decided on the medium you will need to consider the next aspect of the practical production process.

The audience

Who is your target audience? It is no use saying that you will make a magazine about stock-car racing based on the fact that you go to a meeting every week and really enjoy it. Market research may suggest that there is insufficient demand for such a magazine as fans of stock-car racing prefer watching it to reading a magazine about it, and are already well catered for via the web. Equally it is not necessarily a good idea to aim your product at a young teenage audience – it is likely to be the case that you yourself are too close to that market and objective decision-making may become difficult. In many cases it is in fact far better to identify and isolate a specific audience that you are not a part of so that you can remain that much more objective. Consequently, personal taste and opinion are less likely to get in the way of your decision-making.

You must therefore:

- ■ Identify a target audience
- ■ Research their likes, dislikes and media-consumption habits.

Ideally through your research you will discover an area that you feel is not well represented at present.

Create a questionnaire that you can distribute widely across a spectrum of people. Consider carefully the types of questions you need to ask about their media consumption, but also consider the personal information that you require to make the survey worthwhile. Remember, even if you are looking at a teenage audience of which you may be a part, not everyone will share your tastes, opinions and attitudes. Alternatively, try to assemble a small focus group that is representative of your audience. Ideally it would be helpful if you can go back to this group at different points in the production process and obtain their feedback on what you have come up with. This may involve you in going outside of your school or college to get access to this group of people.

One example of a media product aimed at a particular audience is the 'grey' magazines aimed specifically at the over-sixties. Such magazines can be difficult to find since they tend not to be on newsagents' shelves but are ordered specially – either by a newsagent for known customers or directly by the readers themselves on a subscription basis. However, if you were to look at these magazines you would find that they make certain presumptions about the over-sixties, which may prompt you to think about the (possibly enormous) market of over-sixties who may not feel they are appropriately catered for by these magazines.

Figure 5.1 *Saga* Magazine, aimed at the over-sixties: September 2009

Equally, research into magazines and magazine products, such as their websites and TV channels, aimed at teenage girls may suggest that all of these magazines are in fact very similar. Thus it may be an interesting challenge to produce a magazine for this audience that is totally different from all the others already available. It is not for us to suggest what the contents of such a teenage-girl magazine might be but rather that you examine that area.

You may find it worth your while to interview your family and friends about their media consumption and ask them to suggest ways in which they feel they are not being catered for by existing media products.

The subject matter

The subject material of your production is inevitably linked with its target audience and so must obviously appeal to its intended audience and be in an appropriate medium for this audience. It should also be possible to produce the material within the constraints of the medium that you have decided to employ. For instance, you are unlikely to be able to make a video about a wartime submarine, since your ability to create realistic sets and costumes will be severely limited in a school/college context. However, the possibilities offered by a radio play are almost endless.

You also have to be realistic about the time, money and energy that you have. Do not be over-ambitious – be realistic. For example, if you have decided to target 40-year-old sci-fi film enthusiasts then it is fundamentally unrealistic to decide to make a fiction film, largely because you are unlikely to have the equipment and budget necessary to do so. However, if you think around the problem you might:

- Make a television or radio magazine programme that is about sci-fi films
- Make a trailer/advertising campaign for a new sci-fi film
- Make a parody of a sci-fi film of the 1950s (though note that parody/pastiche is actually a sophisticated skill).

This is a good time to conduct a brainstorming session. Sit down with your group and jot down all the ideas that you have about a possible production. Allow yourself around 15 to 20 minutes to do this, then take a 15-minute break. Return and discuss carefully what you have written down and begin to examine the links between the various ideas.

One other point at this stage is important – how many people are to work on your production? In terms of the final assessment there is a lot to be said for working with your own individual ideas. The production is very much an investigation, in the same way that an academic essay might be. Many productions, however, are collaborative efforts. What is important is to show that your work has a clear sense of direction and a well-defined input from you as an individual. One solution is to work collaboratively with classmates in supporting each student's individual project. Where you do get support, specifically technical guidance, be sure to acknowledge this. You will be asked before your work is submitted to sign it to authenticate that it is your own work and that you have acknowledged any additional support you have received. It is a good idea to be honest about this.

The three stages of the production process

The production process may be usefully broken down into three stages:

- Pre-production
- Production
- Post-production.

Pre-production

Having made all the decisions about the nature of your product, you now enter the phase that is absolutely necessary to all media products. In the real world it is a rare individual who is allowed a completely free rein to go out and do whatever s/he sees fit at the time 'because it feels right'. Nowadays, whatever the product, an awful lot of work goes into the pre-production stage.

RESEARCHING SIMILAR MEDIA

Whatever the media you are working in it is almost inevitable that there are other products out there which cover the same area. You need to investigate your 'rivals' and 'competitors' to see what they are doing, investigate their subject material, research how well they seem to target their audience, and look at what works and what does not. Look in particular at how rival products are presented to the audience – study the opening sequences if visual, the front pages if print. What assumptions are the producers making about their audience? Do you want to alter these assumptions and, if you do, then how are you going to do this?

For instance, it seems that children's television presenters are required to be fairly 'wacky' and shout a lot, while the camera never stops moving. Children's television also seems to assume that the majority of children are only interested in boy bands and computer games and, it would appear, very little else.

So what would you change if your area was children's television? Again, you would need to watch a considerable amount of this genre before you could begin to form any conclusions – but remember that you should not be afraid to accept the things that work and rethink the things that seem to you not to work.

This is really about genre expectations and, while accepting the importance of these expectations, it is also important to confront and challenge them (and to be able to articulate the reasoning behind any decision that you make).

We tend to assume that we know what is best for everyone and also that public taste is fairly uniform throughout the country. The truth is that even large-scale media productions can have varying success throughout different regions in the country. What works in London will not necessarily work in Taunton or Doncaster. It is also the case that not all teenage girls necessarily enjoy the same things – and the same is true of teenage boys.

You could say that at present the teenage magazine market tends to play safe by creating an identikit picture of a typical teenager (see section on representation, p. 101) and then creating magazines based on that image. This works to an extent – sales figures are high – but there are still many teenagers nationwide who do not buy magazines because there is simply nothing that caters for them. This could be an interesting area for you to explore.

Having decided upon your medium, subject material and audience you now have to go out and investigate the real nature of your target audience.

- What media products do they consume?
- What in particular do they enjoy about them?
- Which aspects of their favourite texts do they most appreciate?
- But most fundamentally – what more do they want?
- How could the product(s) be improved?
- What other types of products would they like to see created for them?

This is very much what happens in the real media world. Media producers tend to build a profile of their consumers and it can be a very detailed profile, based not just on sex, age and class but also encompassing such things as geographical location, family circumstances, jobs, consumption patterns and preferences.

It is important to ensure that this research does not only take place in your classroom or indeed school. Whatever the nature of your target audience, you should spread your net as far and as wide as possible in an attempt to get a truly representative feel for the subject. This has pitfalls none the less, but as broad a survey as possible gives you more evidence upon which to format and create your eventual product.

This might seem to be stating the obvious, but no one can just produce a media artefact without first researching the subject matter. Whatever the nature of the production you are developing, it is absolutely essential that you have thought about and planned exactly what the subject matter and content will be. It is often the case that students use material that they have found and borrowed from other sources – for instance, those who decide to create a girls' magazine often think it is enough simply to copy out articles that they have found in existing publications. This of course undercuts everything that we have discussed above. It suggests to the readers (and ultimately these are the examiners) that you have not really thought about the nature of your audience or considered the results of all the research that you should have done.

This is even more the case when creating an audio-visual product. Your job is not simply to copy what is already out there, but to develop it and take it further.

There are secondary sources – by which we mean finding out information from books in the library or perhaps from interesting websites – but to make any production come alive you also need to investigate primary sources – interviewing people who are prepared to debate the issues that you are investigating in your production, for example. All this needs careful planning and advance preparation.

ORGANISING

One of the really important skills you should have learned the need for at AS is that of organisation. Now you have to get organised. Prepare yourself and the people who may have agreed to help you so that everyone has a job to do. It is very important that everyone else knows exactly what that job involves. It is also vital that everyone knows when each of the different tasks is going to be done *and* the final date for completion of the project. This holds true for whatever medium you have decided to work in. All of this information needs to be itemised on paper and distributed throughout the group (as well as a copy being ready for submission at the end of the course).

Whatever the eventual product you have decided to create, there is still yet more planning to do. It is important that you do not start work without having a clear idea of what the finished product will look like. This involves serious consideration of the actual contents and the look of the final product. For instance, a front cover of a magazine does not just happen. It involves taking into account all the research work that has gone on before and attempting to create a cover that will:

- Appeal to the target audience
- Give an idea about what is contained within the front cover
- Demonstrate awareness of the generic rules of the sort of magazine it is
- Have some immediate visual appeal – always remember that in theory you are competing with all the magazines that are already out there.

Similarly, you will need to produce a mock-up of the magazine – as you would in real life – in which you are able to demonstrate what will actually be in it, and also suggest the order in which the editorial material, advertisements and illustrations will appear. This is also your opportunity to start experimenting with the look/ style/format of the magazine.

If you are making a video then what you should *not* do is to just go out and start filming. You will need to produce a script and an accompanying shotlist so that you have a basic idea of what the final product will look like. You will also need to prepare careful plans of what will be shot, when and where, who in the group will be needed, when people will be available (especially if you are interviewing members of the public) and what will be needed (props, costumes, equipment).

While this may not necessarily all be true of a documentary, even then there are only a few documentary filmmakers who simply go out with a camera and see what happens. They are much more likely to have decided in the first place who they want to interview, where, when, what they want to ask them, and also (if the truth be told) what sort of light they want to show them in.

This preparation work may not be the most exciting part of the production process – and there will always be members of the group who just want to get on and do it – but at the end of the day all your planning will save you a great deal of time, and also prevent you from making a lot of mistakes. It should mean that the final product is delivered on time – which of course in the real media world is incredibly important.

Production

There are two very important primary stages to the production process. Perhaps the most important is that of familiarisation with the technology available to you, to remind yourself exactly what the equipment you are using is capable of doing for you.

When you feel comfortable again with the equipment, when you know its capabilities and your own limitations, when everyone has agreed on their tasks, when everyone knows what they are doing and when everyone feels confident and prepared . . . then you can begin!

You will have been given a deadline – do everything that you can to keep to this. In the best of all possible worlds you will have constructed a plan that is built around the deadlines set by your teacher/lecturer. Stick to it wherever possible.

However, things will not always go strictly according to plan. Computers will crash. Raw footage that your were especially proud of will get erased. It will be raining on the day that you have organised to shoot outside. The music department will have double-booked the recording studio in which you were going to record the soundtrack. These are the kinds of things that can lead to total despondency. However, if you have a well-organised plan then it is not too difficult to look ahead and work out exactly what you can do in the meantime. There is always too much to do and not enough time to do it in. So if the item you were going to work on on any given day suddenly becomes impossible to do, there should always be an alternative section or task that you can be working on.

Remember, too, to hold frequent 'progress-report meetings'. These are important for several reasons. You should constantly assess how things are going, give everyone an opportunity to come up with new ideas or complaints and also ensure that the entire production is still on track.

You may well have a plan but there is another important point to make at this stage. There is always the possibility that, no matter how good your plan, things will not necessarily work out as you had hoped. No matter how you see events in your head, in reality they may not be a success. There can be any number of reasons for this. Perhaps the sun was shining in the wrong direction. Maybe the colour printer did not have sufficient contrast, thereby making the shades of the same basic colour merge into one. Or an actor vital to the scene you have prepared to shoot did not turn up.

In cases like these you will have to be prepared to improvise, and perhaps alter direction completely. Interestingly, this can sometimes work to your advantage – often what you had least expected turns out to be the best option. This flexibility is important. You have a plan but something better turns up. When it does, seize the opportunity (but remember to note it down because it will be very relevant for your commentary).

Here are some other tips to bear in mind while working on your production:

1. Keep everything. That front cover may not seem right at the time but you may change your mind after you have tried and failed to improve on it. It will also be very useful as evidence when you explain the developmental process in your commentary. Equally, all the video material you create may come in useful when editing. Shoot, watch and log it all, every day if possible.
2. Bear in mind at all times that it is your ideas, and your attempts to get your ideas into concrete form, that matter. You are not professionals working full-time on the job. You will be rewarded for making a genuine attempt at something, even though it may seem to you to be a failure (as long as it is recorded in your log/commentary).
3. Never lose sight of the pre-production research that you did – and which should in any case have taken up much of your time. You will almost certainly be working within a genre – keep in mind at all times the conventions of that genre and its likely audience. Your audience needs to be entertained and challenged, otherwise your product has failed.
4. Even though you may be striving for originality, the chances of achieving it are pretty slight. For instance, if you are working within a particular magazine genre and want to create a product that is totally original (and has the potential to be a fantastic financial success) you should always bear in mind that there are people employed in the media world who are paid huge sums of money each year to try to dream up similar ideas. And they rarely succeed either. It is a good idea to be as ambitious as possible, but that ambition needs to be tempered with a dose of reality. This is a cruel way of suggesting that even though your end-product might not be all you had hoped it might be, it will probably have a great deal of merit – and why give all your best ideas to an examiner for nothing? Save the really good ones until you are working!
5. Keep a log/diary. You will forget what happened six weeks ago. The practicalities of media production are important. It is not simply about ideas but also about technique and about coping with external pressures to get the whole thing finished. This process needs to be articulated in your commentary. If corners are cut due to budgetary or time constraints then you will need to explain how you coped and how it affected what you achieved.

An important point to bear in mind when you are engaged in production work is the way in which media production and consumption have come increasingly to overlap. The distinction between producer and consumer in which monolithic institutions produce while the rest of us sit at home, in cinemas or on trains and buses and consume has become much more blurred. It is true that most media output is still controlled by large corporations, but, as you will read elsewhere in this book, there are many opportunities for individuals to create their own media products and to broadcast or circulate these products using new media technologies. Many of you are probably already engaged in doing so, perhaps using a social networking site or maybe creating your own films, music videos, webpages, or animations for consumption on the web. This is obviously an ideal opportunity for you to develop further your production skills. An even greater advantage is that it allows you to access an audience in a way that is probably easier than ever before. With an audience comes the potential for feedback. The web offers you a great opportunity to find out precisely what people out there think about your products. Provided you are thick-skinned enough, you will be able to read how people react to what you have done. That leaves you with the opportunity to do one of two things:

- Modify your product in line with the comments people have made
- Ignore what they say and don't change anything.

The important thing is that you take heed of what people say and evaluate the validity and value of their comments.

Post-production

All media products need to be marketed and advertised. They do not sell themselves. Many candidates simply produce an artefact and leave it at that. It is very important that you consider the presentation of your product very carefully. There is little point in working very hard on your video production and then delivering the finished product in a shabby, unmarked DVD case. The same is often true of a radio production. Similarly, do not present a magazine that is unkempt, badly bound or a second-generation copy that is hard to read.

First appearances count for a great deal – and not only on the high street. If the product has been well packaged and looks clean and smart, then it is much more likely to be considered a success. Therefore, if you have made a DVD, package it in a clean cover and create a proper insert that fits the genre of the piece and gives suitable information about the product on the back for those who need to know. Bear in mind that the DVD should look as if it could compete with all the other videos on the shelf in the local video hire shop.

Equally, if your product is print-based then it needs to look good so that people browsing in a newsagent will be tempted to pick it up. At all times bear in mind the opposition on the newsagent's shelves and think carefully about the audience you are trying to attract.

You will have spent a long time considering the look of your front page, but the product as a whole needs to be kept pristine. Think very carefully about the different forms of binding available to you. Consider laminating each page and creating a rather firmer wrap-around front cover so that it always stays in one piece. (Remember that you are not being marked for the type of binding that you employ.) Indeed, some candidates in the past have dispensed completely with the pretence of binding their product and have simply placed each page within a plastic folder – and explained why they have done so in their rationale. This ensures that your product will be marked looking its best.

Further reading

Bignell, J. and Orlebar, J. (2005) *The Television Handbook* Abingdon: Routledge
Dewdney, A. and Ride, P. (2006) *The New Media Handbook* Abingdon: Routledge
Fleming, C. (2009) *The Radio Handbook* Abingdon: Routledge
Keeble, R. (2005) *The Newspapers Handbook* Abingdon: Routledge
Lee-Wright, P. (2009) *The Documentary Handbook* Abingdon: Routledge
McKay, J. (2005) *The Magazines Handbook* Abingdon: Routledge
Powell, H. *et al.* (2009) *The Advertising Handbook* Abingdon: Routledge

PASSING MEST4: MEDIA RESEARCH AND PRODUCTION

6

The components

Critical investigation (2000 words or equivalent, 42 marks)

Linked production (38 marks)

Rationale: what are the aims of the coursework unit?

In this unit you will also have the chance to:

■ Explore an area of the media which you have chosen and are particularly interested in
■ Work independently on a research area of your choice
■ Produce your own linked production work.

The spirit of this unit may be found in the following key terms; a successful investigation and production will demonstrate these qualities.

AUTONOMY the ability to work independently and make your own decisions (the active student discussed in the Introduction), based on the study and evaluation of different critical and creative approaches.

SYNTHESIS the process of drawing together different ideas, perspectives and media forms into an argument or discussion. At A2 you have to synthesise theory and production, emphasising the links between the two (see documentary case study and the link between academic theory and practice, p. 266).

Autonomy and synthesis are part of a synoptic assessment which is central to A2 study.

Synoptic assessment

MEST4 is a synoptic unit – it draws on all the knowledge and skills you have developed at AS and A2 including the key theoretical concepts, research skills, technical and creative ability.

What does it mean to be synoptic?

The first step in developing a synoptic approach is providing a synopsis of your subject, drawing together everything that you have covered so far on the course. The next stage is to use that synopsis to develop your knowledge and understanding further.

A synoptic approach should:

■ Be based on knowledge, understanding and skills specified in the MEST4 unit but also draw on those in previously studied units. Part of the skill of a synoptic approach is to select relevant areas from previous study – and not just to mention everything!
■ Demonstrate the ability to construct, evaluate and support an argument. It isn't enough to have the subject knowledge; you must also demonstrate the skills of critical thinking and apply this to the investigation and the linked production.
■ Engage with ideas, issues and debates which go beyond the limits of the knowledge, skills and understanding studied on the course. At MEST4 this might include linking your research to relevant cross-cultural factors and the effects of globalisation on the media.

The critical investigation: what is it?

The specification states that the critical investigation must:

- Be text based
- Have a clearly defined focus
- Explore a text, theme or debate relevant to the contemporary media landscape in dcpth
- Include research and evaluation of a variety of primary and secondary sources.

Choosing your topic area for critical investigation and linked production

Choosing an area for your research can be one of the most enjoyable aspects of the project. It is a chance to investigate an area which you are interested in; to set the agenda for your own studies. To select an area which is appropriate the first stage is to check that your focus text/s fulfils the following criteria:

- Is it contemporary – rather than historical (i.e. was it broadcast/published/ released etc. in the past five years)?
- Can it be defined as a media text? The definition will be through form, technology, platform, audience.
- Is it a text which is easily available for you to study?

Skills for individual work

For this unit you need to work independently on your research and production. Therefore you need to consider how you can work most effectively:

- Draw up a timeline or timetable which includes your deadlines and the amount of time you will have to work on the project.
- Be realistic about the amount of time you will have – do you have time in class? Do you need access to specialist equipment or are there aspects you can work on at home?
- Will you need training to use software programs, etc.?
- Working individually doesn't mean that you have to work in isolation – discuss your ideas with your teacher or other members of the class.
- Perhaps you could form a group with other people in the class to provide feedback and evaluate ideas.
- Although you have sole responsibility for the production it is very likely that you will need to 'employ' other people to appear in your work (particularly for still and moving images).

Restrictions to the critical investigation

It is important that your investigation shows critical autonomy, independent thought and research; therefore you should not base your investigation around one of the two pre-set topics for MEST3.

There are a variety of ways to choose your area for investigation and linked production. The following examples illustrate different ways of developing your initial thoughts and testing your ideas within the context of the relevant media concepts, debates and issues.

1. CHOOSING THROUGH TEXT

One way of approaching this project is to choose a media text with which you are familiar and interested in researching further. A mind map can be a useful framework for constructing an initial review of the text (Figure 6.1).

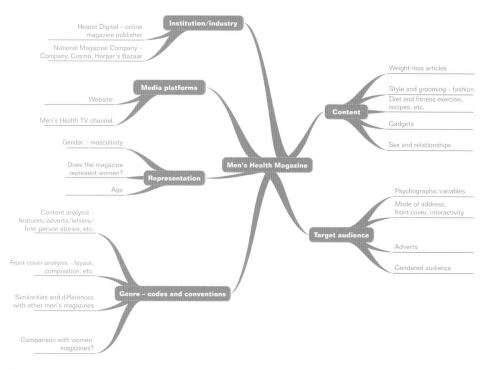

Figure 6.1 *Men's Health* Magazine: a mind map about choosing a text

Once you've completed the outline of your initial areas you can start to narrow down the research to conform to the requirements of the investigation. Study the mind map on *Men's Health* and, using a table, organise the different areas into the relevant concepts – genre, representation, narrative, institution, audience, etc. It is clear that there are a variety of relevant approaches which could be developed here.

Remember! You cannot focus on one of the topic areas for MEST3.

Possible critical investigation titles

An investigation into the genre conventions of men's magazines (*Men's Health* and *GQ*). How are these conventions used to target an audience in a shrinking market?

Strengths and weaknesses

This area is clearly focused around the texts which will allow for an in-depth analysis and prevent the research becoming too generalised. Genre conventions is an area covered extensively at AS – will there be enough to differentiate this as an A2 project? The use of analysis to then consider the position of the magazines in the contemporary media landscape – considering audience and institution – would move it to a higher level.

Possible linked production

Individual project – the front cover, contents page and sample feature for a new men's magazine which challenges the typical genre conventions.

Title

How has the publication and distribution of men's lifestyle magazines responded to developments in new technologies?

Strengths and weaknesses

This area would provide the opportunity to address issues of globalisation in the context of media industries – as recommended in the specification. You will need to select specific examples (e.g. the online magazine) to keep the research textually focused.

Possible linked production

Individual project – home page for a launch edition of a men's magazine with links to other media platforms.

2. CHOOSING THROUGH GENRE

A different way of approaching your selection would be to start with a genre that you're interested in (e.g. the TV crime drama: Figure 6.2).

Once you have a range of possible texts, you can start to categorise them further. This will help you to decide how suitable a programme might be for your research

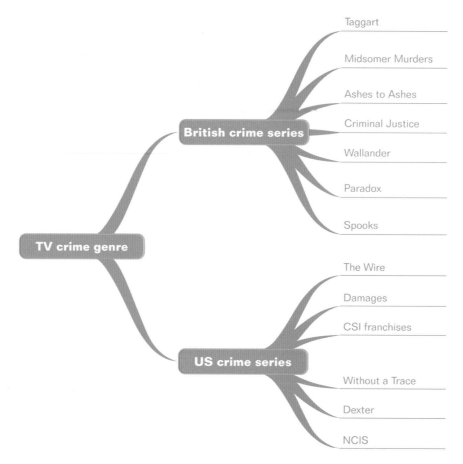

Figure 6.2 A mind map about choosing through genre

as well as develop your ideas. This process could be done through a thought shower, mind map or use of a table:

Form

Series	Serial/mini-series	Franchise	Hybrid genre
Taggart, The Wire Midsomer Murders, Dexter, Without a Trace NCIS, Spooks, CSI, Ashes to Ashes, Wallander	*Damages, Criminal Justice, Paradox*	*Ashes to Ashes, CSI Miami, CSI New York*	*Paradox* (crime/s-f) *Spooks* (crime/spy thriller)

Subject

Police	Government agency	PI	Other
Taggart, The Wire Midsomer Murders, Ashes to Ashes, Criminal Justice, Paradox, Wallander	*Spooks, NCIS, Without a Trace, Dexter, CSI*	None	*The Wire, Criminal Justice* (judicial system), *Damages* (lawyers)

Character focus

Central hero	Group	Pair	Other
Midsomer Murders, Wallander	*Taggart, Spooks, NCIS, Without a Trace, CSI*	*Ashes to Ashes, Paradox*	*Dexter* – anti-hero; *The Wire* – focus on different groups (police, drug dealers, gangsters, etc.); *Damages* – hero and villain roles unclear; *Criminal Justice* – focus on police, lawyers, social worker.

Although this clearly isn't a scientific sample of the contemporary crime series, reflecting on your categories will raise some interesting points. In relation to the above tables these would include the following:

- None of the programmes features private investigators (something which used to be very popular). Following this up suggests some other examples: *The No.1 Ladies' Detective Agency* (BBC, series of films, none scheduled), *Mayo* (BBC, comedy/crime drama, 2006–7), *Rosemary and Thyme* (ITV, gardening detectives, 2003–7).
- Following on from this, *Harper's Island* (US, 2009, shown on BBC3) has an 'amateur' detective and is an interesting genre hybrid (thriller/slasher).
- A common characteristic of the genre seems to be a long-running series (often spawning franchises) centred on the police – or other official government agency – who work in a group.
- Programmes which seem unconventional are: *Criminal Justice, Damages, The Wire, Dexter* in broadcast form, structure and content.

Figure 6.3 *Criminal Justice* and *The Wire*: examples of the crime genre

Testing a proposed area: a critical investigation into the narrative structure of *Criminal Justice*

Does this work as an area of research?

Positives	Problems
It's a contemporary text – Series 2 broadcast 2009	Is it available – DVD? iPlayer?
Format – series broadcast over five nights – lends itself to narrative analysis	Will I need to include Series 1 in the research? They are stand alone but also linked
This format is a new – but becoming more common – type of scheduling; lends itselfto discussion of contemporary media issues	Does it make it difficult to focus on a specific episode?
Storyline developed through variety of points of view, providing a real depth fornarrative analysis	How to handle all the different narrative elements (plus context, theory, issues) in the limited word count?

Conclusions

■ Problems seem to come from the variety and depth of the area, which suggests that this would be an appropriate area to investigate.

Structure the area of investigation by selecting areas of the concept (narrative) which are relevant:

■ *Criminal Justice* follows one crime and examines how it affects all those involved – the accused, victim, police, lawyers, social services

> ▤ The plot is structured over a series of five episodes
> ▤ Each series is self-contained but some of the same characters appear across series.
>
> Therefore relevant areas would include open and closed narratives and audience positioning.

3. CHOOSING THROUGH FORM

The aim of MEST4 is to synthesise theory and production which means that it is just as valid to begin with your choice of practical production and to develop your critical investigation from that; the most important consideration is to ensure that there is a clear link between the research and the production (and vice versa).

An example of this approach is worked through in the diagram shown in Figure 6.4.

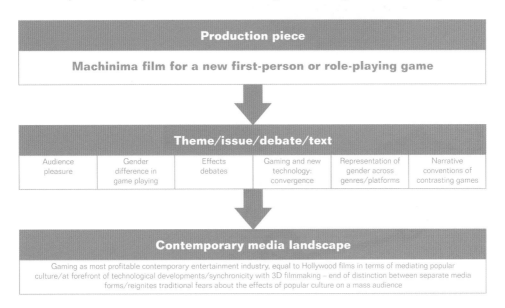

Figure 6.4 Diagram of choosing through form

4. CHOOSING THROUGH ISSUE

It may be that you are interested in exploring a particular media issue or debate further and the critical investigation is an ideal opportunity to do this. One of the stimulating aspects of studying the media is how often theoretical approaches learnt in the classroom are apparent in debates in political, social and cultural arenas. This can provide an excellent opportunity to test some of these critical approaches in the context of extensive research and debate. The most frequent examples of this come within approaches to audience – such as effects theory – and deal with some of the most controversial areas of the media. Recent examples include:

■ **A climate of change: environmentally friendly advertising claims on the rise** (http://www.asa.org.uk/). The Advertising Standards Authority provides research and resources as a context to its guidance and adjudications on UK advertising. This particular report is in response to the increasing use of environmental claims by a range of advertisers, and considers the problems of judging their accuracy and truthfulness.

Figure 6.5 An example of an advert offering environmental claims

■ **Parents too busy to help children learn to talk** (http://www.guardian.co.uk/society/2010/jan/04/parents-busy-children-learn-talk). A survey published by the government's 'communications champion' suggests that children's linguistic development is damaged by video games and screen culture of all kinds.

- **BBC1 has too few over-fifties viewers:** 'The Older Faces Audit' conducted by market research consultants (PCP) found that the over-fifties were under-represented on the BBC in comparison with other channels.
- **Lads' magazines should be restricted to curb sexualisation of children:** Press coverage of one of the conclusions of a Home Office report into young people and the media with particular reference to the effects of 'sexualised' images (http://www.homeoffice.gov.uk/documents/Sexualisation-young-people.pdf). For more on this report see Identity (p. 156).

All of these areas could be the starting point for an investigation leading to a linked production. Different approaches could include:

- Analyse the media coverage of a particular report. How do different programmes, publications, etc. shape the findings to a particular agenda or audience?
- Develop your own response to the findings: this might be to support or counter the conclusions. How would you provide evidence for your views?
- Examine the different research approaches used. Do you think they are effective for analysing all forms of media? Could you usefully replicate any of the research?
- Developing a product which 'solves' the 'problems' identified by researchers (using environmental claims in advertising, foregrounding communication skills in a video game, etc.).

The critical investigation: form and content

The critical investigation is a form of academic research and therefore it is important to follow the conventions of good academic practice. Investigations must include a detailed bibliography/list of references citing primary and secondary sources. This must be an integral part of your research – not an afterthought – if you are to achieve a higher level mark for the investigation. The mark scheme states that evidence of research must be "employed in the investigation and detailed in the bibliography" at Levels 3 and 4. Even Level 1 includes the need for a "bibliography to be present".

Investigations can be presented as either:

- A written (word-processed) report
- A DVD commentary (approximately 10 minutes) which summarises your research findings through interview, commentery and analysis of existing material
- A wiki-based investigation (at least four pages).

Remember: the emphasis for the assessment of the investigation is always on the content (your research) rather than the form. In other words, even if you have a beautifully designed and perfectly functioning wiki you will only get lower level marks if the content is thin.

Sample case study

Suggested titles

1. An investigation into the use of hybrid conventions of film documentary with specific reference to *Man on Wire* (2008).
2. *Documentaries are just another form of fiction but masquerade as truth.* An analysis of the representation of reality in film documentary.
3. Construction of narrative in C4 short documentaries – how does the audience respond to fictional forms in non-fiction texts?
4. How does C4 use documentary strands to target audiences and fulfil its remit? Analyse with reference to C4's 'shock documentaries'.
5. *Audiences no longer respond to fictional texts but demand authenticity.* An investigation into the reasons for the increasing domination of documentary formats in UK TV schedules.

Linked productions

- Produce a documentary 'portrait' for the Channel 4 3MW series.
- The first three minutes of a feature-length hybrid documentary.
- An extract from a new reality TV show for a specific channel.

Initial research

The following suggest some of the ways you could begin your research for the critical investigation. These approaches would also work for any film, TV programme, etc.

Man on Wire (James Marsh, 2008)

Synopsis (taken from the official website)

On 7 August 1974, a young Frenchman Philippe Petit stepped out on a wire illegally rigged between New York's Twin Towers, then the world's tallest buildings. After nearly an hour dancing on the wire, he

---

was arrested, taken for psychological evaluation, and brought to jail before he was finally released. Following six and a half years of dreaming of the Towers, Petit spent eight months in New York City planning the execution of the coup . . . a unique and magnificent spectacle that became known as the artistic crime of the century.

As a starting point, research relevant institutional information to provide a foundation for your investigation.

Institutional context: production, distribution and exhibition.

Source	Type of source	Information	Outcomes/next step
manonwire. com	Secondary research official website.	Production context, multiple production companies: Magnolia, Wall to Wall, Discovery, BBC, UK Film Council.	Suggests low-budget, niche audience film. Co-production by TV and film companies typical of contemporary media production. Why did the Film Council award lottery money? Research distributors and producers – go to industry websites.
Imdb.com	Secondary research media industry website.	Magnolia Pictures (US) is the distributor. BBC production through *Storyville* strand. Directed by James Marsh – previous films include hybrid documentaries such as *Wisconsin Death*	Magnolia distributes low-budget British and US features and documentary – often with a social agenda. Go to *Storyville* website for information on other documentaries. Watch previous films (but both too old for a contemporary research investigation).

continued

Source	Type of source	Information	Outcomes/next step
		Trip, Burger and the King Exhibition: 43 screens (UK) In US opened on two screens, building to 93 after Oscar win.	Limited exhibition will be evidence for type of audience. Oscar win characteristic of the number of awards received.
http://www.bbc.co.uk/bbcfour/documentaries/storyville/	Secondary research media industry website.	*Storyville* is a series of documentaries about international people and events shown on BBC4.	*Man on Wire* funded through the licence fee (PSB). Many of the *Storyville* documentaries are portraits of individuals – famous and anonymous. May be a useful comparison text.
http://www.ukfilmcouncil.org.uk/new cinemafund		Funded with money from the New Cinema Fund which aims to 'encourage unique ideas, innovative approaches and original voices'.	This definition would be a way to discuss the techniques used in the film.

3MW

3 Minute Wonders are a series of shorts from new directors who haven't yet made a film for broadcast TV. The films are often – but not always – documentaries and are shown four nights a week after the Channel 4 7 p.m. news. The films are connected by subject, but they also have to be able to stand alone and be understood in isolation.

There is an archive of films on the *3 Minute Wonder* website, which will give you a chance to research a range of examples (http://www.channel4.com/culture/microsites/0–9/3mw/index.html).

Typical of the types of documentaries made for *3MW* is the series *Nursing Britain*. Each of the four films follows the experiences of a foreign NHS worker either newly arrived or long established. Through the focus on an individual, these portraits also explore wider social and cultural issues such as Britain as a multicultural society or the future of the NHS. The series on the Aylesbury Estate in South London (on C4 July 2007/available on YouTube) constructed a portrait of estate life through the stories of different residents, while placing their experiences in the context of 10 years of a Blair government.

The commissioning editor of the *3MW* series states:

> **❝** I'm actively searching for directors with **unique** perspectives **who want to tell stories in new, exciting, non-traditional** ways. I'm interested in ideas that feel timely and connected to something happening in the outside world. . . . It's also important that the trajectory of the films feels absolutely suited to the three minutes so the **form and structure of the film is crucial** to me. **❞**

How does this link to practical production?

This reference to the content and style of the films is something you should take into account in your production. Research this by watching a range of *3MW* films and note how they tell stories in 'new and exciting ways' – this might be to do with the form or perhaps a subject which hasn't been covered elsewhere. (Note also the similarity to the stated aims of the Film Council in funding films like *Man on Wire* referred to earlier.)

RELEVANT THEORETICAL APPROACHES

- Genre
- Defining types of documentary
- Representation and realism.

What is a documentary?

Whichever theoretical area you choose to investigate, you will need to develop a definition of the term 'documentary'. Defining the documentary has become increasingly complicated with the development of new styles of documentary and hybrid forms (e.g. documentary drama, reality TV), but there are still some characteristics that we expect from a text in order for it to be defined as a documentary. It will be:

- Non-fiction
- About the real (historical, political, cultural, etc. events) world

continued

- Informative, educational
- Based on observation rather than intervention
- Unstaged
- Filmed in a particular style (e.g. interviews, voice-over, handheld camera).

Even these few characteristics are likely to provoke questions and debate as you continue your study.

Documentary style and realism

One of the important areas to analyse is that of realism and documentary form. This is central to defining the documentary and therefore will be essential whether your main focus is **genre** (realism is one of the genre conventions of documentary), **representation** (how do documentaries represent the real world?) or **narrative** (how do documentaries use realist techniques to shape the real world into a story for the audience?).

Read the following quote about the relationship between realism and the real world:

> " **Realism is a construction, therefore it is impossible to achieve a perfect match between events in the real world and the text that represents them.** "

(Kilborn and Izod, 1997)

This suggests that:

- Realism is a style of filmmaking – just as Hollywood narrative and film noir are styles

Figure 6.6
A scene from *Man on Wire*

- Realism involves a series of choices on the part of the filmmaker (it is a construction)
- Documentaries can never directly reflect reality (it is impossible to achieve a perfect match).

Secondary research: documentary realism

Develop your secondary research by following up the Kilborn and Izod quote opposite. Their book *An Introduction to Television Documentary – Confronting Reality* provides an overview of the key definitions and debates in the area. Begin by selecting the most relevant sections, chapters, pages, etc. (e.g. Part 1, Chapter 2, *How Real Can You Get? Realism and Documentary*).

How does this link to the practical production?

These questions of realism will have a practical application in your own documentary production; it is worth reflecting on how you would go about tackling the challenge of representing the real world on film. As a documentary-maker, ask yourself the following questions:

- To what extent can film (fiction or non-fiction) reflect the real world?
- How would you try to capture the real world on film? What techniques would you use?
- What would be some of the obstacles to showing the real world?
- What are some of the differences between the real world as you experience it and the real world as shown on film?
- Which films have you seen (fiction or non-fiction) which you think represent reality accurately? What techniques were used?

Once we start to consider documentaries in this way we can analyse the role of the documentary-maker. If they aren't just reflecting reality then they must be shaping it somehow – perhaps to manipulate the way in which the audience responds to the film. In this way documentaries share many characteristics with fiction films.

Objectivity and subjectivity

Can a documentary (or documentary-maker) ever be objective? There is often the assumption that a documentary must 'show both sides of the story', but if a documentary is a construction can it ever be objective? Do you think objectivity is even something which documentary-makers should aim for? When making your own documentary consider how the following

continued

affects objectivity: choice of subject, the use of editing, what is left in and what is excluded.

Defining modes of documentary

The term 'documentary' covers a variety of different styles of filmmaking, subject matter, aims and exhibition. There have been some attempts in academic study to categorise different documentaries into groups. This is a similar approach to grouping fiction films into genres but here the groups are referred to as documentary 'modes'. Many documentaries will feature conventions from more than one mode (rather like hybrid genres) and there are overlaps across the different modes.

Another way of using the modes is to think about the role or position of the documentary-maker and therefore the role of the audience.

GROUP A: EXPOSITORY, OBSERVATIONAL

These modes attempt to hide the role of the filmmaker and emphasises the filmmaker's interpretation of the world.

GROUP B: PARTICIPATORY, REFLEXIVE, PERFORMATIVE

These modes foreground the role of the filmmaker and shift the emphasis to the way in which the audience interprets the documentary.

Figure 6.7 Michael Moore in *Capitalism: A Love Story*

Secondary research: Bill Nichols and modes of documentary

Bill Nichols is one of the key theorists in the study of documentary and identified the modes of documentary representation which have since been debated, argued over and added to. In *Representing Reality* (1991) Nichols identified four dominant groups in documentary: expository, observational, interactive and reflexive. In *Blurred Boundaries* (1994) this was expanded to include poetic as an early form (1920s) and performative as a recent development in documentary style.

Nichols' work is sometimes attacked for being rigid and prescriptive. He does, however, emphasise that the modes tend to be combined and altered in individual films and that older categories do not disappear with the introduction of new modes.

Development of modes

Why do new modes of representation within documentary emerge? Nichols identifies the modes as developing chronologically and in reaction to the limitations of the previous mode.

In studying the development of new modes it is apparent that there are a range of contextual factors which affect this development – new technology, institutions and audience. Rather than initially defining them through techniques and conventions it is helpful to introduce the concept of different modes of representation in terms of understanding the role of the documentary-maker.

How does this link to the practical production?

As a documentary-maker will you appear on screen or remain behind the camera?

continued

If you do appear on screen there are a variety of different approaches you can use: you could be an interviewer or a 'presenter' of factual information, or you might develop a persona in a similar way to Nick Broomfield or Michael Moore. Whatever role you choose should be appropriate to the type of documentary you're making; it should develop from the aim of your documentary.

Primary research: comparing different roles and modes

To analyse the different functions available to documentary-makers look at a range of contrasting documentaries. Some suggestions:

The World's . . . and Me (available to watch at http://www.channel4.com/programmes/the-worlds-and-me). Channel 4 TV series in which comedian Mark Dolan visits 'extraordinary' children – strongest, smallest, cleverest, etc.

The Red Lion: Part of Channel 4's long-running Cutting Edge series of documentaries, *The Red Lion* is by the respected documentary-maker Sue Bourne who examines British pub culture by visiting over 600 Red Lion pubs (available to watch at http://www.channel4.com/programmes/the-red-lion).

Être et Avoir: Documentary which follows a single-class school in rural France for a year. This uses many of the techniques of observational documentary – particularly hiding the presence of the documentary-maker (available on DVD or an extensive selection of clips are on YouTube).

For each documentary consider:

- What is the role of the filmmaker?
- Is the audience aware of their presence? If so, how?
- Do you think the role of the documentary-maker fits the subject matter?
- Do different documentary styles attract different types of audience?
- Which of the documentaries you have watched seems more or less mediated?

Mediation refers to the way in which documentary-makers record and represent the real world on film. The analysis of these techniques illustrates the different ways documentary is constructed – rather than being a direct recording of reality. Analysing these techniques in existing documentaries will also help you in considering your own approach to documentary-making. When constructing an analysis of the techniques it can be helpful to use a table with prompts.

Primary research

Title of documentary, director, year: *Man on Wire* (James Marsh, 2008). Sequence for analysis: Opening/pre-credit sequence (approximately eight minutes).

Mediation techniques	Identification/ description	Function/effect
Types of shots Static or mobile? Handheld camera? Long takes?	1. Emphasis on mid shots of people and close-ups of objects.	1. Hides the identity of the actors in the reconstruction – makes it easier for the viewer to think it's Philippe. Close-ups on objects emphasise the meticulous planning of the stunt.
	2. Some camera movement but slow and smooth – zooms and pans, not handheld.	2. Fluid camera movement creates the impression that the viewer is there – looking around the room, etc.
	3. Variety of shot lengths, changes in tempo of editing.	3. The increase in tempo creates tension and suspense – similar to a fiction film technique.
Sound List the different types of sound – diegetic and non-diegetic.	4. Soundtrack (Michael Nyman).	4. Music is electronic, insistent, repetition of a theme adds to the tension of the sequence. (Use of Nyman for soundtrack also signals the film as 'alternative' 'artistic' because of the other films his music has been used in.)
	5. Sound effects – hammering nails into the coffin, etc.	5. Sound effects intensify Philippe's memory of the event – placing the viewer at the scene.
	0. Richard Nixon press conference: 'I'm not a crook'.	0. Nixon's defence makes the viewer consider whether Philippe is a criminal or not.

continued

Mediation techniques	Identification/ description	Function/effect
Interviews Who is interviewed? How are the interviews conducted? What information do they provide?	7. Philippe, interview responses also used as voice-over.	7. The main interviewee is the subject of the film – the 'man on wire'. Therefore we know he survived the walk between the Towers (takes away some of the suspense?), getting a firsthand account of the event (a version of it).
	8. Jean-Louis, Jean-François, Annie (group members and ex-girlfriend). David aka Donald, Alan aka Albert (sometime group members).	8. Other views of Philippe and his plan come from his close (ex?) friends which will provide a more complete picture. Already tensions are apparent through reference to arguments. Use of aliases reinforces heist genre. All the interviewees use emotional and subjective language: 'we're going to get caught', 'we're not going to die', 'could no longer go on living'. Creates immediacy – firsthand knowledge.
	9. All interviews conducted with subjects seated, minimal *mise-en-scène*.	9. Minimal *mise-en-scène* gives little indication of the interviewees' status, current situation, etc., making us focus on their past experiences.
Archive material What different type of film footage/ material is used?	10. Black and white reconstruction of preparations for the walk.	10. Use of black and white identifies this as something happening in the past. Iconography is reminiscent of a heist movie which provides tension for the viewer and makes the characters seem like outlaws

Mediation techniques	Identification/ description	Function/effect
Is it pre-existing ('found') or made especially for the documentary?	11. Silent film pastiche of Philippe's early life.	(suggests the documentary-maker's view). 11. The use of an irising effect links this to a silent film but also suggests it is Philippe's memory of an event (rather than objective). The style of filmmaking presents Philippe as a magician – someone extraordinary (how he sees himself?).
	12. Archive footage of the construction of the Twin Towers. Photos of Philippe as a boy.	12. The footage of the construction of the Twin Towers is shown in split screen with the photos of Philippe in the other half – this firmly links the two – they seem to come into existence together.
Documentary-maker Do they appear on screen? If so, describe their persona. Is the audience aware of the documentary-maker in any other way?	13. Documentary-maker doesn't appear; we don't hear the questions asked of the interviewees (if it's the documentary-maker asking them?).	13. Because the documentary-maker (James Marsh) doesn't appear on screen it means the viewer can concentrate on Philippe – there isn't a competing presence.
	14. Aware of the documentary-maker in the extreme mediation of different film styles.	14. The film language itself is foregrounded – aware of *Man on Wire* as a film made by a director – not a direct reflection of reality.

As the above table suggests, *Man on Wire* is extreme in the use of mediation techniques. There is almost no observational or expository-style documentary-making in it. The reasons for this may range from stylistic and artistic to practical:

continued

- The viewer knows that Philippe survived his walk; therefore the suspense and tension are constructed through the conventions of a crime film or heist.
- There is almost no footage of the walk itself – the documentary-maker has to find other ways of creating a sense of awe in the viewer.
- Much of the reconstruction draws on a theatrical style which fits with Philippe's persona as a showman.
- The constant mix of diverse styles also seems to reflect Philippe's endless energy.

How does this link to the practical production?

Although it is unlikely that the subject of your documentary will have done anything as unique as Philippe in *Man on Wire* there are elements of the documentary which will be applicable to planning a style of your own.

- Think about representing the personality and characteristics of your subject through the style of filmmaking.
- If you have interviews in your documentary consider the *mise-en-scène* – do you want to provide clues to the audience about the interviewee or keep a blank background?
- Photos may be used to develop the narrative – in this case Philippe's ongoing obsession with the Twin Towers – not just to show the viewer what someone looked like.
- Remember that although this is a documentary you may still use techniques associated with fiction films – if it's justified. Here the opening of the documentary withholds information from the viewer to create a disorientating but gripping start.

Research and practical production

Brief for Practical Production: Produce a 3MW documentary which creates a **portrait of an individual or group** within a wider **social, cultural or geographical** context.

You need to do this in *three* minutes.

Secondary research and practical skills

In preparation for your work, consider studying some of the many books which are now available on documentary-making. These provide practical suggestions and guidance on how to produce a successful documentary. Some suggestions:

Directing the Documentary by Michael Rabiger (Focal Press, 2004)

The Shut Up and Shoot Documentary Guide: *A Down and Dirty DV Production* by Anthony Artis (Focal Press, 2007)

There are also some very useful websites providing professional and amateur help and experience. One which should be of particular use to you is the 4Docs website (http://www.channel4.com/culture/microsites/F/fourdocs/video/video3.html).

The site includes a **wiki** which gives tips on obtaining funding, the legal issues relevant to documentary, what equipment to use and the latest online developments. The basis of the wiki is information provided by 4Docs, but a wiki is a collaborative website and therefore includes contributions from its users to create an up-to-date resource. There is also a **blog** on the site which gives details of documentary competitions and festivals as well as highlighting new documentary releases and TV screenings.

Primary research and practical production

In preparation for constructing your own film watch the *3MW* film *Pockets* (available at 4Docs).

Pockets takes a simple, clearly focused idea – what people have in their pockets – and presents it in a striking, uncluttered way. The film seems to work because it:

- Uses an everyday experience which most people can relate to.
- Chooses a variety of people in terms of age, gender, ethnicity, appearance, etc.
- Links form and content: using extreme close-ups of objects and faces, bringing the foreground into focus while the background is less clear, extra lighting used to focus on the subject matter.
- Leaves some things unsaid; rather than explaining everything for the audience (sometimes people explain the meaning behind their objects; sometimes the audience is left to think about what significance they might have).
- Uses non-diegetic sound sparingly.

How does this link to the practical production?

Pockets provides an excellent example of how attention to detail in framing, composition and editing is vital to creating a successful film – particularly when working in 'miniature' (three minutes). It also shows the importance of a strong, interesting idea:

- How might you apply the approaches in *Pockets* to your own film?

Resources

Broadcast documentary

Pockets (James Lee 2008)

The Red Lion (Sue Bourne, C4, 2009)

The World's . . . . and Me (C4, 2009)

Film documentary

Être et Avoir (Nicholas Philibert, 2004)

Man on Wire (James Marsh, 2008)

Websites

3MW (http://www.channel4.com/culture/microsites/0–9/3mw/index.html)

Four Docs (http://www.4docs.org.uk/)

Storyville (http://www.bbc.co.uk/bbcfour/documentaries/storyville/). Home page of BBC's international documentary strand includes interviews, articles on Storyville documentaries, and links to available programmes on iPlayer.

Books

The following are specialist, academic sources:

Cousins, M. and Macdonald, K. (eds) *Imagining Reality* (Faber, 2005)
Kilborn, R. and Izod, J. *An Introduction To Television Documentary – Confronting Reality* (Manchester University Press, 1997)
Nichols, B. *Introduction to Documentary* (Indiana University Press, 2002)
—— *Representing Reality* (Indiana University Press, 1991)
—— *Blurred Boundaries* (Indiana University Press, 1994)

Overviews and summaries of debates around documentaries may be found in a range of media and film studies textbooks, for example:

Artis, A. *The Shut Up and Shoot Documentary Guide: A Down and Dirty DV Production* (Focal Press, 2007)
Casey Benyahia *et al. A2 Film Studies: The Essential Introduction* (2nd edn, Routledge, 2009)
Cook, P. (ed.) *The Cinema Book* (3rd edn, BFI, 2008)
Nelmes, J. (ed.) *An Introduction to Film Studies* (3rd edn, Routledge, 2007)
Rabiger, M. *Directing the Documentary* (Focal Press, 2004)

GLOSSARY

360-degree content producing news across all platforms.

Alternative representations a representation that is different from the dominant representation, often with different values from the dominant ideology and often made by non-mainstream media companies.

Anchoring when a caption is placed in an open text to anchor meaning.

Base in Marxist terminology, the base refers to the economic core upon which a society is organised. It is the central means by which wealth is created and distributed among the people within that society.

Bourgeoisie the Marxist name for those who own or control the means of production or services; the middle classes.

Bricolage the dictionary usefully defines it as "a construction made of whatever materials are at hand; something created from a variety of available things", which is precisely how postmodernists use it, though the constructions are of meaning. 'Bricoleurs' in French are tinkers, people who travel around collecting other people's unwanted items.

Capitalism the economic system in which a society is focused upon the pursuit of capital (wealth). In Britain and other Western countries, capitalism may be said to be at the heart of the economic base. The main criticism is that it does not seek to create wealth for all people. For there to be wealthy people, others have to remain poor. Therefore critics of capitalism argue that while it is good at creating wealth, the unavoidable consequence of capitalism is inequality: the rich get richer and the poor get poorer. As capitalism has spread across the world, this inequality is no longer confined to within a country but is seen on a global scale.

Citizen journalism citizen journalism means that ordinary people as well as professional journalists are creating the news.

Closed and open texts a text with only one possible meaning is said to be a closed text whereas a more ambiguous text with more than one possible interpretation is an open text. An open text may also be called *polysemic*, literally meaning many signs.

Deconstruction studying a media text by 'taking it apart' to examine its constituent elements and explaining each element.

Democracy power belongs to all of the people.

Distribution the distributor is an organisation which mediates between the producer and exhibitor to make the text available for consumption by an audience (e.g. in film the distributor is the link between a film producer and the exhibitor (cinema, DVD, TV, etc.), who ensures that the film is seen by the widest audience possible). In media the term 'distribution' also refers to the *marketing* and advertising of media texts.

Dominant ideology a set of values that reflects and reinforces the values of those in power.

Dominant representation the representation that comes to dominate the media; it is repeated in the media over time.

False consciousness a term which suggests that the working classes are not being fully aware of the exploitation they endure at the hands of the ruling class. It is regarded as a reason why those who are exploited do not rise up and rebel against the ruling elite.

Freedom of expression everyone has a right to express their own views, but often within certain laws or regulations.

Juxtaposition placing two contrasting elements next to each other in order to increase the impact of each (e.g. darkness seems to be darker when it is placed next to brightness and in a film, or a sudden increase in volume makes it seem much louder due to the contrast).

Mediation the media comes between the audience and the original source; it mediates.

Preferred reading the most likely interpretation of an open text.

Production the production stage refers to the developers or producers of a media text (e.g. Hollywood as the producer of blockbusters, the BBC as the producer of TV news programmes).

Proletariat the name Marx gave to those who work the means of production and provide the services offered in a society: the working classes.

Self-representation when a group represent themselves in the media.

Semiotics the study of signs and their meanings. First used by Ferdinand de Saussure in his Course in General Linguistics at the University of Geneva (1906–11), semiotics is an important part of media study as it is a device by which meanings are attached to the signs we see in media texts.

Stereotype a simple, generalised and exaggerated representation. A few characteristics, usually negative, are presumed to belong to the whole group.

Superstructure this is the name Marxists give to the institutions which exist in a society other than those associated with the economy, which would be part of the base. These institutions include religions, the law, education, the political system and the media. Marxists believe not only that these institutions are shaped by the economic base, but also that the superstructure helps to legitimise the base and ensure its future as the economic system of that society.

User-generated content media content shown by the mainstream media that is produced by the users or audience.

BIBLIOGRAPHY

Abercrombie, N. (1996) *Television and Society*, Polity Press.

Barthes, R. (1977) 'Rhetoric of the image', in R. Barthes, *Image, Music, Text*, edited and translated by S. Heath, Hill and Wang.

Bennett, P., Slater, J. and Wall, P. (2005) *A2 Media Studies: The Essential Introduction*, Routledge.

Berger, J. (1972) *Ways of Seeing*, Penguin.

Blumer, J. and Katz, E. (1975) *The Uses of Mass Communication: Current Perspectives on Gratification Research*, Sage.

Butler, J. (1990) *Gender Trouble: Feminism and the Subversion of Identity*, Routledge.

Chomsky, N. (1988) *Manufacturing Consent: The Political Economy of the Mass Media*, Pantheon Books.

Chomsky, N. (2004) *Hegemony and Survival: America's Quest for Global Dominance*, Penguin Books.

Cohen, S. (2002) *Folk Devils and Moral Panics: The Creation fo Mods and Rockers*, McKibbon and Kee.

Coleman, S. (nd) 'Review of government communication: from the megaphone to the Radar screen', http://www.gcreview.gov.uk/evidence/coleman.pdf, accessed 1 November 2004.

Doty, A. (1995) 'There's something queer here', in C.K. Creekmur and A. Doty (eds) *Out in Culture: Gay, Lesbian and Queer Essays on Popular Culture*, Duke University Press.

Doty, A. (1998) 'Queer theory', in J. Hill and P. Church Gibson (eds) *The Oxford Guide to Film Studies*, Oxford University Press.

Dyer, R. (1993) *The Matter of Images: Essays on Representation*, Routledge.

Dyer, R. (2002) *Only Entertainment*, Routledge.

Fiske, J. (1989) *Reading the Popular*, Routledge.

Freidan, B. (1963 Reprinted 2010) *The Feminine Mystique*, Penguin Classics.

Gauntlett, D. (2008) *Media, Gender and Identity*, Routledge.

Gelder, K. (1994) *Reading the Vampire*, Routledge.

Giddens, A. (1993) *Sociology*, Polity Press.

Giddens, A. (1999) *Runaway World: How Globalization is Reshaping Our Lives*, Profile.

Gramsci, A. (1971) *Selections From the Prison Notebook*, edited and translated by Quintin Hoare and Goffrey Nowell Smith, Lawrence & Wishart.

Graner-Ray, S. (2003) *Gender Inclusive Game Design: Expanding The Market*, Charles River Media.

Greer, G. (1970) *The Female Eunuch*, MacGibbon, & Kee.

Gross, L. (1989) 'Out of the mainstream: sexual minorities and the mass media', in L. Seiter *et al.* (eds) *Remote Control: Television, Audiences and Cultural Power*, Routledge.

Hall, S. (1997) *Representation: Cultural Representations and Signifying Practices*, Sage.

Harcup, T. and O'Neill, D. (2001) 'What is news? Galtung and Ruge revisited', in P. Rayner, P. Wall and S. Kruger (2003) *Media Studies: The Essential Resource*, Routledge.

Herman, E. and Chomsky, N. (1988) *Manufacturing Consent: The Political Economy of The Mass Media*, Pantheon Books.

Herman, H.S. and Chomsky, N. (1994) *Manufacturing Consent: The Political Economy Model of the Media*, Vintage.

Jenkins, H. (2003) 'Interactive audiences', in V. Nightingale and K. Ross (eds) *Media and Audiences: New Perspectives*, Open University Press.

Levy, A. (2005) *Female Chauvinist Pigs: Women and the Rise of Raunch Culture*, Pocket Books.

Lyotard, J.F. [1979] (1984) *The Postmodern Condition*, Manchester University Press.

McKee, R. (1997) Five-part narrative taken from McKee's story seminar at Northern Alberta Institute of Technology.

McLuhan, M. (1964) *Understanding Media*, Routledge.

McRobbie, A. (1991) *Feminism and Youth Culture: From Jackie to Just 17*, Macmillan.

McRobbie, A. (2005) *The Aftermath of Feminism The Aftermath of Feminism: Gender, Culture and Social Change*, Sage.

Medhurst, A. (1998) 'Tracing desires: sexuality and media texts', in A. Briggs and P. Cobley (eds) *The Media: An Introduction*, Longman.

Morley, D. (1980) *The Nationwide Audience*, BFI Publishing.

Mulvey, L. [1975] (2003) 'Visual pleasure and narrative cinema', in W. Brooker and D. Jermyn (eds) *The Audience Studies Reader*, Routledge.

Papadopoulos, L. (2010) *Sexualisation of Young People Review* (http://www.homeoffice. gov.uk/documents/Sexualisation-young-people.pdf).

Perkins, T. (1997) 'Rethinking stereotypes', in M. Barrett *et al.* (eds) *Ideology and Cultural Production*, Croom Helm.

Poole, E. (2000) 'Media representations and British Muslims', *Dialogue Magazine*.

Postman, N. (1985) *Amusing Ourselves to Death*, Methuen.

Ross, K. (2000) 'Whose image? TV criticism and black minority viewers', in S. Cottle (ed.) *Ethnic Minorities and the Media*, Open University Press.

Ross, K. and Nightingale, V. (2003) *Media and Audiences: New Perspectives*, Open University Press.

Said, E. (1978) *Orientalism*, Pantheon Books.

Storey, J. (ed.) (1998) *Cultural Theory and Popular Culture: An Introduction*, University of Georgia Press.

Todorov, T. (1969). *Grammaire du Décameron*, Mouton.

Williams, R. (1977) *Marxism and Literature*, Oxford University Press.

Winship, J. (1987) *Inside Women's Magazines*, Pandora.

Wolf, N. (1991) *The Beauty Myth: How Images of Beauty Are Used Against Women*, Anchor.

Woodward, K. (1997) 'Concepts of identity and difference', in K. Woodward (ed.) *Identity and Difference*, Sage.

Useful online resources

Race, Representation and the Media Report www.channel4.com
www.guardian.co.uk
www.mediaed.org
www.heromachine2.
www.youtube.com
www.asa.org.uk
www.zeeuk.com
www.manchester.gov.uk
www.nwda.co.uk
www.asiansoundradio.co.uk
www.unityradio.fm
www.manchestereveningnews.co.uk
www.manchestermule.co.uk
www.salfordstar.com
www.screenonline.org
www.youtube.com/shows
www.homeoffice.gov.uk/documents/Sexualisation-young-people.pdf
www.vgfreedom.blogspot.com
www.lacan.com/zizekchro1.htm
www.indymedia.org.uk
www.theory.org.uk

INDEX

Note: page numbers in italics denote figures where they are separated from their textual reference

Media Studies: The Essential Resource

Edited by Philip Rayner, Peter Wall and Stephen Kruger

A unique collection of resources for all those studying the media at university and pre-university level, this book brings together a wide array of material including advertisements, political cartoons and academic articles, with supporting commentary and explanation to clarify their importance to Media Studies. In addition, activities and further reading and research are suggested to help kickstart students' autonomy.

The book is organized around three main sections: Reading the Media, Audiences, and Institutions and is edited by the same teachers and examiners who brought us the hugely successful *AS Media Studies: The Essential Introduction*.

This is an ideal companion or standalone sourcebook to help students engage critically with media texts. Its key features include:

- further reading suggestions
- a comprehensive bibliography
- a list of web resources.

ISBN13: 978–0–415–29172–9 (hbk)
ISBN13: 978–0–415–29173–6 (pbk)
ISBN13: 978–0–203–64440–9 (ebk)

Available at all good bookshops
For ordering and further information please visit:
www.routledge.com

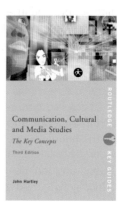

Communication Studies: The Essential Resource

Edited by Andrew Beck, Peter Bennett and Peter Wall

This book brings together a huge range of material including academic articles, film scripts and interplanetary messages adrift on space probes with supporting commentary to clarify their importance to the field. *Communication Studies: The Essential Resource* is a collection of essays and texts for all those studying communication at university and pre-university level.

Individual sections address:

- texts and meanings in communication
- themes in personal communication
- communication practice
- culture, communication and context
- debates and controversies in communication.

Edited by the same teachers and examiners who brought us *AS Communication Studies: The Essential Introduction*, this volume will help communications students to engage with the subject successfully. Its key features include:

- suggested further activities at the end of each chapter
- a glossary of key terms
- a comprehensive bibliography with web resources.

ISBN13: 978–0–415–28792–0 (hbk)
ISBN13: 978–0–415–28793–7 (pbk)

Available at all good bookshops
For ordering and further information please visit:
www.routledge.com

Multimedia Journalism: A Practical Guide

Andy Bull

Multimedia Journalism offers clear advice on working across multiple media platforms and includes guides to creating and using video, audio, text and pictures.

This textbook contains all the essentials of good practice that are the bedrock to being a successful multimedia journalist and is supported by an immersive website at **www.multimedia-journalism.co.uk** which demonstrates how to apply the skills covered in the book, gives many examples of good and bad practice, and keeps the material constantly up to date and in line with new hardware, software, methods of working and legislation as they change. The book is fully cross-referenced and interlinked with the website, which offers the chance to test your learning and send in questions for industry experts to answer in their masterclasses.

Split into three levels – getting started, building proficiency and professional standards – this book builds on the knowledge attained in each part, and ensures that skills are introduced one step at a time until professional competency is achieved. This three stage structure means it can be used from initial to advanced level to learn the key skill areas of video, audio, text, and pictures and how to combine them to create multimedia packages. Skills covered include:

- Writing news reports, features, email bulletins and blogs
- Building a website using a content management system
- Measuring the success of your website or blog
- Shooting, cropping, editing and captioning pictures
- Recording, editing and publishing audio reports and podcasts
- Shooting and editing video, creating effective packages
- Streaming live video reports
- Creating breaking news tickers and using Twitter
- Using and encouraging user-generated content
- Interviewing and conducting advanced online research
- Subediting, proofreading and headlining, including search engine optimisation
- Geo-tagging, geo-coding and geo-broadcasting
- Scripting and presenting bulletins.

ISBN13: 978–0–415–47822–9 (hbk)
ISBN13: 978–0–415–47823–6 (pbk)
ISBN13: 978–0–203–86603–0 (ebk)

Available at all good bookshops
For ordering and further information please visit:
www.routledge.com

Film: The Essential Study Guide

Edited by Ruth Doughty and Deborah Shaw .

Providing a key resource to new students, *Film: The Essential Study Guide* introduces all the skills needed to succeed on a film studies course.

This succinct, accessible guide covers key topics such as:

- Using the library
- Online research and resources
- Viewing skills
- How to watch and study foreign language films
- Essay writing
- Presentation skills
- Referencing and plagiarism
- Practical filmmaking

Including exercises and examples, *Film: The Essential Study Guide* helps film students understand how study skills are applicable to their learning and gives them the tools to flourish in their degree.

ISBN13: 978–0–415–43700–4 (pbk)
ISBN 3: 978–0–203–00292–6 (ebk)

Available at all good bookshops
For ordering and further information please visit:
www.routledge.com

Film Studies: The Essential Resource

Peter Bennett, Andrew Hickman, Peter Wall

Film Studies: The Essential Resource is a collection of resource material for all those studying film at university and pre-university level. The Resource brings together a wide variety of material ranging from academic articles; advertisements; websites; interviews with directors and actors; magazines and newspapers.

Individual sections address:

- Codes – examines the language of film, production, narrative and canon.
- Concepts – considers genre, the auteur, stars and realism.
- Contexts – covers themes of textual analysis, theoretical perspectives, industry and audience.
- Cinemas – investigates Hollywood, British cinema, national cinemas and alternative takes.

With each extract introduced and contextualized by the editors, and suggestions for further activities and further reading included, *Film Studies: The Essential Resource* is the perfect resource to kick-start students' autonomy.

ISBN13: 978–0–415–36567–3 (hbk)
ISBN13: 978–0–415–36568–0 (pbk)

Available at all good bookshops
For ordering and further information please visit:
www.routledge.com

Horror

Brigid Cherry

Horror cinema is a hugely successful, but at the same time culturally illicit, genre that spans the history of cinema. It continues to flourish with recent cycles of supernatural horror and torture porn that span the full range of horror styles and aesthetics. It is enjoyed by audiences everywhere, but also seen as a malign influence by others.

In this Routledge Film Guidebook audience researcher and film scholar Brigid Cherry provides a comprehensive overview of the horror film and explores how the genre works.

Examining the way horror films create images of gore and the uncanny through film technology and effects, Cherry provides an account of the way cinematic and stylistic devices create responses of terror and disgust in the viewer.

Horror examines the way these films construct psychological and cognitive responses and how they speak to audiences on an intimate personal level, addressing their innermost fears and desires. Cherry further explores the role of horror cinema in society and culture, looking at how it represents various identity groups and engages with social anxieties, and examining the way horror sees, and is seen by, society.

A range of national cinemas both historical and recent are discussed, including canonical films such as:

- The Curse of Frankenstein
- Night of the Living Dead
- Ginger Snaps
- Suspiria
- Halloween
- The Evil Dead
- Candyman
- Saw
- Ringu
- Nosteratu

This introduction to horror cinema is the perfect guide for any student new to the genre or wishing to study in more depth.

ISBN13: 9–78–0–415–45667–8 (hbk)
ISBN13: 9–78–0–415–45668–5 (pbk)
ISBN13: 9–78–0–203–88218–4 (ebk)

AQA Religious Ethics for AS and A2

Structured directly around the specification of the AQA, this is the definitive textbook for students of Advanced Subsidiary or Advanced Level courses. It covers all the necessary topics for Religious Ethics in an enjoyable student-friendly fashion. Each chapter includes:

AQA
RELIGIOUS ETHICS FOR
AS AND A2

JILL OLIPHANT
EDITED BY
JON MAYLED AND ANNE TUNLEY

- A list of key issues
- AQA specification checklist
- Explanations of key terminology
- Helpful summaries
- Self-test review questions
- Exam practice questions

To maximise students' chances of success, the book contains a section dedicated to answering examination questions. It comes complete with lively illustrations, a comprehensive glossary, full bibliography and a companion website.

Jill Oliphant teaches Religious Studies at Angley School in Kent. She is also an experienced examiner.

Jon Mayled has been a Chief Examiner for Religious Studies. He is a freelance writer and editor.

Anne Tunley is Head of Religious Studies at Gateways School in Leeds and an experienced examiner.

ISBN 978–0–415–54933–2 (paperback)

Available at all good bookshops
For ordering and further information please visit
www.routledge.com